The universe :
523.1 UNI

THE UNIVERSE

A Historical Survey of Beliefs, Theories, and Laws

An Explorer's Guide to the Universe

THE UNIVERSE

A Historical Survey of Beliefs, Theories, and Laws

Edited by Erik Gregersen, Associate Editor, Astronomy and Space Exploration

Britannica®
Educational Publishing

IN ASSOCIATION WITH

ROSEN
EDUCATIONAL SERVICES

Published in 2010 by Britannica Educational Publishing
(a trademark of Encyclopædia Britannica, Inc.)
in association with Rosen Educational Services, LLC
29 East 21st Street, New York, NY 10010.

Distributed exclusively by Rosen Educational Services.
For a listing of additional Britannica Educational Publishing titles, call toll free (800) 237-9932.

First Edition

Britannica Educational Publishing
Michael I. Levy: Executive Editor
Marilyn L. Barton: Senior Coordinator, Production Control
Steven Bosco: Director, Editorial Technologies
Lisa S. Braucher: Senior Producer and Data Editor
Yvette Charboneau: Senior Copy Editor
Kathy Nakamura: Manager, Media Acquisition
Erik Gregersen: Associate Editor, Astronomy and Space Exploration

Rosen Educational Services
Jeanne Nagle: Senior Editor
Nelson Sá: Art Director
Nicole Russo: Designer
Introduction by Alexandra Hanson-Harding

Library of Congress Cataloging-in-Publication Data

The universe: a historical survey of beliefs, theories, and laws / edited by Erik Gregersen.—
1st ed.
    p. cm.—(An explorer's guide to the universe)
"In association with Britannica Educational Publishing, Rosen Educational Services."
Includes index.
ISBN 978-1-61530-026-6 (library binding)
1. Cosmology—History—Popular works. 2. Astronomy—History—Popular works. I.
Gregersen, Erik.
QB982.U554 2010
523.1—dc22
                                                                    2009040645

Manufactured in the United States of America

On the cover: Theories and beliefs about the cosmos have been nearly as vast as the universe itself, covering everything from the birth of a single star to the discovery of objects such as the Galaxy Triplet ARP 274 (pictured). *NASA, ESA, and M. Livio and the Hubble Heritage Team (STScI/AURA)*

CONTENTS

23

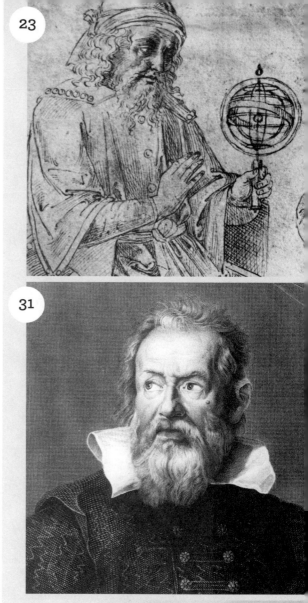

31

45

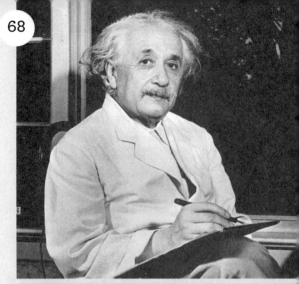
68

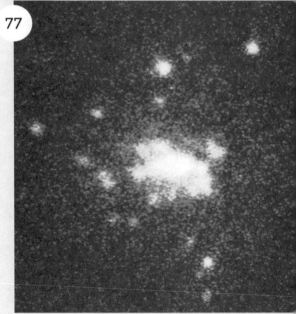
77

90

Chapter 6: Ancient and Early Astronomers 109

CHAPTER 7: NOTABLE ASTRONOMERS OF THE 19TH CENTURY   137

139

153

155

CHAPTER 8: 20TH-CENTURY ASTRONOMERS 162

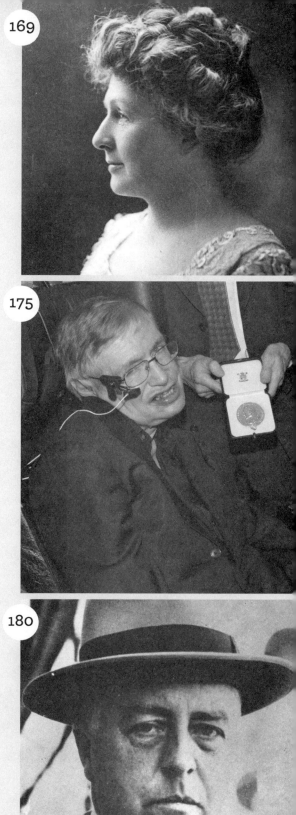

169

175

180

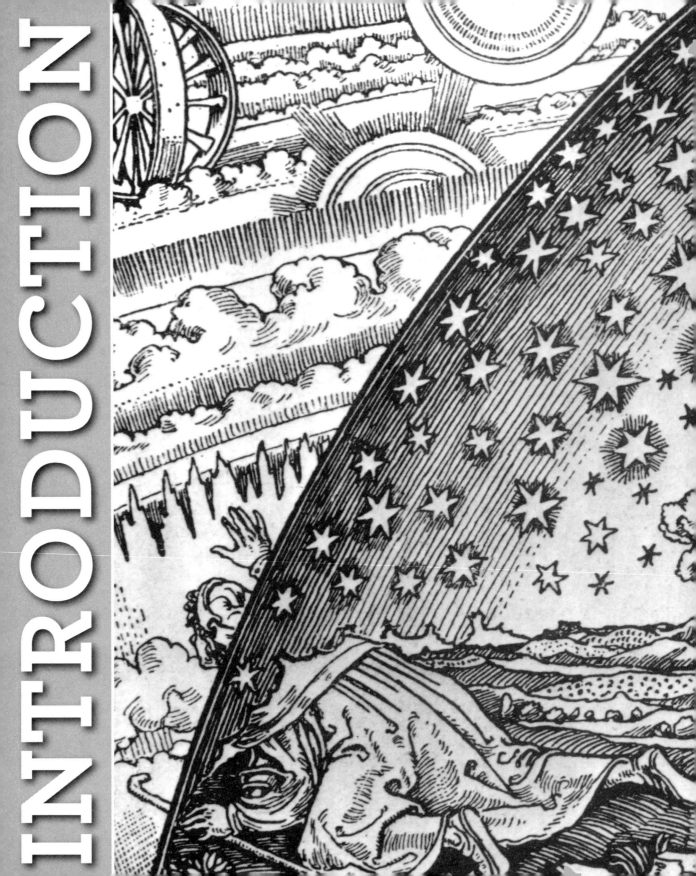

INTRODUCTION

Albert Einstein (1879–1955) didn't seem like anyone's idea of a genius when he was young. He didn't talk until he was three. He hated his strict school, and one teacher told him, "You will never amount to anything." Rebellious, he cut so many classes in college he was only able to pass his exams by using other people's notes. Later in life, he couldn't find a teaching job and had to settle for working as an examiner at a patent office. He seemed to be going nowhere. And yet his theories of special and general relativity, which revealed new ideas about the nature of the universe, were some of the greatest achievements of the 20th century.

Einstein was by no means the only visionary to ponder the universe, as this book amply shows. The exceptional men and women who made the cognitive leaps (and leaps of faith) that have led to a greater understanding of the universe are found in these pages—their lives, their beliefs, and the often painstaking work that proved their theories. Readers also will learn about the ways people have viewed the sky through history, from observing the patterns of the Moon to using high-tech equipment to studying the tiniest particles that make up the fabric of the universe.

For instance, ancient agrarian cultures used the heavens to help them to keep track of seasons and learn when to plant their crops. Armed with the knowledge that the Moon affected the tides, and the Sun separated day and night, they theorized that the stars and planets affected Earth, too, and developed astrology. Ancient civilizations also used the stars to develop the calendar, and early sailors and nomads used their understanding of the constellations to guide them on their travels.

Early theories of the universe depicted Earth as a pillar at the center of everything, around which the Sun, Moon, and planets circled. The Greeks were experts at geography—they calculated the radius of Earth by using the Sun—and mathematics, but they used reason to avoid coming to some obvious conclusions. By the time of Aristotle (384–322 BCE), hundreds of years later, they believed Earth was in the shape of a ball, but still thought that the Sun, stars, and planets passed around Earth. Aristotle believed that there could only be a finite number of stars, because they all passed around Earth every 24 hours. He was incorrect. Even though certain mathematical and geographic equations involving the heavens were available to him, he believed that Earth had to be the centre of the universe, because he could not imagine that humans could live on

For centuries, humans have speculated about what lies beyond Earth's firmament. This inquisitiveness has led to many discoveries, from which sprang several known laws of the universe. Hulton Archive/Getty Images

a planet that moved and rotated around the Sun.

Aristotle's view of the universe became doctrine in the Catholic Church and stayed so through the Middle Ages. But during the Renaissance, many people began to question old ideas. Polish astronomer Nicolaus Copernicus (1473–1543) deduced that Earth revolved around the Sun, which meant that Earth wasn't the centre of the world. Copernicus was so afraid of the Catholic Church's reaction that he was reluctant to put his theory in writing. His book, *De revolutionibus orbium coelestium*, was not published until he was on his death bed in 1543.

Galileo Galilei (1564–1642) was also part of the Copernican revolution. Galileo believed that careful observation was more helpful in understanding the sky than Aristotle's use of logical deduction. Using telescopes with lenses he ground himself, which were much more powerful than other lenses of the time, he noted the phases of the Moon and observed more stars than the naked eye had thus far revealed. His observations also revealed four moons of Jupiter—a discovery that meant Earth was not unique in its possession of a moon. In 1632, Galileo published a book called *Dialogue Concerning the two Chief World Systems*, which confirmed Copernicus's idea that Earth moved around the Sun, not the other way around. For his views, he was summoned from his sickbed at age 70 and put on trial by the Catholic Church, which resulted in his being put

under house arrest for the remainder of his life.

At Trinity College, Isaac Newton (1642–1727) studied the works of Copernicus and Galileo. Credited with the invention of calculus, Newton also studied the ways prisms refract light. However, he is most noted for his theory of universal gravitation. According to this theory, later explained in *Philosophiae Naturalis Principia Mathematica* (1687), each body in the universe is pulled toward the force of gravity. The larger the bodies, the stronger the attraction, but the farther apart the bodies are, the smaller the force. For example, the gravitational attraction of a star is exactly one quarter that of a similar star at half the distance. Because all of these bodies operate on each other all the time, it also shows that the universe can not be static. This law explained how gravity keeps planets in their orbits, and allowed scientists to predict the orbits of Earth, the Moon, and the planets with great accuracy.

The 18th and 19th centuries had their fair share of celestial theorists and revelations as well. English astronomer William Herschel (1738–1822) discovered Uranus, and German astronomer Friedrich Wilhelm Bessel (1874–1846) became the first to accurately measure the distance of a star. But it was during the 20th century that the study of astronomy took another giant leap forward in the person of Albert Einstein. In 1905, Einstein published his theory of special relativity. In this theory, Einstein showed

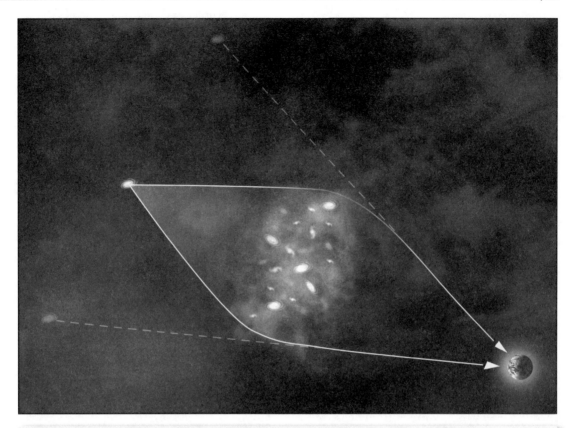

Gravity from intervening celestial bodies, such as a galactic cluster (pictured), redirects light rays, causing them to "bend." Such gravitational lensing is at the root of Einstein's theory of general relativity. BSIP/Photo Researchers, Inc.

that nothing can move faster than the speed of light, and that light moves at a constant speed through empty space. Because measurements of time are altered by the frame of reference of an observer, time is not absolute. Einstein gave the world a whole different way to imagine the universe. Instead of three dimensions, there were four—space and time could be seen as part of a deeper structure called space-time.

In 1915, Einstein took Newton's law of gravitation a step further with his theory of general relativity. According to this theory, the gravity of the stars, planets, and other matter curves the flat plane of the universe back upon itself in a four-dimensional way. Not only that, but gravity can cause matter and light to change, too. For instance, a beam of light that passes near a large planet would be bent by the planet's gravity.

At about the same time that Einstein was experimenting with gravity, American astronomer Edwin Hubble (1889–1953) was dealing with distance. By studying faint, fluctuating patches of light in the night sky, Hubble was able to measure the distance to Cepheid stars in what was thought to be a nearby nebulous cloud. His findings proved that not only was the nebula farther away than suspected, but that the cloud was actually a distant galaxy—one of several Hubble would study over the course of his career.

Then Hubble went on to make an even more important discovery. Through the use of spectrographs, astronomers had concluded that light from celestial objects such as stars that were moving toward an observer on Earth would move toward the blue end of the spectrum (called blueshifts) and those that were moving away concentrated on the red end (redshifts). Almost all the galaxies Hubble observed had redshifts and were moving away from the Milky Way. In fact, every galaxy was hurrying away from every other galaxy at speeds of thousands of miles per second. That meant that instead of being one size, the universe was actually expanding. Building on the work of scientists who had come before, he created Hubble's law, a mathematical formula that showed that the farther away a heavenly body was, the faster it appeared to be hurrying away.

This discovery gave rise to another question. If the universe is expanding, what is it expanding from? According to the hot big bang theory, approximately 13.7 billion years ago, all the matter and energy of the universe was contained in one tiny ball. That ball didn't hang in space—there was no space. There was also no time. Then, in one moment, the universe exploded into being and began to expand rapidly.

Scientists theorized that high temperatures associated with the big bang should leave the universe filled with radiation that would turn into microwaves, a form of energy found in the radio spectrum. Yet no one was able to prove the theory. In the 1960s, two scientists, Arno Penzias (1933–) and Robert Wilson, (1936–) were conducting experiments with an advanced satellite antenna for Bell Labs. They were distracted by a crackling hiss from deep space that they couldn't silence no matter how they positioned the antenna. Penzias and Wilson had found the Cosmic Microwave Background (CMB). They won the 1978 Nobel Prize in Physics for their work.

Through the centuries, other noteworthy individuals have laboured to expand humankind's understanding of the universe, many of whom are also

Measuring the distance to Cepheid stars, like those in the Andromeda Galaxy, much as Edwin Hubble had years ago, is still the best way to understand the scale of the universe. B.J. Mochejska (Warsaw University), The DIRECT Project, FLWO, MDM/NASA Images

profiled in this book. Of note are scientists such as Gian Domenico Cassini (1625–1712), who is noted for a number of discoveries. His earthbound experiments centred on hydraulics. In the celestial realm, Cassini focused his attention first on the Sun, then the planets that revolve around it. His observations led to a more precise value for the Martian parallax, and he is credited with discovering four of Saturn's moons (Iapetus, Rhea, Tethys, and Dione). He also was among the first to notice that there was a gap between Saturn's rings—a space that was named for him, the Cassini Division.

In 1933, Fritz Zwicky (1898–1974) inferred the existence of dark matter. Dark matter is matter that can't be seen—it can only be detected by the gravitational effect that it has on visible matter. Scientists now believe that about a quarter of the total energy density of the universe is composed of dark matter.

Astronomical excellence has not been the domain of men alone. Among the women astronomers whose work paved the way for a greater understanding of universal theories is Annie Jump Cannon (1863–1941). She brought order to the study of the stars through the creation of the Harvard classification system, which classified stellar spectra based on temperature. Cannon's work resulted in the classification of hundreds of thousands of stars, and the discovery of hundreds more. She is the first woman to become an officer in the American Astronomical Society.

The totality of the universe is perhaps unknowable. But the theories, beliefs, and laws examined in this book—which represent the life's work of many incredible individuals—offer the best understanding humankind has been able to achieve thus far. It is awe-inspiring to ponder what advances the dreamers and visionaries of the 21st century will bring.

CHAPTER 1

IN THE BEGINNING

Humanity has traveled a long road since societies imagined Earth, the Sun, and the Moon as the main objects of creation, with the rest of the universe being formed almost as an afterthought. Today it is known that Earth is only a small ball of rock in a space of unimaginable vastness and that the birth of the solar system was probably only one event among many that occurred against the backdrop of an already mature universe. This humbling lesson has unveiled a remarkable fact, one that endows the minutest particle in the universe with a rich and noble heritage: events that occurred in the first few minutes of the creation of the universe turn out to have had a profound influence on the birth, life, and death of galaxies, stars, and planets. Indeed, a line can be drawn from the forging of the matter of the universe in a primal "big bang" to the gathering on Earth of atoms versatile enough to serve as the basis of life. The intrinsic harmony of such a worldview has great philosophical and aesthetic appeal, and it may explain why public interest in the universe has always endured.

EARLIEST CONCEPTIONS OF THE UNIVERSE

All scientific thinking on the nature of the universe can be traced to the distinctive geometric patterns formed by the stars in the night sky. Even prehistoric people must have noticed that, apart from a daily rotation (which is now understood to arise from the spin of Earth), the stars did not seem to move with respect to one another: the stars appear "fixed." Early nomads found that knowledge of the constellations could guide their travels, and they developed stories to help them remember the relative positions of the stars in the night sky. These stories became the mythical tales that are part of most cultures.

When nomads turned to farming, an intimate knowledge of the constellations served a new function—an aid in time-keeping, in particular for keeping track of the seasons. People had noticed very early that certain celestial objects did not remain stationary relative to the "fixed" stars. Instead, during the course of a year, they moved forward and backward in a narrow strip of the sky that contained 12 constellations constituting the signs of the zodiac. Seven such wanderers were known to the ancients: the Sun, the Moon, Mercury, Venus, Mars, Jupiter, and Saturn. Foremost among the wanderers was the Sun. Day and night came with its rising and setting, and its motion through the zodiac signaled the season

to plant and the season to reap. Next in importance was the Moon. Its position correlated with the tides, and its shape changed intriguingly over the course of a month. The Sun and Moon had the power of gods; why not then the other wanderers? This probably led to the astrological belief that the positions of the planets (from the Greek word *planetes*, "wanderers") in the zodiac could influence worldly events and even cause the rise and fall of kings. In homage to this belief, Babylonian priests devised the week of seven days, whose names even in various modern languages (for example, English, French, or Norwegian)

Constellations were originally a navigational aide. Early travelers attributed shapes to certain star groupings, then gave these figures backstories in an effort to remember each constellation's position in the night sky.
© Corbis

can still easily be traced to their origins in the seven planet-gods.

ASTRONOMICAL THEORIES OF THE ANCIENT GREEKS

The apex in the description of planetary motions during classical antiquity was reached with the Greeks, who were of course superb geometers. Like their predecessors, Greek astronomers adopted the natural picture, from the point of view of an observer on Earth, that Earth lay motionless at the centre of a rigidly rotating celestial sphere (to which the stars were "fixed"), and that the complex to-and-fro wanderings of the planets in the zodiac were to be described against this unchanging backdrop. They developed an epicyclic model that would reproduce the observed planetary motions with quite astonishing accuracy. The model invoked small circles on top of large circles, all rotating at individual uniform speeds, and it culminated about 140 CE with the work of Ptolemy, who introduced the ingenious artifact of displaced centres for the circles to improve

In this depiction by an unknown artist, Ptolemy demonstrates his conception of the universe on a three-dimensional sphere. The Ptolemaic model was a refinement of previous attempts to explain the nature of the universe. Hulton Archive/Getty Images

the empirical fit. Although the model was purely kinematic and did not attempt to address the dynamical reasons for why the motions were as they were, it laid the groundwork for the paradigm that nature is not capricious but possesses a regularity and precision that can be discovered from experience and used to predict future events.

The application of the methods of Euclidean geometry to planetary astronomy by the Greeks led to other schools of thought as well. Pythagoras (c. 570–? BCE), for example, argued that the world could be understood on rational principles ("all things are numbers"); that it was made of four elements—earth, water, air, and fire; that Earth was a sphere; and that the Moon shone by reflected light. In the 4th century BCE Heracleides Ponticus, a follower of Pythagoras, taught that the spherical Earth rotated freely in space and that Mercury and Venus revolved about the Sun. From the different lengths of shadows cast in Syene and Alexandria at noon on the first day of summer, Eratosthenes (c. 276–194 BCE) computed the radius of Earth to an accuracy within 20 percent of the modern value. Starting with the size of Earth's shadow cast on the Moon during a lunar eclipse, Aristarchus of Samos (c. 310–230 BCE) calculated the linear size of the Moon relative to Earth. From its measured angular size, he then obtained the distance to the Moon. He also proposed a clever scheme to measure the size and distance of the Sun. Although flawed, the method did enable him to deduce that the Sun is much larger than Earth. This deduction led Aristarchus to speculate that Earth revolves about the Sun rather than the other way around.

THE PTOLEMAIC SYSTEM

The Ptolemaic system is a mathematical model of the universe formulated by the Alexandrian astronomer and mathematician Ptolemy in about 150 CE and recorded by him in his Almagest *and* Planetary Hypotheses. *It is a geocentric cosmology. That is, it starts by assuming that Earth is stationary and at the centre of the universe. The "natural" expectation for ancient societies was that the heavenly bodies (Sun, Moon, planets, and stars) must travel in uniform motion along the most "perfect" path possible, a circle. However, the paths of the Sun, Moon, and planets as observed from Earth are not circular. Ptolemy's model explained this "imperfection" by postulating that the apparently irregular movements were a combination of several regular circular motions seen in perspective from a stationary Earth. The principles of this model were known to earlier Greek scientists, including the mathematician Hipparchus (c. 150 BCE), but they culminated in an accurate predictive model with Ptolemy. The resulting Ptolemaic system persisted, with minor adjustments, until Earth was displaced from the centre of the universe in the 16th and 17th centuries by the Copernican system and by Kepler's laws of planetary motion.*

The first principle of the Ptolemaic model is eccentric motion. A body traveling at uniform speed on a circular path with Earth at its centre will sweep out equal angles in equal times from a terrestrial perspective. However, if the path's centre is displaced from Earth, the body will sweep out equal angles in unequal times (again, from a terrestrial perspective), moving slowest when farthest from Earth (apogee) and fastest when nearest Earth (perigee). With this simple eccentric model Ptolemy explained the Sun's varying motion through the zodiac. Another version of the model, suitable for the Moon, had the direction of the line from apogee to perigee gradually shift.

In order to explain the motion of the planets, Ptolemy combined eccentricity with an epicyclic model. In the Ptolemaic system each planet revolves uniformly along a circular path (epicycle), the centre of which revolves around Earth along a larger circular path (deferent). Because one half of an epicycle runs counter to the general motion of the deferent path, the combined motion will sometimes appear to slow down or even reverse direction (retrograde). By carefully coordinating these two cycles, the epicyclic model explained the observed phenomenon of planets retrograding when at perigee. Ptolemy enhanced the effect of eccentricity by making the epicycle's centre sweep out equal angles along the deferent in equal times as seen from a point that he called the equant. The centre of the deferent was located midway between the equant and Earth.

Although the Ptolemaic system successfully accounted for planetary motion, Ptolemy's equant point was controversial. Some Islamic astronomers objected to such an imaginary point, and later Nicolaus Copernicus (1473–1543) objected for philosophical reasons to the notion that an elementary rotation in the heavens could have a varying speed—and added further circles to the models to achieve the same effect. Nevertheless, the equant would eventually lead Johannes Kepler (1571–1630) to the correct elliptical model as expressed by his laws of planetary motion.

Ptolemy believed that the heavenly bodies' circular motions were caused by their being attached to unseen revolving solid spheres. For example, an epicycle would be the "equator" of a spinning sphere lodged in the space between two spherical shells surrounding Earth. He discovered that if he represented the motions of the Sun, the Moon, and the five known planets with spheres, he could nest them inside one another with no empty space left over and in such a manner that the solar and lunar distances agreed with his calculations. (His estimate of the Moon's distance was roughly correct, but his figure for the solar distance was only about a twentieth of the correct value.) The largest sphere, known as the celestial sphere, contained the stars and, at a distance of 20,000 times Earth's radius, formed the limit of Ptolemy's universe.

Through Islamic astronomers, Ptolemy's nested spheres became a standard feature of medieval cosmology. When Copernicus proposed a heliocentric model—with Earth and planets all orbiting the Sun—he was compelled to abandon the notion that there is no empty space between the spheres. After Tycho Brahe (1546–1601) demonstrated that the comet of 1577 would have had to pass through several of these invisible spheres, the hypothesis of solid spheres also became untenable.

Unfortunately, except for the conception that Earth is a sphere (inferred from Earth's shadow on the Moon always being circular during a lunar eclipse), these ideas failed to gain general acceptance. The precise reasons remain unclear, but the growing separation between the empirical and aesthetic branches of learning must have played a major role. The unparalleled numerical accuracy achieved by the theory of epicyclic motions for planetary movement lent great empirical validity to the Ptolemaic system. Henceforth, such computational matters could be left to practical astronomers without the necessity of having to ascertain the physical reality of the model. Instead, absolute truth was to be sought through the Platonic ideal of pure thought. Even the Pythagoreans fell into this trap. The depths to which they eventually sank may be judged from the story that they discovered and then tried to conceal the fact that the square root of 2 is an irrational number (i.e., cannot be expressed as a ratio of two integers).

THE SYSTEM OF ARISTOTLE AND ITS IMPACT ON MEDIEVAL THOUGHT

The systematic application of pure reason to the explanation of natural phenomena reached its extreme development with Aristotle (384-322 BCE), whose great system of the world later came to be regarded as the synthesis of all worthwhile knowledge. Aristotle argued that humans could not inhabit a moving and rotating Earth without violating common sense perceptions. Moreover, in his theory of impetus, all terrestrial motion—presumably including that of Earth itself—would grind to a halt without the continued application of force. He took for granted the action of friction because he would not allow the seminal idealization of a body moving through a void ("nature abhors a vacuum"). Thus, Aristotle was misled into equating force with velocity rather than, as Sir Isaac Newton was to show much later, with (mass times) acceleration. Celestial objects were exempt from dynamical decay because they moved in a higher stratum whereby a perfect sphere was the natural shape of heavenly bodies and uniform rotation in circles was the natural state of their motion. Indeed, primary motion was derived from the outermost sphere, the seat of the unchangeable stars and of divine power. No further explanation was needed beyond the aesthetic one. In this scheme, the imperfect motion of comets had to be postulated as meteorological phenomena that took place within the imperfect atmosphere of Earth.

The great merit of Aristotle's system was its internal logic, a grand attempt to unify all branches of human knowledge within the scope of a single self-consistent and comprehensive theory. Its great weakness was that its rigid arguments rested almost entirely on aesthetic grounds. It lacked a mechanism by which empirical knowledge gained from experimentation or observation could be used to test, modify, or reject the fundamental principles underlying the theory. Aristotle's system had the fundamental philosophical drive of modern science without its flexible procedure of self-correction that allows the truth to be approached in a series of successive approximations.

With the fall of the Roman Empire in 476 CE, much of what was known to the Greeks was lost or forgotten—at least to Western civilizations. (Hindu astronomers still taught that Earth was a sphere and that it rotated once daily.) The Aristotelian system, however, resonated with the teachings of the Roman Catholic Church during the Middle Ages, especially in the writings of St. Thomas Aquinas in the 13th century. Later, during the period of the Counter-Reformation in the 16th and early 17th century, it ascended to the status of religious dogma. Thus the notion of an Earth-centred universe become gradually enmeshed in the politics of religion. Also welcome in an age that insisted on a literal interpretation of the Scriptures was Aristotle's view that the living species of Earth were fixed for all time. What was not accepted was Aristotle's argument on logical grounds that the world was eternal, extending infinitely into the past and the future even though it had finite spatial extent. For the church, there was definitely a creation event, and infinity was reserved for God, not space or time.

CHAPTER 2

THE COPERNICAN REVOLUTION

The Renaissance brought a fresh spirit of inquiry to the arts and sciences. Explorers and travelers brought home the vestiges of classical knowledge that had been preserved in the Muslim world and the East, and in the 15th century Aristarchus's heliocentric hypothesis again came to be debated in certain educated circles. The boldest step was taken by the Polish astronomer Nicolaus Copernicus, who hesitated for so long in publication that he did not see a printed copy of his own work until he lay on his deathbed in 1543. Copernicus recognized more profoundly than anyone else the advantages of a Sun-centred planetary system. By adopting the view that Earth circled the Sun, he could qualitatively explain the to-and-fro wanderings of the planets much more simply than Ptolemy. For example, at certain times in the motions of Earth and Mars around the Sun, Earth would catch up with Mars's projected motion, and then that planet would appear to go backward through the zodiac. Unfortunately in his Sun-centred system, Copernicus continued to adhere to the established tradition of using uniform circular motion, and if he adopted only one large circle for the orbit of each planet, his calculated planetary positions would in fact be quantitatively poorer in comparison with the observed positions of the planets than tables based on the Ptolemaic system. This defect could be partially corrected by providing additional smaller circles, but then much of the beauty and simplicity of Copernicus' original system would be lost. Moreover, though the Sun was now removed from the list of planets and Earth added, the Moon still needed to move around Earth.

GALILEO

The Italian natural philosopher, astronomer, and mathematician Galileo Galilei's discoveries with the telescope revolutionized astronomy and paved the way for the acceptance of the Copernican heliocentric system, but his advocacy of that system eventually resulted in an Inquisition process against him. His formulation of (circular) inertia, the law of falling bodies, and parabolic trajectories marked the beginning of a fundamental change in the study of motion. His insistence that the book of nature was written in the language of mathematics changed natural philosophy from a verbal, qualitative account to a mathematical one in which experimentation became a recognized method for discovering the facts of nature.

Galileo was born in Pisa, Tuscany, on Feb. 15, 1564, the oldest son of Vincenzo Galilei, a musician who made important contributions to the theory and practice of music. He may have also performed some experiments with Galileo in 1588–89 on the relationship between pitch and the tension of strings. In the early 1570s the family moved to Florence, where the Galilei family had lived for generations. In his middle teens Galileo attended the monastery school at Vallombrosa, near Florence, and then in 1581 matriculated at the University of Pisa, where he was to study medicine. However, he became enamoured with mathematics and decided to make the mathematical subjects and philosophy his profession, against the protests of his father. Galileo then began to prepare himself to teach Aristotelian philosophy and mathematics, and several of his lectures have survived. In 1585 Galileo left the university without having obtained a degree, and for several years he gave private lessons in the mathematical subjects in Florence and Siena. During this period he designed a new form of hydrostatic balance for weighing small quantities and wrote a short treatise, *La bilancetta* ("The Little Balance"), which circulated in manuscript form. He also began his studies on motion, which he pursued steadily for the next two decades.

In 1588 Galileo applied for the chair of mathematics at the University of Bologna but was unsuccessful. His reputation was, however, increasing, and later that year he was asked to deliver two lectures to the Florentine Academy, a prestigious literary group, on the arrangement of the world in Dante's *Inferno*. He also found some ingenious theorems on centres of gravity (again, circulated in manuscript) that brought him recognition among mathematicians and the patronage of Guidobaldo del Monte (1545–1607), a nobleman and author of several important works on mechanics. As a result, he obtained the chair of mathematics at the University of Pisa in 1589. There, according to his first biographer, Vincenzo Viviani (1622–1703), Galileo demonstrated, by dropping bodies of different weights from the top of the famous Leaning Tower, that the speed of fall of a heavy object is not proportional to its weight, as Aristotle had claimed. The manuscript tract *De motu* (*On Motion*), finished during this period, shows that Galileo was abandoning Aristotelian notions about motion and was instead taking an Archimedean approach to the problem. But his attacks on Aristotle made him unpopular with his colleagues, and in 1592 his contract was not renewed. His patrons, however, secured him the chair of mathematics at the University of Padua, where he taught from 1592 until 1610.

Although Galileo's salary was considerably higher there, his responsibilities as the head of the family (his father had died in 1591) meant that he was chronically pressed for money. His university salary could not cover all his expenses, and he therefore took in well-to-do boarding students whom he tutored privately in such subjects as fortification. He also sold a proportional compass, or sector, of his own devising, made by an artisan whom he employed in his house. Perhaps because of these financial problems, he did not marry, but he did have an arrangement with a Venetian woman, Marina Gamba, who bore him two daughters and a son. In the midst of his busy life, Galileo continued his research on motion, and by

1609, he had determined that the distance fallen by a body is proportional to the square of the elapsed time (the law of falling bodies) and that the trajectory of a projectile is a parabola, both conclusions that contradicted Aristotelian physics.

At this point, however, Galileo's career took a dramatic turn. In the spring of 1609 he heard that in the Netherlands an instrument had been invented that showed distant things as though they were nearby. By trial and error, he quickly figured out the secret of the invention and made his own three-powered spyglass from lenses for sale in spectacle makers' shops. Others had done the same. What set Galileo apart was that he quickly figured out how to improve the instrument, taught himself the art of lens grinding, and produced increasingly powerful telescopes. In August of that year he presented an eight-powered instrument to the Venetian Senate (Padua was in the Venetian Republic). He was rewarded with life tenure and a doubling of his salary.

Galileo was now one of the highest-paid professors at the university. In the fall of 1609 he began observing the heavens with instruments that magnified up to 20 times. In December he drew the Moon's phases as seen through the telescope, showing that the Moon's surface is not smooth, as had been thought, but is rough and uneven. In January 1610 he discovered four moons revolving around Jupiter. He also found that the telescope showed many more stars than are visible with the naked eye. These discoveries

The Italian natural philosopher, astronomer, and mathematician Galileo made fundamental contributions to the sciences of motion, astronomy, and strength of materials, as well as development of the scientific method. Hulton Archive/Getty Images

were earthshaking, and Galileo quickly produced a little book, *Sidereus Nuncius* (*The Sidereal Messenger*), in which he described them. He dedicated the book to Cosimo II de Medici (1590–1621), the grand duke of his native Tuscany, whom he had tutored in mathematics for several summers, and he named the moons of Jupiter after the Medici family—the Sidera Medicea, or "Medicean Stars." Galileo was rewarded with an appointment as mathematician and philosopher of the grand duke of Tuscany, and in the fall of 1610 he returned in triumph to his native land.

Galileo was now a courtier and lived the life of a gentleman. Before he left Padua he had discovered the puzzling appearance of Saturn, later to be shown as caused by a ring surrounding it. In Florence he discovered that Venus goes through phases just as the Moon does. Although these discoveries did not prove that Earth is a planet orbiting the Sun, they undermined Aristotelian cosmology: the absolute difference between the corrupt earthly region and the perfect and unchanging heavens was proved wrong by the mountainous surface of the Moon, the moons of Jupiter showed that there had to be more than one centre of motion in the universe, and the phases of Venus showed that it (and, by implication, Mercury) revolves around the Sun. As a result, Galileo was confirmed in his belief, which he had probably held for decades but which had not been central to his studies, that the Sun is the centre of the universe and that Earth is a planet, as

Copernicus had argued. Galileo's conversion to Copernicanism would be a key turning point in the scientific revolution.

Galileo published a book on the subject of floating bodies in 1612, which led to several printed attacks on his theories. After this brief controversy Galileo again turned his attention to the heavens and entered a debate with Christoph Scheiner (1573–1650), a German Jesuit and professor of mathematics at Ingolstadt, about the nature of sunspots (of which Galileo was an independent discoverer). This controversy resulted in Galileo's *Istoria e dimostrazioni intorno alle macchie solari e loro accidenti* ("History and Demonstrations Concerning Sunspots and Their Properties," or "Letters on Sunspots"), which appeared in 1613. Against Scheiner, who, in an effort to save the perfection of the Sun, argued that sunspots are satellites of the Sun, Galileo argued that the spots are on or near the Sun's surface, and he bolstered his argument with a series of detailed engravings of his observations.

Galileo's increasingly overt Copernicanism began to cause trouble for him. In 1613 he wrote a letter to his student Benedetto Castelli (c. 1577–1643) in Pisa about the problem of squaring the Copernican theory with certain biblical passages. Inaccurate copies of this letter were sent by Galileo's enemies to the Inquisition in Rome, and he had to retrieve the letter and send an accurate copy. Several Dominican fathers in Florence lodged complaints against

Galileo in Rome, and Galileo went to Rome to defend the Copernican cause and his good name. Before leaving, he finished an expanded version of the letter to Castelli, now addressed to the grand duke's mother and good friend of Galileo, the dowager Christina. In his *Letter to the Grand Duchess Christina*, Galileo discussed the problem of interpreting biblical passages with regard to scientific discoveries but, except for one example, did not actually interpret the Bible. That task had been reserved for approved theologians in the wake of the Council of Trent (1545–63) and the beginning of the Catholic Counter-Reformation.

But the tide in Rome was turning against the Copernican theory. In 1615, when the cleric Paolo Antonio Foscarini (*c.* 1565–1616) published a book arguing that the Copernican theory did not conflict with scripture, Inquisition consultants examined the question and pronounced the Copernican theory heretical. Foscarini's book was banned, as were some more technical and nontheological works, such as Johannes Kepler's *Epitome of Copernican Astronomy*. Copernicus's own 1543 book, *De revolutionibus orbium coelestium libri vi* ("Six Books Concerning the Revolutions of the Heavenly Orbs"), was suspended until corrected. Galileo was not mentioned directly in the decree, but he was admonished by Robert Cardinal Bellarmine (1542–1621) not to "hold or defend" the Copernican theory. An improperly prepared document placed in the Inquisition files at this time states that Galileo was admonished "not to hold, teach, or defend" the Copernican theory "in any way whatever, either orally or in writing."

Galileo was thus effectively muzzled on the Copernican issue. Only slowly did he recover from this setback. Through a student, he entered a controversy about the nature of comets occasioned by the appearance of three comets in 1618. After several exchanges, mainly with Orazio Grassi (1583–1654), a professor of mathematics at the Collegio Romano, he finally entered the argument under his own name. *Il saggiatore* (*The Assayer*), published in 1623, was a brilliant polemic on physical reality and an exposition of the new scientific method. Galileo here discussed the method of the newly emerging science, arguing:

> *Philosophy is written in this grand book, the universe, which stands continually open to our gaze. But the book cannot be understood unless one first learns to comprehend the language and read the letters in which it is composed. It is written in the language of mathematics, and its characters are triangles, circles, and other geometric figures without which it is humanly impossible to understand a single word of it.*

He also drew a distinction between the properties of external objects and the sensations they cause in us—for example, the distinction between primary and secondary qualities. Publication of *Il saggiatore* came at an auspicious moment, for Maffeo Cardinal Barberini (1568–1644), a friend, admirer, and patron of Galileo for a decade, was named Pope Urban VIII as the book was going to press. Galileo's friends quickly arranged to have it dedicated to the new pope. In 1624 Galileo went to Rome and had six interviews with Urban VIII. Galileo told the pope about his theory of the tides (developed earlier), which he put forward as proof of the annual and diurnal motions of Earth. The pope gave Galileo permission to write a book about theories of the universe but warned him to treat the Copernican theory only hypothetically. The book, *Dialogo sopra i due massimi sistemi del mondo, tolemaico e copernicano* (*Dialogue Concerning the Two Chief World Systems, Ptolemaic & Copernican*), was finished in 1630, and Galileo sent it to the Roman censor. Because of an outbreak of the plague, communications between Florence and Rome were interrupted, and Galileo asked for the censoring to be done instead in Florence. The Roman censor had a number of serious criticisms of the book and forwarded these to his colleagues in Florence. After writing a preface in which he professed that what followed was written hypothetically, Galileo had little trouble getting the book through the Florentine censors, and it appeared in Florence in 1632.

In the *Dialogue*'s witty conversation between Salviati (representing Galileo), Sagredo (the intelligent layman), and Simplicio (the dyed-in-the-wool Aristotelian), Galileo gathered together all the arguments (mostly based on his own telescopic discoveries) for the Copernican theory and against the traditional geocentric cosmology. As opposed to Aristotle's, Galileo's approach to cosmology is fundamentally spatial and geometric. Earth's axis retains its orientation in space as Earth circles the Sun, and bodies not under a force retain their velocity—although this inertia is ultimately circular. But in giving Simplicio the final word, that God could have made the universe any way he wanted to and still made it appear to us the way it does, he put Pope Urban VIII's favourite argument in the mouth of the person who had been ridiculed throughout the dialogue.

Reaction against the book was swift. The pope convened a special commission to examine the book and make recommendations. The commission found that Galileo had not really treated the Copernican theory hypothetically and recommended that a case be brought against him by the Inquisition. Galileo was summoned to Rome in 1633. During his first appearance before the Inquisition, he was confronted with the 1616 edict recording that he was forbidden to discuss the Copernican theory. In his defense Galileo produced a letter from Cardinal Bellarmine, by then dead, stating that he was admonished only not to hold or defend the theory. The case was at somewhat of an impasse, and, in what can only be called a plea bargain,

Galileo confessed to having overstated his case. He was pronounced to be vehemently suspect of heresy and was condemned to life imprisonment and was made to abjure formally. There is no evidence that at this time he whispered, "Eppur si muove" ("And yet it moves").

It should be noted that Galileo was never in a dungeon or tortured. During the Inquisition process, he stayed mostly at the house of the Tuscan ambassador to the Vatican and for a short time in a comfortable apartment in the Inquisition building. After the process he spent six months at the palace of Ascanio Piccolomini (c. 1590–1671), the archbishop of Siena and a friend and patron, and then moved into a villa near Arcetri, in the hills above Florence. He spent the rest of his life there. Galileo's daughter Sister Maria Celeste, who was in a nearby nunnery, was a great comfort to her father until her untimely death in 1634.

Galileo was then 70 years old. Yet he kept working. In Siena he had begun a new book on the sciences of motion and strength of materials. There he wrote up his unpublished studies that had been interrupted by his interest in the telescope in 1609 and pursued intermittently since. The book was spirited out of Italy and published in Leiden, Netherlands, in 1638 under the title *Discorsi e dimostrazioni matematiche*

THE HELIOCENTRIC SYSTEM

In the heliocentric system the Sun is assumed to lie at or near a central point (e.g., of the solar system or of the universe) while Earth and other bodies revolve around it. In the 5th century BCE the Greek philosophers Philolaus and Hicetas speculated separately that Earth was a sphere revolving daily around some mystical "central fire" that regulated the universe. Two centuries later, Aristarchus of Samos extended this idea by proposing that Earth and other planets moved around a definite central object, which he believed to be the Sun.

The heliocentric, or Sun-centred, model of the solar system never gained wide support because its proponents could not explain why the relative positions of the stars seemed to remain the same despite Earth's changing viewpoints as it moved around the Sun. In the 2nd century CE, Claudius Ptolemy of Alexandria suggested that this discrepancy could be resolved if it were assumed that Earth was fixed in position, with the Sun and other bodies revolving around it. As a result, Ptolemy's geocentric (Earth-centred) system dominated scientific thought for some 1,400 years.

In 1444, Nicholas of Cusa again argued for the rotation of Earth and of other heavenly bodies, but it was not until the publication of Nicolaus Copernicus's De revolutionibus orbium coelestium libri VI *("Six Books Concerning the Revolutions of the Heavenly Orbs") in 1543 that the heliocentric system began to be reestablished. It was Galileo's support of this model that resulted in his trial before the Inquisition in 1633.*

intorno a due nuove scienze attenenti alla meccanica (*Dialogues Concerning Two New Sciences*). Galileo here treated for the first time the bending and breaking of beams and summarized his mathematical and experimental investigations of motion, including the law of falling bodies and the parabolic path of projectiles as a result of the mixing of two motions, constant speed and uniform acceleration. By then Galileo had become blind, and he spent his time working with a young student, Vincenzo Viviani, who was with him when he died on Jan. 8, 1642.

THE INFINITE UNIVERSE

In February 1584, years before Galileo's discoveries, the Italian philosopher Giordano Bruno was invited by Fulke Greville, a member of Sir Philip Sidney's circle, to discuss his theory of the movement of Earth with some Oxford doctors—but the discussion degenerated into a quarrel. A few days later he started writing his Italian dialogues, which constitute the first systematic exposition of his philosophy. There are six dialogues, three cosmological—on the theory of the universe—and three moral. In the *Cena de le Ceneri* (1584; "The Ash Wednesday Supper"), he not only reaffirmed the reality of the heliocentric theory but also suggested that the universe is infinite, constituted of innumerable worlds substantially similar to those of the solar system. In the same dialogue he anticipated Galileo by maintaining that the Bible should be followed for its moral teaching but not for its astronomical implications. In the *De la causa, principio e uno* (1584; *Concerning the Cause, Principle, and One*) he elaborated the physical theory on which his conception of the universe was based: "form" and "matter" are intimately united and constitute the "one." Thus, the traditional dualism of the Aristotelian physics was reduced by him to a monistic conception of the world, implying the basic unity of all substances and the coincidence of opposites in the infinite unity of Being. In the *De l'infinito universo e mondi* (1584; *On the Infinite Universe and Worlds*), he developed his cosmological theory by systematically criticizing Aristotelian physics.

KEPLER'S LAWS OF PLANETARY MOTION

It was the German astronomer Johannes Kepler, a contemporary of Galileo, who would provide the crucial blow that assured the success of the Copernican revolution. Of all the planets whose orbits Copernicus had tried to explain with a single circle, Mars had the largest departure (the largest eccentricity, in astronomical nomenclature). Consequently, Kepler arranged to work with the foremost observational astronomer of his day, Tycho Brahe of Denmark, who had accumulated over many years the most precise positional measurements of this planet. When Kepler finally gained access to the data, upon Tycho's death, he painstakingly tried to fit the observations to one curve after another. The work was especially difficult because he had to assume an orbit for Earth before he could self-consistently subtract the effects of its motion. Finally, after many close calls and rejections, he hit upon a simple, elegant solution—an ellipse with the Sun at one focus. The other planets also fell into place. This triumph was followed by others, notable among which was Kepler's discovery of his so-called three laws of planetary motion. Kepler announced his first two laws in the year 1609 and a third law nearly a decade later, in 1618. Kepler himself never numbered these laws or specially distinguished them from his other discoveries. The empirical victory secure, the stage was set for Newton's matchless theoretical campaigns.

Kepler's three laws of planetary motion can be stated as follows: (1) All planets move about the Sun in elliptical orbits, having the Sun as one of the foci. (2) A radius vector joining any planet to the Sun sweeps out equal areas in equal lengths of time (the "area law"). (3) The squares of the sidereal periods (of revolution) of the planets are directly proportional to the cubes of their mean distances from the Sun (the "harmonic law"). Knowledge of these laws, especially the second, proved crucial to Isaac Newton in 1684–85, when he formulated his famous law of gravitation between Earth and the Moon and between the Sun and the planets, postulated by him to have validity for all objects anywhere in the universe. Newton showed that the motion of bodies subject to central gravitational force need not always follow the elliptical orbits specified by the first law of Kepler but can take paths defined by other, open conic curves. The motion can be in parabolic or hyperbolic orbits, depending on the total energy of the body. Thus, an object of sufficient energy—e.g., a comet—can enter the solar system and leave again without returning. From Kepler's second law, it may be observed further that the angular momentum of any planet about an axis through the Sun and perpendicular to the orbital plane is also unchanging.

The usefulness of Kepler's laws extends to the motions of natural and artificial satellites as well as to unpowered spacecraft in orbit in stellar systems or near planets. As formulated by Kepler, the laws do not, of course, take into account the gravitational interactions (as perturbing effects) of the various planets on each other. The general problem of accurately predicting the motions of more than two bodies under their mutual attractions is quite complicated. Analytical solutions of the three-body problem are unobtainable except for some special cases. It may be noted that Kepler's laws apply not only to gravitational but also to all other inverse-square-law forces and, if due allowance is made for relativistic and quantum effects, to the electromagnetic forces within the atom.

JOHANNES KEPLER

(b. Dec. 27, 1571, Weil der Stadt, Württemberg [Ger.]—d. Nov. 15, 1630, Regensburg)

Johannes Kepler's discovery of the three major laws of planetary motion turned Nicolaus Copernicus's Sun-centred system into a dynamic universe, with the Sun actively pushing the planets around in noncircular orbits.

Among Kepler's many other achievements, he provided a new and correct account of how vision occurs, and he developed a novel explanation for the behaviour of light in the newly invented telescope. Although Kepler's scientific work was centred first and foremost on astronomy, that subject was classified as part of a wider subject of investigation called "the science of the stars." The science of the stars was regarded as a mixed science consisting of a mathematical and a physical component and bearing a kinship to other like disciplines, such as music (the study of ratios of tones) and optics (the study of light).

Kepler came from a very modest family. He was one of the beneficiaries of a ducal scholarship that xmade possible his attendance at the University of Tübingen, where he began his studies in 1589. Kepler had planned to become a theologian.

At Tübingen, the professor of mathematics was Michael Maestlin. Maestlin was, privately, one of the few adherents of the Copernican theory. Maestlin lent Kepler his own heavily annotated copy of Copernicus's 1543 book, De revolutionibus orbium coelestium libri vi *("Six Books Concerning the Revolutions of the Heavenly Orbs"). Kepler sensed intuitively that Copernicus had hit upon an account of the universe that contained the mark of divine planning—literally a revelation.*

The ideas that Kepler would pursue for the rest of his life were already present in his first work, Mysterium cosmographicum *(1596; "Cosmographic Mystery"). In 1595, it struck him suddenly that the spacing among the planets might be explained by circumscribing and inscribing each orbit with one of the five regular polyhedrons. Since Kepler knew Euclid's proof that there can be five and only five such mathematical objects, he decided that such self-sufficiency must betoken a perfect idea. If the ratios of the mean orbital distances agreed with the ratios obtained from circumscribing and inscribing the polyhedrons, then, Kepler felt confidently, he would have discovered the architecture of the universe. Remarkably, Kepler did find agreement within 5 percent, with the exception of Jupiter, at which, he said, "no one will wonder, considering such a great distance."*

Kepler posited that a single force from the Sun accounts for the increasingly long periods of motion as the planetary distances increase. Kepler did not yet have an exact mathematical description for this relation, but he intuited a connection. A few years later he acquired William Gilbert's groundbreaking book De Magnete, Magneticisque Corporibus, et de Magno Magnete Tellure *(1600; "On the Magnet, Magnetic Bodies, and the Great Magnet, the Earth"), and he immediately adopted Gilbert's theory that Earth is a magnet. From this Kepler generalized to the view that the universe is a system of magnetic bodies in which the rotating Sun sweeps the planets around. The solar force, attenuating inversely with distance in the planes of the orbits, was the major physical principle that guided Kepler's struggle to construct a better orbital theory for Mars.*

But there was something more: the standard of empirical precision that Kepler held for himself was unprecedented for his time. The great Danish astronomer Tycho Brahe (1546–1601) had set himself the task of amassing a completely new set of planetary observations. In 1600 Tycho invited Kepler to join his court at Castle Benátky near Prague. When Tycho died suddenly in 1601, Kepler quickly succeeded him as imperial mathematician to Holy Roman emperor Rudolf II. The relatively great intellectual freedom possible at Rudolf's court was now augmented by Kepler's unexpected inheritance of a critical resource: Tycho's observations. Without data of such precision to back up his solar hypothesis, Kepler would have been unable to discover his "first law" (1609), that Mars moves in an elliptical orbit.

After Galileo built a telescope in 1609 and announced hitherto-unknown objects, Kepler responded with three important treatises. These works provided strong support for Galileo's discoveries, and Galileo, who had never been especially generous to Kepler, wrote to him, "I thank you because you were the first one, and practically the only one, to have complete faith in my assertions."

Finally, Kepler published the first textbook of Copernican astronomy, Epitome Astronomiae Copernicanae *(1618–21;* Epitome of Copernican Astronomy*). The title mimicked Maestlin's traditional-style textbook, but the content could not have been more different. The* Epitome *began with the elements of astronomy, but then gathered together all the arguments for Copernicus's theory and added to them Kepler's harmonics and new rules of planetary motion. This work would prove to be the most important theoretical resource for the Copernicans in the 17th century.*

The last decade of Kepler's life was filled with personal anguish. In October 1630 Kepler left for Regensburg in hopes of collecting interest on some Austrian bonds. But soon after arriving, he became seriously ill with fever, and on November 15, he died. His grave was swept away in the Thirty Years' War.

TYCHONIC SYSTEM

The Tychonic system was a scheme for the structure of the solar system put forward in 1583 by the Danish astronomer Tycho Brahe. He retained from the ancient Ptolemaic system the idea of Earth as a fixed centre of the universe around which the Sun and Moon revolved, but he held that, as in the newer system of Copernicus, all other planets revolved around the Sun. In both the Tychonic and the Ptolemaic systems, an outer sphere containing the fixed stars was considered to revolve every day around Earth. The Tychonic theory

TYCHO BRAHE

(b. Dec. 14, 1546, Knudstrup, Scania, Den.—d. Oct. 24, 1601, Prague)

Tycho Brahe was a Danish astronomer whose work in developing astronomical instruments and in measuring and fixing the positions of stars paved the way for future discoveries.

Tycho's father was a privy councillor and later governor of the castle of Helsingborg. His wealthy and childless uncle, Jørgen, abducted Tycho at a very early age and, after the initial shock was overcome, raised him at his castle in Tostrup, Scania. The uncle financed the youth's education, which began with the study of law at the University of Copenhagen in 1559–62.

Several important natural events turned Tycho from law to astronomy. The first was the total eclipse of the Sun predicted for Aug. 21, 1560. Such a prediction seemed audacious and marvelous to a 14-year-old student, but when Tycho witnessed its realization, he never forgot the event. His subsequent student life was divided between his daytime lectures on jurisprudence, in response to the wishes of his uncle, and his nighttime vigil of the stars.

In 1562 Tycho's uncle sent him to the University of Leipzig, where he studied until 1565. Another significant event in Tycho's life occurred in August 1563, when he made his first recorded observation, a conjunction, or overlapping, of Jupiter and Saturn. Almost immediately he found that the existing almanacs and ephemerides, which record stellar and planetary positions, were several days off in predicting this event. In his youthful enthusiasm Tycho decided to devote his life to accurate observations of the heavens.

Between 1565 and 1570 (some sources list the date as 1572) he traveled widely throughout Europe, acquiring mathematical and astronomical instruments. After inheriting the estates of his father and of his uncle Jørgen, Tycho settled in Scania in around 1571 and constructed a small observatory. Here occurred the third and most important astronomical event in Tycho's life. On Nov. 11, 1572, he suddenly saw a "new star," brighter than Venus and where no star was supposed to be, in the constellation Cassiopeia. He carefully observed the new star and showed that it lay beyond the Moon and therefore was in the realm of the fixed stars. To the world at the time, this was a disquieting discovery, because the intellectual community protected itself against the uncertainties of the future by confidence in the Aristotelian doctrine of inner and continuous harmony of the whole world. This harmony was ruled by the stars, which were regarded as perfect and unchanging. The news that a star could change dramatically, together with the reports of the Copernican theory that the Sun, not Earth, was the centre of the universe, shook confidence in the immutable laws of antiquity and suggested that the chaos and imperfections of Earth were reflected in the heavens. Tycho's discovery of the new star in Cassiopeia in 1572 marked his transformation from a Danish dilettante to an astronomer with a European reputation.

The new star had caused Tycho to rededicate himself to astronomy. One immediate decision was to establish a large observatory for regular observations of celestial events. His plan to establish this observatory in Germany prompted King Frederick II to keep him in Denmark by granting him title in 1576 to the island of Ven, together with financial support for the observatory and laboratory buildings. Tycho called the observatory Uraniborg, after Urania, the Muse of astronomy.

Uraniborg fulfilled the hopes of Tycho's king and friend, Frederick II, that it would become the centre of astronomical study and discovery in northern Europe. But Frederick died in 1588, and under the rule of his son, Christian IV, Tycho's influence dwindled. Most of his income was stopped. Spoiled by Frederick, Tycho had become both unreasonably demanding of more money and less inclined to carry out the civic duties required by his income from state lands.

At odds with the three great powers—king, church, and nobility—Tycho left Ven in 1597, and he settled in Prague in 1599 under the patronage of Emperor Rudolf II, who also later supported the astronomer Johannes Kepler.

The major portion of Tycho's lifework—making and recording accurate astronomical observations—had already been done at Uraniborg. To his earlier observations, he added a comprehensive study of the solar system and his proof that the orbit of the comet of 1577 lay beyond the Moon. What Tycho accomplished, using only his simple instruments and practical talents, remains an outstanding accomplishment of the Renaissance.

A chance planetary observation in his university days sparked Tycho Brahe's interest in astronomy. He went on to record an invaluable comprehensive study of the solar system. Hulton Archive/Getty Images

Tycho attempted to continue his observations at Prague with the few instruments he had salvaged from Uraniborg, but the spirit was not there, and he died in 1601, leaving all his observational data to Kepler, his pupil and assistant. With these data Kepler laid the groundwork for the work of Sir Isaac Newton.

explained the observed variations of phase of Venus, for which the Ptolemaic system had no explanation.

A system somewhat similar to Tycho's had been proposed in the 4th century BCE by the Greek philosopher Heracleides Ponticus, who thought that at least Mercury and Venus (it is uncertain if Heracleides included other planets) went around the Sun.

CHAPTER 3

Newton's Impact and 19th-Century Advancements

Two towering achievements paved the way for Sir Isaac Newton's conquest of the dynamical problem of planetary motions: his discoveries of the second law of mechanics and of the law of gravitation. The second law of mechanics (that the change of velocity of a body times its mass is proportional to the force impressed) asserted how any body moves when it is subjected to external forces. The law of gravitation asserted that two massive bodies attract one another with a force directly proportional to the product of their masses and inversely proportional to the square of their distance. By pure mathematical deduction, Newton showed that when these two general laws were applied to the celestial realm, the result was Kepler's three laws of planetary motion. This brilliant coup completed the Copernican program to replace the old worldview with an alternative that was far superior, both in conceptual principle and in practical application. In the same stroke of genius, Newton unified the mechanics of heaven and Earth and initiated the era of modern science.

NEWTON'S LAW OF GRAVITATION

Newton's law of gravitation states that any particle of matter in the universe attracts any other with a force varying directly as the product of the masses and inversely as the square of the distance between them. In symbols, the magnitude of the attractive force F is equal to G (the gravitational constant, a number the size of which depends on the system of units used and which is a universal constant) multiplied by the product of the masses (m_1 and m_2) and divided by the square of the distance R: $F = G(m_1 m_2)/R^2$. Isaac Newton put forward the law in 1687 and used it to explain the observed motions of the planets and their moons, which had been reduced to mathematical form by Johannes Kepler early in the 17th century.

In formulating the law of gravitation and the second law of mechanics, Newton asserted as postulates the notions of absolute space (in the sense of Euclidean geometry) and absolute time (a mathematical quantity that flows in the universe without reference to anything else). A kind of relativity principle did exist ("Galilean relativity") in the freedom to choose different inertial frames of reference—i.e., the form of Newton's laws was unaffected by motion at constant velocity with respect to the "fixed stars." However, Newton's scheme unambiguously sundered space and time as fundamentally separate entities. This step was necessary for progress to be made. It was such a wonderfully accurate approximation to the truth for describing motions that are slow compared with the speed of light that Newton's scheme withstood all tests for more than two centuries.

CONTRIBUTIONS OF EDMOND HALLEY

It was the English astronomer Edmond Halley who used Newton's laws to predict that a certain comet last seen in 1682 would reappear 76 years later. When Halley's Comet returned on Christmas night in 1758, many years after the deaths of both Newton and Halley, no educated person could ever again seriously doubt the power of mechanistic explanations for natural phenomena. Nor would anyone worry again that the unruly excursions of comets through the solar system would smash the crystalline spheres that earlier thinkers had mentally constructed to carry planets

Scientist and astronomer Edmund Halley is the namesake of the famous comet whose return he predicted but didn't live to see. Hulton Archive/Getty Images

and the other celestial bodies through the heavens. The attention of professional astronomers now turned increasingly toward an understanding of the stars.

Halley was born on Nov. 8, 1656, at Haggerston, Shoreditch, near London, and he began his education at St. Paul's School, London. He had the good fortune to live through a period of scientific revolution that established the basis of modern thought. He was four years old when the monarchy was restored under Charles II. Two years later the new monarch granted a charter to the informal organization of natural philosophers originally called the "invisible college," which then became known officially as the Royal Society of London. Halley entered Queen's College, Oxford, in 1673 and there was introduced, by letter, to John Flamsteed, who was appointed astronomer royal in 1676. On one or two occasions Halley visited the Royal Greenwich Observatory, where Flamsteed did his work, and there was encouraged to study astronomy.

Influenced by Flamsteed's project of using the telescope to compile an accurate catalog of northern stars, Halley proposed to do the same for the Southern Hemisphere. With financial assistance from his father and an introduction to the East India Company from King Charles II, he sailed in November 1676 in a ship of that company (having left Oxford without his degree) for the island of St. Helena—the southernmost territory under British rule, in the South Atlantic. Bad weather frustrated his full expectations. But, when he embarked for home in January 1678, he had recorded the celestial longitudes and latitudes of 341 stars, observed a transit of Mercury across the Sun's disk, made numerous pendulum observations, and noticed that some stars apparently had become fainter since their observation in antiquity. Halley's star catalog, published late in 1678, was the first such work to be published containing telescopically determined locations of southern stars, and it established his reputation as an astronomer. In 1678 he was elected a fellow of the Royal Society and, with the intercession of the King, was granted the M.A. degree from Oxford University.

HALLEY AND NEWTON

In 1684 Halley made his first visit to Sir Isaac Newton in Cambridge, an event that led to his prominent role in the development of the theory of gravitation. Halley was the youngest of a trio of Royal Society members in London that included Robert Hooke, the inventor and microscopist, and Sir Christopher Wren, the famous architect, both of whom, with Newton at Cambridge, were attempting to find a mechanical explanation for planetary motion. Their problem was to determine what forces would keep a planet in forward motion around the Sun without either flying off into space or falling into the Sun. Since these men were dependent upon their scientific stature for both livelihood and sense of achievement, each had a personal interest in being the first to find a solution. This desire for priority, a propelling motive in science, was the cause of much lively discussion and competition among them.

Although Hooke and Halley had reasoned that the force keeping a planet in orbit must decrease as the inverse of the square of its distance from the Sun, they were not able to deduce from this hypothesis a theoretical orbit that would match the observed planetary motions—despite the incentive of a prize offered by Wren. Halley then visited Newton, who told him he had already solved the problem—the orbit would be an ellipse—but that he had mislaid his calculations to prove it. Encouraged by Halley, Newton then expanded his studies on celestial mechanics into one of the greatest masterpieces produced by the mind of man, the *Principia*. The Royal Society decided that "Mr. Halley undertake the business of looking after it, and printing it at his own charge," which he proceeded to do. He consulted with Newton, tactfully subdued a priority dispute between Newton and Hooke, edited

An engraving based on Godfrey Kneller's portrait of Sir Isaac Newton, c. 1702. Newton's theories started a new era in the astronomy. Hulton Archive/Getty Images

the text of the *Principia*, wrote laudatory verse in Latin for the preface to honour its author, corrected the proofs, and saw it through the press in 1687.

PRINCIPIA

About 1679, Newton began to ascribe puzzling phenomena—chemical affinities, the generation of heat in chemical reactions, surface tension in fluids, capillary action, the cohesion of bodies, and the like—to attractions and repulsions between particles of matter. But late in 1679, not long after he had embraced the concept, another application of the idea of attractions and repulsions was suggested in a letter from Hooke, who was seeking to renew correspondence. Hooke mentioned his analysis of planetary motion. Newton suggested an experiment to demonstrate the rotation of Earth: Let a body be dropped from a tower. Because the tangential velocity at the top of the tower is greater than that at the foot, the body should fall slightly to the east. He sketched the path of fall as part of a spiral ending at the centre of Earth. This was a mistake, as Hooke pointed out. According to Hooke's theory of planetary motion, the path should be elliptical, so that if Earth were split and separated to allow the body to fall, it would rise again to its original location. Newton did not like being corrected, least of all by Hooke, but he had to accept the basic point. He corrected Hooke's figure, however, using the assumption that gravity is constant. Hooke then countered by replying that, although Newton's figure was correct for constant gravity, his own assumption was that gravity decreases as the square of the distance. Several years later, this letter became the basis for Hooke's charge of plagiarism. He was mistaken in the charge. His knowledge of the inverse square relation rested only on intuitive grounds. He did not derive it properly from the quantitative statement of centripetal force and Kepler's third law, which relates the periods of planets to the radii of their orbits. Moreover, unknown to him, Newton had so derived the relation more than ten years earlier.

Nearly five years later, in August 1684, Newton was visited by Edmond Halley, who was also troubled by the problem of orbital dynamics. Upon learning that Newton had solved the problem, Halley extracted Newton's promise to send the demonstration. Three months later he received a short tract entitled De Motu *("On Motion"). Already Newton was at work improving and expanding it. In two and a half years, the tract* De Motu *grew into* Philosophiae Naturalis Principia Mathematica, *which is not only Newton's masterpiece but also the fundamental work for the whole of modern science.*

The mechanics of the Principia *was an exact quantitative description of the motions of visible bodies. It rested on Newton's three laws of motion: (1) that a body remains in its state of rest unless it is compelled to change that state by a force impressed on it, (2) that the change of motion (the change of velocity times the mass of the body) is proportional to the force impressed, and (3) that to every action there is an equal and opposite reaction. The analysis of circular motion in terms of these laws yielded a formula of the quantitative measure, in terms of a body's velocity and mass, of the centripetal force necessary to divert a body from its rectilinear path into a given circle. When Newton substituted this formula into Kepler's third law, he found that the centripetal force holding the planets in their given orbits about the Sun must decrease with the square of the planets' distances from the Sun. Because the satellites of Jupiter also obey Kepler's third law, an inverse square centripetal force must also attract them to the centre of their orbits. Newton was able to show that a similar relation holds between Earth and its Moon. Newton concluded that one and the same force, governed by a single quantitative law, is operative in all three cases. From the correlation of the Moon's orbit with the measured acceleration of gravity on the surface of Earth, he applied the ancient Latin word* gravitas *(literally, "heaviness" or "weight") to it. The law of universal gravitation, which he also confirmed from such further phenomena as the tides and the orbits of comets, states that every particle of matter in the universe attracts every other particle with a force that is proportional to the product of their masses and inversely proportional to the square of the distance between their centres.*

When the Royal Society received the completed manuscript of Book I in 1686, Hooke raised the cry of plagiarism, a charge that cannot be sustained in any meaningful sense. On the other hand, Newton's response to it reveals much about him. Hooke would have been satisfied with a generous acknowledgment. It would have been a graceful gesture to a sick man already well into his decline, and it would have cost Newton nothing. Newton, instead, went through his manuscript and eliminated nearly every reference to Hooke.

Tracking Comets and Stars

Continuing his pioneering work in observational astronomy, in 1705 Halley published *A Synopsis of the Astronomy of Comets,* in which he described the parabolic orbits of 24 comets that had been observed from 1337 to 1698. He showed that the three historic comets of 1531, 1607, and 1682 were so similar in characteristics that they must have been successive returns of the same visitant—now known as Halley's Comet—and accurately predicted its return in 1758.

In 1716 he devised a method for observing transits of Venus across the disk of the Sun—predicted for 1761 and 1769—in order to determine accurately, by solar parallax, the distance of Earth from the Sun. In 1718, by comparing recently observed star positions with data recorded in the ancient Greek astronomer Ptolemy's *Almagest,* he found that Sirius and Arcturus had slightly shifted their positions with respect to their neighbours. This was the discovery of what modern astronomers call proper motion. (Halley incorrectly announced proper motions for two other stars, Aldebaran and Betelgeuse, but for these was misled by errors in the ancient star positions.) In 1720 Halley succeeded Flamsteed as astronomer royal at Greenwich, where he made observations, such as timing the transits of the Moon across the meridian, which he hoped would eventually be useful in determining longitude at sea.

HALLEY'S COMET

Halley's Comet was the first comet whose return was predicted and, almost three centuries later, the first to be photographed up close by spacecraft. The comet was sighted late in 1758, passed perihelion (closest distance to the Sun) in March 1759, and was named in Halley's honour. Its periodic returns demonstrated that it was in orbit around the Sun and, thus, that at least some comets are members of the solar system.

Dozens of earlier passages of Halley's Comet were later calculated and checked against historical records of comet sightings. Its earliest recorded appearance, witnessed by Chinese astronomers, was in 240 BCE. Its closest approach to Earth took place in April 837. It was the large, bright comet seen during the Norman Conquest of England (1066) and shown in the Bayeux Tapestry of that time. Its passage in 1301 appears to have inspired the form of the Star of Bethlehem that the Italian painter Giotto used in his The Adoration of the Magi. *Its passages have taken place about 76 years apart on average, but the gravitational influence of the planets on the comet's orbit have caused the orbital period to vary by a year or two from one reappearance to the next. During the comet's return in 1910, Earth probably passed through part of its tail, which was millions of kilometres in length, with no apparent effect.*

As predicted, the comet passed Earth in November–December 1985, reached perihelion on Feb. 9, 1986, and came closest to Earth on April 11, 1986. Its passage was observed by two Japanese spacecraft (Sakigake and Suisei), two Soviet spacecraft (Vega 1 and Vega 2), and a European Space Agency spacecraft (Giotto). Close-up images of the comet's nucleus made by Giotto show an oblong object with dimensions of about 15 × 8 km (9 × 5 miles). As expected, the nucleus proved to be a mixture of frozen water, other volatile ices, and rocky (silicate) particles. This was covered with an irregular crust having several large vents from which jets of steam, other gases, and dust escaped. Surprisingly, the crust turned out to be very black, apparently from a surface coating of less-volatile carbon compounds. High heat absorption by the dark surface was thought to explain a temperature of 350 K (170 °F, 80 °C) measured for the comet when it was 0.9 AU (135 million km [84 million miles]) from the Sun. As the comet rotated on its axis, the rate of dust and gas emission were observed to increase on the sunward side and then to drop off quickly as that side turned toward the darkness. Dust particles shed during the comet's slow disintegration over the millennia are distributed along its orbit. The passage of Earth through this debris stream every year is responsible for the Orionid and Eta Aquarid meteor showers in October and May, respectively.

Halley's Comet is next expected to return to the inner solar system in 2061.

Halley's Comet, 1986. NASA/National Space Science Data Center

THE DISCOVERIES OF WILLIAM HERSCHEL

In the effort to understand the stars, the British astronomer William Herschel and his son John led the assault. The construction of ever more powerful reflecting telescopes allowed them during the late 1700s and early 1800s to measure the angular positions and apparent brightnesses of many faint stars.

William Herschel was born on Nov. 15, 1738, in Hannover. Herschel's father was an army musician. Following the same profession, the boy played in the band of the Hanoverian Guards. After the French occupation of Hanover in 1757, he escaped to England, where at first he earned a living by copying music. But he steadily improved his position by becoming a music teacher, performer, and composer. Then, in 1766, he was appointed organist of a fashionable chapel in Bath, the well-known spa.

By this time, the intellectual curiosity he had acquired from his father led him from the practice to the theory of music, which he studied in Robert Smith's *Harmonics*. From this book he turned to Smith's *A Compleat System of Opticks*, which introduced him to the techniques of telescope construction and whetted his appetite for viewing the night sky. Combining obstinacy with boundless energy, William was not content to observe the nearby Sun, Moon, and planets, as did nearly all astronomers of his day. He was determined to study the distant celestial bodies as well, and he realized he would need telescopes with large mirrors to collect enough light—larger, in fact, than opticians could supply at reasonable cost. He was soon forced to grind his own mirrors. They were ground from metal disks of copper, tin, and antimony in various proportions. In 1781 William's ambitions outran the capacities of the local foundries, and so he prepared to cast molten metal into disks in the basement of his own home. The first mirror cracked on cooling, and on the second attempt, the metal ran out onto the flagstones, after which even William accepted temporary defeat. His later and more successful attempts produced ever larger mirrors of superb quality—his telescopes proved far superior even to those used at the Greenwich Observatory. He also made his own eyepieces, the strongest with a magnifying power of 6,450 times.

At Bath, he was helped in his researches by his brother Alexander, who had come from Hanover, and his sister, Caroline, who was his faithful assistant through much of his career. News of this extraordinary household began to spread in scientific circles. He made two preliminary telescopic surveys of the heavens. Then, in 1781, during his third and most complete survey of the night sky, William came upon an object that he realized was not an ordinary star.

It proved to be the planet Uranus, the first planet to be discovered since prehistoric times. William became famous almost overnight. His friend Dr. William Watson, Jr., introduced him to the Royal

In an attempt to better observe individual stars in distant nebulae, William Herschel built a series of increasingly powerful telescopes, including a 40-foot (12.2-metre) behemoth that was a marvel of its age. MPI/ Hulton Archive/Getty Images

Society of London, which awarded him the Copley Medal for the discovery of Uranus, and elected him a Fellow. In 1782 Watson also helped him to secure an annual pension of £200 from George III. William could give up music and devote himself exclusively to astronomy. At this time he was appointed as an astronomer to George III, and the Herschels moved to Datchet, near Windsor Castle.

Although he was 43 years old when he became a professional astronomer, William worked night after night to develop a "natural history" of the heavens. A fundamental problem for which Herschel's big telescopes were ideally suited concerned the nature of nebulae, which appear as luminous patches in the sky. Some astronomers thought they were nothing more than clusters of innumerable stars the light of which blends to form a milky appearance. Others held that some nebulae were composed of a luminous fluid. When William's interest in nebulae developed in the winter of 1781–82, he quickly found that his most powerful telescope could resolve into stars several nebulae that appeared "milky" to less well- equipped observers. He was convinced that other nebulae would eventually be resolved into individual stars with more powerful instruments. This encouraged him to argue in 1784 and 1785 that all nebulae were formed of stars and that there was no need to postulate the existence of a mysterious luminous fluid to explain the observed facts. Nebulae that could not yet be resolved must be very

distant systems, he maintained. Since they seem large to the observer, their true size must indeed be vast—possibly larger even than the star system of which the Sun is a member. By this reasoning, William was led to postulate the existence of what later were called "island universes" of stars.

In order to interpret the differences between these star clusters, it was natural for William to emphasize their relative densities, which he did by contrasting a cluster of tightly packed stars with others in which the stars were widely scattered. These formations showed that attractive forces were at work. With the passage of time, he maintained, widely scattered stars would no doubt condense into one or more tightly packed clusters. In other words, a group of widely scattered stars was at an earlier stage of its development than one whose stars were tightly packed. Thus, William made change in time, or evolution, a fundamental explanatory concept in astronomy. In 1785 he developed a cosmogony—a theory concerning the origin of the universe: the stars originally were scattered throughout infinite space, in which attractive forces gradually organized them into even more fragmented and tightly packed clusters. Turning then to the system of stars of which the Sun is part, he sought to determine its shape on the basis of two assumptions: (1) that with his telescope he could see all the stars in our system, and (2) that within the system the stars are regularly spread out. Both of these assumptions he subsequently had to abandon. But in his studies he gave the first major example of the usefulness of stellar statistics in that he could count the stars and interpret this data in terms of the extent in space of the Galaxy's star system. Other astronomers, cut off from the evidence by the modest size of their telescopes and unwilling to follow William in his bold theorizing, could only look on with varying degrees of sympathy or skepticism.

In 1787 the Herschels moved to Old Windsor, and the following year to nearby Slough, where William spent the rest of his life. Night after night, whenever the Moon and weather permitted, he observed the sky in the company of Caroline, who recorded his observations. On overcast nights, William would post a watchman to summon him if the clouds should break. Often in the daytime, Caroline would summarize the results of their work while he directed the construction of telescopes, many of which he sold to supplement their income. His largest instrument, too cumbersome for regular use, had a mirror made of speculum metal, with a diameter of 122 centimetres (48 inches) and a focal length of 12 metres (40 feet). Completed in 1789, it became one of the technical wonders of the 18th century.

William's achievement, in a field in which he became a professional only in middle life, was made possible by his own total dedication and the selfless support of Caroline. He seems not to have considered the possibility of marriage until after the 1786 death of a friend and neighbour, John Pitt, whose widow, Mary, was a charming and pleasant woman. Before long, William proposed marriage. He and Mary would live in the Pitt house, while Caroline would remain at Observatory House in Slough. But Mrs. Pitt was shrewd enough to realize that William's commitment would be to Observatory House, which they made their principal home after their marriage on May 8, 1788. William continued his labour in astronomy, but as the rigours of observing took their toll on William's health, he came to appreciate more and more the comforts that Mary's sensible management brought to his home.

William's grand concept of stellar organization received a jolt on Nov. 13, 1790, when he observed a remarkable nebula, which he was forced to interpret as a central star surrounded by a cloud of "luminous fluid." This discovery contradicted his earlier views. Hitherto William had reasoned that many nebulae that he was unable to resolve (separate into distinct stars), even with his best telescopes, might be distant "island universes" (such objects are now known as galaxies). He was able, however, to adapt his earlier theory to this new evidence by concluding that the central star he had observed was condensing out of the surrounding cloud under the forces of gravity. In 1811, he extended his cosmogony backward in time to the stage

CAROLINE HERSCHEL

(b. March 16, 1750, Hannover, Hanover—d. Jan. 9, 1848, Hannover)

German-born British astronomer Caroline Lucretia Herschel was noted for her contributions to the astronomical researches of her brother, Sir William Herschel. She executed many of the calculations connected with his studies and, on her own, detected by telescope three nebulae in 1783 and eight comets from 1786 to 1797.

Caroline assisted her mother in the management of the household until 1772, when her brother, William, took her to Bath, Eng., where he had established himself as a teacher of music. Once settled in Bath, Caroline trained and performed successfully as a singer. Both she and William gave their last public musical performance in 1782, when her brother accepted the private office of court astronomer to George III. In addition to keeping house for her brother and grinding and polishing mirrors, she began executing the laborious calculations that were connected with his observations. As her interest grew, she swept the heavens with a small Newtonian reflector and made her own observations and astronomical discoveries. In 1787 the king gave her an annual pension of £50 in her capacity as her brother's assistant. In 1798 she presented to the Royal Society an Index to Flamsteed's observations, together with a catalog of 560 stars omitted from the British Catalogue and a list of the errata in that publication.

She returned to Hannover after William's death in 1822 and soon completed the cataloging of 2,500 nebulae and many star clusters. In 1828 (when she was 77) the Astronomical Society awarded Caroline its gold medal for an unpublished revision and reorganization of their work. She lived some 20 years longer and continued to receive the respect and admiration of both scientists and the general public.

when stars had not yet begun to form out of the fluid.

This example of William's theorizing is typical of his thinking: an unrivaled wealth of observations interpreted by means of bold though vulnerable assumptions. For example, in dealing with the structural organization of the heavens, he assumed that all stars were equally bright, so that differences in apparent brightness are an index only of differences in distances. Throughout his

career he stubbornly refused to acknowledge the accumulating evidence that contradicted this assumption. Herschel's labours through 20 years of systematic sweeps for nebulae (1783–1802) resulted in three catalogs listing 2,500 nebulae and star clusters that he substituted for the 100 or so milky patches previously known. He also cataloged 848 double stars—pairs of stars that appear close together in space, and measurements of the comparative brightness of stars.

He observed that double stars did not occur by chance as a result of random scattering of stars in space but that they actually revolved about each other. His 70 published papers include not only studies of the motion of the solar system through space and the 1800 announcement of the discovery of infrared rays, but also a succession of detailed investigations of the planets and other members of the solar system. William Herschel died on Aug. 25, 1822, in Slough, Buckinghamshire.

THE HERSCHEL LEGACY

In 1814 John Herschel began to study for the bar in London, but he was not happy with his choice and discontinued his studies in the summer of 1815 when he became seriously ill. After convalescence he returned to Cambridge as a mathematics teacher. He left Cambridge again in 1816 to assist his renowned father in astronomical research. Through his work with his father, he gained the full benefit of the aged astronomer's unrivaled experience in the construction and use of large telescopes. This apprenticeship laid the foundation of John's subsequent achievements. In 1820 he was among the founders of the Royal Astronomical Society. In later years, John made important contributions to chemistry and the physics of light and particularly to mathematics, for which he was awarded the Copley Medal of the Royal Society in 1821.

John Herschel's first major task in astronomy was the reobservation of the double stars cataloged by his father. The movements of these pairs of stars around each other offered the best hope of investigating the gravitational forces operating in the universe. John was fortunate to find in James South a collaborator who was able to afford the refined instruments best suited for this work. The catalog that they compiled between 1821 and 1823 and published in the *Philosophical Transactions* in 1824 earned them the Gold Medal of the Royal Astronomical Society and the Lalande Prize in 1825 from the Paris Academy of Sciences. This work was their only joint undertaking.

Herschel served as secretary of the Royal Society in 1824–27. He married in 1829, and in 1831 he was knighted.

John Herschel's sense of obligation to complete his father's work in astronomy led him to consider a journey to the Southern Hemisphere to survey the skies not visible in England. In 1832 he began planning his expedition. The revision and extension of his father's catalogs, which he carried out at Observatory House, beginning in 1825, was brought to completion and published in 1833. In November of that year, John and his family set sail for the Cape of Good Hope with a large reflecting telescope for observing faint nebulae, similar in size to William's favourite instrument. He also possessed a refracting telescope for observing double stars.

The family established their home at Feldhausen, a Dutch farmhouse southeast of Cape Town. John spent four years of intense scientific activity, the clear southern skies allowing much more rapid progress in observing than was possible in England. When the family embarked for home in March 1838, John had recorded the locations of 68,948 stars and had amassed long catalogs of nebulae and double stars. He had also described many details of the Great Nebula in the constellation Orion, as well as the Magellanic Clouds—actually two galaxies visible only in the Southern Hemisphere—and had observed Halley's Comet and the satellites of Saturn. In addition, his descriptions of sunspot activities and his measuring of solar radiation by means of a device he had invented contributed to the development of systematic studies of the Sun as an important part of astrophysics. Upon his return he was made a baronet (1838) and was lionized by the scientific world.

TAKING ASTRONOMY
TO A NEW LEVEL

Friedrich Wilhelm Bessell (1784–1846) was a German astronomer whose measurements of positions for about 50,000 stars and rigorous methods of observation (and correction of observations) took astronomy to a new level of precision. He was the first to accurately measure the parallax, and hence the distance, of a star other than the Sun.

The achievements of Bessel were possible only because he first established the real framework of the universe by making accurate measurements of the positions and motions of the nearest stars, making corrections for various measuring errors caused by imperfections in his telescopes and by disturbances in the atmosphere. He reduced, or systematized, the observations of the English astronomer James Bradley, correcting for the effects of instrumental errors in the mean positions of 3,222 stars and publishing the results in *Fundamenta Astronomiae* (1818). This work marked the beginning of modern astrometry (positional astronomy). The uniform system of reduction that Bessel established in *Tabulae Regiomontanae* (1830; "Königsberg Tables") long remained standard.

Having established exact positions for thousands of individual stars at his observatory in Königsberg, he was ready to observe exceedingly small but highly significant motions, relative to one another, among them. Choosing 61 Cygni, a star barely visible to the naked eye and known to possess a relatively high velocity in the plane of the sky, Bessel showed in 1838 that, after correcting for this, the star apparently moved in an ellipse every year. This back and forth motion, called the annual parallax, could only be interpreted as being caused by the motion of Earth around the Sun. Astronomers had known for centuries that such an effect must occur, but Bessel was the first to demonstrate it accurately.

(Russian astronomer Friedrich Struve had announced an inaccurate value of Vega's parallax in 1837.) Bessel's parallax of about one-third of a second of arc corresponds to a distance from Earth to 61 Cygni of about 10.3 light-years, though Bessel did not express it this way. (The nearest star known is Alpha Centauri, 4.3 light-years away.) Olbers, presented with these conclusions on his 80th birthday, thanked Bessel and said the gift "put our ideas about the universe for the first time on a sound basis." Bessel was honoured for this achievement by the Royal Astronomical Society of London and others.

Another major discovery by Bessel was that the two bright stars Sirius and Procyon execute minute motions that could be explained only by assuming that they had invisible companions disturbing their motions. The existence of such bodies, now named Sirius B and Procyon B, was confirmed with more powerful telescopes after Bessel's death. An important share in the discovery of the planet Neptune also belongs to Bessel. In a paper read in 1840, he called attention to exceedingly small irregularities in the orbit of Uranus, which he had observed and concluded were caused by an unknown planet beyond.

Bessel was a scientist whose works laid the foundations for a better determination than any previous method had allowed of the scale of the universe and

GEODESY

The scientific discipline concerned with the precise figure of Earth and its determination and significance is called geodesy. Until the advent of satellites, all geodesic work was based on land surveys made by triangulation methods employing a geodesic coordinate system (one used to study the geometry of curved surfaces). It is now possible to use satellites in conjunction with the land-based system to refine knowledge of Earth's shape and dimensions. This endeavour is sometimes termed satellite geodesy.

In geodesy, Friedrich Wilhelm Bessel's contributions include a correction in 1826 to the seconds pendulum, the length of which is precisely calculated so that it requires exactly one second for a swing. During 1831–32 he directed geodetical measurements of meridian arcs in East Prussia. In 1841 he deduced a value of $1/_{299}$ for the ellipticity of Earth—i.e., the amount of elliptical distortion by which Earth's shape departs from a perfect sphere. He introduced corrected observations for the so-called personal equation, a statistical bias in measurement characteristic of the observer himself that must be eliminated before results can be considered reliable, and he made a systematic study of the causes of instrumental errors. His own corrected observations were more accurate than any previous ones, and his methods offered the way to great advances in the field.

the sizes of stars, galaxies, and clusters of galaxies. Much credit for the final establishment of a scale for the universe in terms of solar system and terrestrial distances, which depends vitally on accurate measurement of the distances of the nearest stars from Earth, must go to Bessel.

BESSEL FUNCTIONS

Around 1817 Bessel systematically derived a set of mathematical functions during an investigation of solutions of one of Kepler's equations of planetary motion. Particular functions of the set had been formulated earlier by the Swiss mathematicians Daniel Bernoulli, who studied the oscillations of a chain suspended by one end, and Leonhard Euler, who analyzed the vibrations of a stretched membrane.

After Bessel published his findings, other scientists found that the functions appeared in mathematical descriptions of many physical phenomena, including the flow of heat or electricity in a solid cylinder, the propagation of electromagnetic waves along wires, the diffraction of light, the motions of fluids, and the deformations of elastic bodies. One of these investigators, Lord Rayleigh, also placed the Bessel functions in a larger context by showing that they arise in the solution of Laplace's equation when the latter is formulated in cylindrical (rather than Cartesian or spherical) coordinates.

Specifically, a Bessel function is a solution of the differential equation

$$x^2 \frac{d^2 y}{dx^2} + x \frac{dy}{dx} + (x^2 - n^2)\, y = 0,$$

which is called Bessel's equation. For integral values of n, the Bessel functions are

$$J_n(x) = \frac{x^n}{2^n n!} \left[1 - \frac{x^2}{2(2n+2)} + \frac{x^4}{2 \cdot 4(2n+2)(2n+4)} - \cdots \right].$$

The graph of $J_0(x)$ looks like that of a damped cosine curve, and that of $J_1(x)$ looks like that of a damped sine curve.

Certain physical problems lead to differential equations analogous to Bessel's equation. Their solutions take the form of combinations of Bessel functions and are called Bessel functions of the second or third kind.

NEWCOMB'S TABLES AND CONSTANTS

The Canadian-born American astronomer and mathematician Simon Newcomb (1835–1909) prepared ephemerides—tables of computed places of celestial bodies over a period of time—and tables of astronomical constants that were some of the most important astronomical works of the 19th century. Newcomb had little or no formal education. At the age of 16 he was apprenticed to a quack herb doctor in Salisbury, N.B. After two or three years he ran away to join his widowed father who had settled in the United States, in Maryland. In the libraries at Washington, D.C., Simon found the first full opportunity to indulge his intellectual curiosity. After avidly exploring many technical fields he concluded that his principal talent lay in mathematics. He was especially attracted to the *American Ephemeris and Nautical Almanac*, an annual handbook for astronomers, containing predicted positions in the sky of the principal celestial objects and other astronomical phenomena. He thereupon applied for employment in the American Nautical Almanac Office, then at Cambridge, Mass., and became a computer there in 1857. He also enrolled in the Lawrence Scientific School of Harvard University, receiving a degree in 1858. In 1861 he applied for and received a commission in the corps of professors of mathematics in the United States Navy and was assigned to the United States Naval Observatory at Washington. He worked there for more than 10 years determining the positions of celestial objects with the meridian instruments and for two years with a then new 26-inch refractor telescope.

In 1877 Newcomb was put in charge of the American Nautical Almanac Office—then in Washington—where almost at once he commenced the great work that he had had in his mind for some years and that was to occupy the greater part of the rest of his life: the calculation of the motions of the bodies in the solar system. Reaching the compulsory retirement age for captains in 1897, he later received the then unusual distinction of retirement with the rank of rear admiral.

Newcomb's most important work appeared in the *Astronomical Papers Prepared for the Use of the American Ephemeris and Nautical Almanac*, a series of memoirs that he founded in 1879 with the object of giving "a systematic determination of the constants of astronomy from the best existing data, a reinvestigation of the theories of the celestial motions, and the preparation of tables, formulae, and precepts for the construction of ephemerides, and for other applications of the same results." Of 36 articles filling approximately 4,500 quarto pages in the first nine volumes, he was the sole or principal author of 25. Among them were his tables of the Sun, Mercury, Venus, Mars, Uranus, and Neptune, along with tables of Jupiter and Saturn that were devised by George W. Hill, another American astronomer.

These tables were used throughout most of the world for calculating daily positions of the objects from 1901 to 1959, and even afterward for the Sun, Mercury, Venus, and Mars. This series of *Papers* is remarkable for its sustained high quality. Hardly anything in them proved to be incorrect.

Possibly Newcomb's most far-reaching contribution was his inauguration, jointly with A. M. W. Downing—then superintendent of the British Nautical Almanac Office—of a worldwide unified system of astronomical constants. This was later to lead to the outstandingly successful scheme of international collaboration among the principal almanac makers of the world that survived two World Wars with increasing vigour. Newcomb and Downing were impressed by the "confusion which pervaded the whole system of exact astronomy, arising from the diversity of the fundamental data made use of by the astronomers of foreign countries and various institutions in their work." A conference of the directors of the national ephemerides of the United States, Great Britain, France, and Germany, was held in Paris in May 1896. It resolved that beginning with 1901 a certain set of constants—substantially Newcomb's—should be used by all the ephemerides. The decision even included some work of Newcomb's that was not to be finished for several years. A similar conference, held at Paris in 1950, decided unanimously that the system of constants adopted in 1896 was still preferable to any other for practical use.

CHAPTER 4

PERCEPTIONS OF THE 20TH CENTURY

The statistical studies based on the perceptions of the Milky Way Galaxy as a vast stellar system continued into the early 20th century. They culminated with the analysis by the Dutch astronomer Jacobus Cornelius Kapteyn who, like William Herschel before him, used number counts of stars to study their distribution in space. It can be shown for stars with an arbitrary but fixed mixture of intrinsic brightnesses that—in the absence of absorption of starlight—the number N of stars with apparent brightness, energy flux f, larger than a specified level f_o, is given by $N = Af_o^{-3/2}$, where A is a constant, if the stars are distributed uniformly in Euclidean space (space satisfying the principles of Euclidean geometry). The number N would increase with decreasing limiting apparent brightness f_o, because one is sampling, on average, larger volumes of space when one counts fainter sources. Kapteyn found that the number N increased less rapidly with decreasing f_o than the hypothetical value $Af_o^{-3/2}$. This indicated to him that the solar system lay near the centre of a distribution of stars, which thinned in number with increasing distance from the centre. Moreover, Kapteyn determined that the rate of thinning was more rapid in certain directions than in others. This observation, in conjunction with other arguments that set the scale, led him in the first two decades of the 20th century to depict the Milky Way Galaxy (then confused with the entire universe) as a rather small, flattened stratum of stars and gaseous nebulae in which the number of stars decreased

HENRIETTA SWAN LEAVITT

(b. July 4, 1868, Lancaster, Mass., U.S.—d. Dec. 12, 1921, Cambridge, Mass.)

American astronomer Henrietta Swan Leavitt was known for her discovery of the relationship between period and luminosity in Cepheid variables, pulsating stars that vary regularly in brightness in periods ranging from a few days to several months.

Leavitt attended Oberlin College for two years (1886–88) and then transferred to the Society for the Collegiate Instruction of Women (later Radcliffe College), from which she graduated in 1892. Following an interest aroused in her senior year, she became a volunteer assistant in the Harvard Observatory in 1895. In 1902 she received a permanent staff appointment. From the outset she was employed in the observatory's great project, begun by Edward C. Pickering, of determining the brightnesses of all measurable stars. In this work she was associated with the older Williamina Fleming and the more nearly contemporary Annie Jump Cannon.

Leavitt soon advanced from routine work to a position as head of the photographic stellar photometry department. A new phase of the work began in 1907 with Pickering's ambitious plan to ascertain photographically standardized values for stellar magnitudes. The vastly increased accuracy permitted by photographic techniques, which unlike the subjective eye were not misled by the different colours of the stars, depended upon the establishment of a basic sequence of standard magnitudes for comparison. The problem was given to Leavitt, who began with a sequence of 46 stars in the vicinity of the north celestial pole. Devising new methods of analysis, she determined their magnitudes and then those of a much larger sample in the same region, extending the scale of standard brightnesses down to the 21st magnitude. These standards were published in 1912 and 1917.

She then established secondary standard sequences of from 15 to 22 reference stars in each of 48 selected "Harvard Standard Regions" of the sky, using photographs supplied by observatories around the world. Her North Polar Sequence was adopted for the Astrographic Map of the Sky, an international project undertaken in 1913. By the time of her death she had completely determined magnitudes for stars in 108 areas of the sky. Her system remained in general use until improved technology made possible photoelectrical measurements of far greater accuracy. One result of her work on stellar magnitudes was her discovery of 4 novas and some 2,400 variable stars, the latter figure comprising more than half of all those known even by 1930. Leavitt continued her work at the Harvard Observatory until her death.

Leavitt's outstanding achievement was her 1912 discovery that in a certain class of variable stars, the Cepheid variables, the period of the cycle of fluctuation in brightness is highly regular and is determined by the actual luminosity of the star. The subsequent calibration of the period-luminosity curve allowed American astronomers Edwin Hubble, Harlow Shapley, and others to determine the distances of many Cepheid stars and consequently of the star clusters and galaxies in which they were observed. The most dramatic application was Hubble's *use in 1924 of a Cepheid variable to determine the distance to the great nebula in Andromeda, which was the first distance measurement for a galaxy outside the Milky Way. Although it was later discovered that there are actually two different types of Cepheid variable, the same method can still be applied separately to each type.*

to 10 percent of their central value at a distance in the plane of about 8,500 light-years from the galactic centre.

SHAPLEY'S CONTRIBUTIONS

In 1917, the American astronomer Harlow Shapley mounted a serious challenge to the Kapteyn universe. Shapley's study of the distances of globular clusters led him to conclude that their distribution centred on a point that lay in the direction of the constellation Sagittarius and at a distance that he estimated to be about 45,000 light-years (50 percent larger than the modern value). Shapley was able to determine the distance to the globulars through the calibration of the intrinsic brightnesses of the Cepheid variables found in them. (Knowing the period of the light variations allowed Shapley to infer the average intrinsic brightness. A measurement of the average apparent brightness then allowed, from the $1/r^2$ law of brightness, a deduction of the distance r.) According to Shapley, the galactic system was much larger than Kapteyn's estimate. Moreover, the Sun was located not at its centre but rather at its radial outskirts (though close to the midplane of a flattened disk). Shapley's dethronement of the Sun from the centre of the stellar system has often been compared

with Copernicus's dethronement of Earth from the centre of the planetary system, but its largest astronomical impact rested with the enormous physical dimensions ascribed to the Galaxy. In 1920 a debate was arranged between Shapley and Heber D. Curtis to discuss this issue before the National Academy of Sciences in Washington, D.C.

The debate also addressed a second controversy—the nature of the so-called spiral nebulae. Shapley and his adherents held that these objects were made up of diffuse gas and were therefore similar to the other gas clouds known within the confines of the Milky Way Galaxy. Curtis and others, by contrast, maintained that the spirals consisted of stars and were thus equivalent to independent galaxies coequal to the Galaxy. A parallel line of thought had been proposed earlier by the philosophers Immanuel Kant and Thomas Wright and by William Herschel. The renewed argument over the status of the spirals grew in part out of an important development that occurred around the turn of the 20th century: the astronomical incorporation of the methods of spectroscopy both to study the physical nature of celestial bodies and to obtain the component of their velocities along the line of sight. By analyzing the properties of spectral lines in the received light (e.g., seeing if the lines were produced by absorption or emission and if the lines were broad or narrow), or by analyzing the gross colours of the observed object, astronomers learned to distinguish between ordinary stars and gaseous nebulae existing in the regions between stars. By measuring the displacement in wavelength of the spectral lines with respect to their laboratory counterparts and assuming the displacement to arise from the Doppler effect, they could deduce the velocity of recession (or approach). The spirals posed interpretative difficulties on all counts. They had spectral properties that were unlike either local collections of stars or gaseous nebulae (because of the unforeseen roles of dust and different populations of stars in the arms, disk, and central bulge of a spiral galaxy). Also, as had been shown by the American astronomer Vesto Slipher, they generally possessed recession velocities that were enormous compared to those then known for any other astronomical object.

The formal debate between Shapley and Curtis ended inconclusively, but history has proved Shapley to be mostly right on the issue of the off-centre position of the solar system and the large scale of the Galaxy. Curtis was mostly right on the issue of the nature of the spirals as independent galaxies, as demonstrated in the work of the Swiss-born U.S. astronomer Robert J. Trumpler in 1930. Kapteyn (and Herschel) had been misled by the effects of the undiscovered but pervasive interstellar dust to think that the stars in the Milky Way thinned

THE DOPPLER EFFECT

When an object both moves and emits sound, there is an apparent difference between the frequency at which sound or light waves leave a source and that at which they reach an observer, caused by the relative motion of the observer and the wave source. This phenomenon is called the Doppler effect and is used in astronomical measurements, in Mössbauer effect studies, and in radar and modern navigation. It was first described in 1842 by Austrian physicist Christian Doppler.

The following is an example of the Doppler effect. As one approaches a blowing horn, the perceived pitch is higher until the horn is reached and then becomes lower as the horn is passed. Similarly, the light from a star, observed from Earth, shifts toward the red end of the spectrum (lower frequency or longer wavelength) if Earth and the star are receding from each other. It shifts toward the violet (higher frequency or shorter wavelength) if they are approaching each other. Because the displacement of the spectrum of an astronomical object is toward longer (red) wavelengths, the change in wavelengths is called a redshift. Distances to objects such as galaxies are often given in terms of their redshifts. The motion that causes the redshift is that of the expansion of the universe.

out with distance much more quickly than they actually do. The effect of interstellar dust was much less important for Shapley's studies because the globular clusters mostly lie well away from the plane of the Milky Way system.

RELATIVISTIC COSMOLOGIES

When one looks to great distances, one is seeing things as they were a long time ago, again because light takes a finite time to travel to Earth. Over such great spans, do the classical notions of Euclid concerning the properties of space necessarily continue to hold? The answer given by Einstein was that, no, the gravitation of the mass contained in cosmologically large regions may warp one's usual perceptions of space and time. In particular, the Euclidean postulate that parallel lines never cross need not be a correct description of the geometry of the actual universe. And in 1917 Einstein presented a mathematical model of the universe in which the total volume of space was finite yet had no boundary or edge. The model was based on his theory of general relativity that utilized a more generalized approach to geometry devised in the 19th century by the German mathematician Bernhard Riemann.

GRAVITATION AND THE GEOMETRY OF SPACE-TIME

The physical foundation of Einstein's view of gravitation, general relativity, lies on two empirical findings that he elevated to the status of basic postulates. The first postulate is the relativity principle: local physics is governed by the theory of special relativity. The second postulate is the equivalence principle: there is no way for an observer to distinguish locally between gravity and acceleration. The motivation for the second postulate comes from Galileo's observation that all objects—independent of mass, shape, colour, or any other property—accelerate at the same rate in a (uniform) gravitational field.

Einstein's theory of special relativity, which he developed in 1905, had as its basic premises (1) the notion (also dating back to Galileo) that the laws of physics are the same for all inertial observers and (2) the constancy of the speed of light in a vacuum—namely, that the speed of light has the same value (3 × 10^{10} centimetres per second [cm/sec], or 2 × 10^5 miles per second [miles/sec]) for all inertial observers independent of their motion relative to the source of the light. Clearly, this second premise is incompatible with Euclidean and Newtonian precepts of absolute space and absolute time, resulting in a program that merged space and time into a single structure, with well-known consequences. The space-time structure of special relativity is often called "flat" because, among other things, the propagation of photons is easily represented on a flat sheet of graph paper with equal-sized squares. Let each tick on the vertical axis represent one light-year (9.46 × 10^{17} cm [5.88 × 10^{12} miles]) of distance in the direction of the flight of the photon, and each tick on the horizontal axis represent the passage of one year (3.16×10^7 seconds) of time. The propagation path of the photon is then a 45° line because it flies one light-year in one year (with respect to the space and time measurements of all inertial observers no matter how fast they move relative to the photon).

The principle of equivalence in general relativity allows the locally flat space-time structure of special relativity to be warped by gravitation, so that (in the cosmological case) the propagation of the photon over thousands of millions of light-years can no longer be plotted on a globally flat sheet of paper. To be sure, the curvature of the paper may not be apparent when only a small piece is examined, thereby giving the local impression that space-time is flat (i.e., satisfies special relativity). It is only when the graph paper is examined globally that one realizes it is curved (i.e., satisfies general relativity).

In Einstein's 1917 model of the universe, the curvature occurs only in space, with the graph paper being rolled up into a cylinder on its side, a loop around the cylinder at constant time having a circumference of $2\pi R$—the total spatial extent of the universe. Notice that the "radius of the universe" is measured in a "direction" perpendicular to the space-time surface of the graph paper. Since the ringed space axis corresponds to one of three dimensions of the actual world (any will do since all directions are equivalent in an isotropic model), the radius of the universe exists in a fourth spatial dimension (not time), which is not part of the real world. This fourth spatial dimension is a mathematical artifice introduced to represent diagrammatically the solution (in this case) of equations for curved three-dimensional space that need not refer to any dimensions other than the three physical ones. Photons traveling in a straight line in any physical direction have trajectories that go diagonally (at 45° angles to the space and time axes) from corner to corner of each little square cell of the space-time grid. Thus, they describe helical paths on the cylindrical surface of the graph paper, making one turn after traveling a spatial distance $2\pi R$. In other words, always flying dead ahead, photons would return to where they started from after going a finite distance without ever coming to an edge or boundary. The distance to the "other side" of the universe is therefore πR, and it would lie in any and every direction. Space would be closed on itself.

Now—except by analogy with the closed two-dimensional surface of a sphere that is uniformly curved toward a centre in a third dimension lying nowhere on the two-dimensional surface—no three-dimensional creature can visualize a closed three-dimensional volume that is uniformly curved toward a centre in a fourth dimension lying nowhere in the three-dimensional volume. Nevertheless, three-dimensional creatures could discover the curvature of their three-dimensional world by performing surveying experiments of sufficient spatial scope. They could draw circles, for example, by tacking down one end of a string and tracing along a single plane the locus described by the other end when the string is always kept taut in between (a straight line) and walked around by a surveyor. In Einstein's universe, if the string were short compared to the quantity R, the circumference of the circle divided by the length of the string (the circle's radius) would nearly equal 2π = 6.2837853 . . . , thereby fooling the three-dimensional creatures into thinking that Euclidean geometry gives a correct description of their world. However, the ratio of circumference to length of string would become less than 2π when the length of string became comparable to R. Indeed, if a string of length πR could be pulled taut to the antipode of a positively curved universe, the ratio would go to zero. In short, at the tacked-down end the string could be seen to sweep out a great arc in the sky from horizon to horizon and back again. Yet, to make the string do this, the surveyor at the other end need only walk around a circle of vanishingly small circumference.

To understand why gravitation can curve space (or more generally, space-time) in such startling ways, consider the following thought experiment that was originally conceived by Einstein. Imagine an elevator in free space accelerating upward, from the viewpoint of a woman in inertial space, at a rate numerically equal to g, the gravitational field at the surface of Earth. Let this elevator have parallel windows on two sides, and let the woman shine a brief pulse of light toward the windows. She will see the photons enter close to the top of the near window and exit near the bottom of the far window because the elevator has accelerated upward in the interval it takes light to travel across the elevator. For her, photons travel in a straight line, and it is merely the acceleration of the elevator that has caused the windows and floor of the elevator to curve up to the flight path of the photons.

Let there now be a man standing inside the elevator. Because the floor of the elevator accelerates him upward at a rate g, he may—if he chooses to regard himself as stationary—think that he is standing still on the surface of Earth and is being pulled to the ground by its gravitational field g. Indeed, in accordance with the equivalence principle, without looking out the windows (the outside is not part of his local environment), he cannot perform any local experiment that would inform him otherwise. Let the woman shine her pulse of light. The man sees, just like the woman, that the photons enter near the top edge of one window and exit near the bottom of the other. And just like the woman, he knows that photons propagate in straight lines in free space. (By the relativity principle, they must agree on the laws of physics if they are both inertial observers.) However, since he actually sees the photons follow a curved path relative to himself, he concludes that they must be bent by the force of gravity. The woman tries to tell him there is no such force at work; he is not an inertial observer. Nonetheless, he has the solidity of Earth beneath him, so he insists on attributing his acceleration to the force of gravity. According to Einstein, they are both right. There is no need to distinguish locally between acceleration and gravity—the two are in some sense equivalent. But if that is the case, then it must be true that gravity—"real" gravity—can actually bend light. And indeed it can, as many experiments have shown since Einstein's first discussion of the phenomenon.

It was the genius of Einstein to go even further. Rather than speak of the force of gravitation having bent the photons into a curved path, it might be more fruitful to think of photons as always flying in straight lines—in the sense that a straight line is the shortest distance between two points—and that what really happens is that gravitation bends space-time. In other words, perhaps gravitation is curved space-time, and photons fly along the shortest paths possible in this curved space-time, thus giving the appearance of being bent by a "force" when one insists on thinking that space-time is flat. The utility of taking this approach is that it becomes automatic that all test bodies fall at the same rate under the "force" of gravitation; they are merely producing their natural trajectories in a background space-time that is curved in a certain fashion independent of the test bodies. What was a minor miracle for Galileo and Newton becomes the most natural thing in the world for Einstein.

To complete the program and to conform with Newton's theory of gravitation in the limit of weak curvature (weak field), the source of space-time curvature would have to be ascribed to mass (and energy). The mathematical expression of these ideas constitutes Einstein's theory of general relativity, one of the most beautiful artifacts of pure thought ever produced. The American physicist John Archibald Wheeler and his colleagues summarized Einstein's view of the universe in these terms:

Curved spacetime tells mass-energy how to move;

mass-energy tells spacetime how to curve.

Contrast this with Newton's view of the mechanics of the heavens:

Force tells mass how to accelerate;

mass tells gravity how to exert force.

Notice therefore that Einstein's worldview is not merely a quantitative modification of Newton's picture (which is also possible via an equivalent route using the methods of quantum field theory) but represents a qualitative change of perspective. And modern experiments have amply justified the fruitfulness of Einstein's alternative interpretation of gravitation as geometry rather than as force. His theory would have undoubtedly delighted the Greeks.

Albert Einstein's development of the special and general theories of relativity allowed for more precise measurements of celestial motion. AFP/Getty Images

Einstein's Model

To derive his 1917 cosmological model, Einstein made three assumptions that lay outside the scope of his equations. The first was to suppose that the universe is homogeneous and isotropic in the large (i.e., the same everywhere on average at any instant in time)—an assumption that the English astrophysicist Edward A. Milne later elevated to an entire philosophical outlook by naming it the cosmological principle. Given the success of the Copernican revolution, this outlook is a natural one. Newton himself had it implicitly in mind when he took the initial state of the universe to be everywhere the same before it developed "ye Sun and Fixt stars."

The second assumption was to suppose that this homogeneous and isotropic universe had a closed spatial geometry. As described above, the total volume of a three-dimensional space with uniform positive curvature would be finite but possess no edges or boundaries (to be consistent with the first assumption).

The third assumption made by Einstein was that the universe as a whole is static—i.e., its large-scale properties do not vary with time. This assumption, made before Hubble's observational discovery of the expansion of the universe, was also natural. It was the simplest approach, as Aristotle had discovered, if one wishes to avoid a discussion of a creation event. Indeed, the philosophical attraction of the notion that the universe on average is not only homogeneous and isotropic in space but also constant in time was so appealing that a school of English cosmologists—Hermann Bondi, Fred Hoyle, and Thomas Gold—would call it the perfect cosmological principle. They would carry its implications in the 1950s to the ultimate refinement in the so-called steady-state theory.

To his great chagrin Einstein found in 1917 that with his three adopted assumptions, his equations of general relativity—as originally written down—had no meaningful solutions. To obtain a solution, Einstein realized that he had to add to his equations an extra term, which came to be called the cosmological constant. If one speaks in Newtonian terms, the cosmological constant could be interpreted as a repulsive force of unknown origin that could exactly balance the attraction of gravitation of all the matter in Einstein's closed universe and keep it from moving. The inclusion of such a term in a more general context, however, meant that the universe in the absence of any mass-energy (i.e., consisting of a vacuum) would not have a space-time structure that was flat (i.e., would not have satisfied the dictates of special relativity exactly). Einstein was prepared to make such a sacrifice only very reluctantly, and, when he later learned of Hubble's discovery of the expansion of the universe and realized that he could have predicted it had he only had more faith in the original form of his equations, he regretted the introduction of the cosmological constant as the "biggest blunder" of his life. Ironically, observations of distant supernovas have shown the existence of dark energy, a repulsive force that is the dominant component of the universe.

DE SITTER'S MODEL

It was also in 1917 that the Dutch astronomer Willem de Sitter recognized that he could obtain a static cosmological model differing from Einstein's simply by removing all matter. The solution remains stationary essentially because

there is no matter to move about. If some test particles are reintroduced into the model, the cosmological term would propel them away from each other. Astronomers now began to wonder if this effect might not underlie the recession of the spiral galaxies.

FRIEDMANN-LEMAÎTRE MODELS

In 1922 Aleksandr A. Friedmann, a Russian meteorologist and mathematician, and in 1927 Georges Lemaître, a Belgian cleric, independently discovered solutions to Einstein's equations that contained realistic amounts of matter. These evolutionary models correspond to big bang cosmologies. Friedmann and Lemaître adopted Einstein's assumption of spatial homogeneity and isotropy (the cosmological principle). They rejected, however, his assumption of time independence and considered both positively curved spaces ("closed" universes) as well as negatively curved spaces ("open" universes). The difference between the approaches of Friedmann and Lemaître is that the former set the cosmological constant equal to zero, whereas the latter retained the possibility that it might have a nonzero value. To simplify the discussion, only the Friedmann models are considered here.

The decision to abandon a static model meant that the Friedmann models evolve with time. As such, neighbouring pieces of matter have recessional (or contractional) phases when they separate from (or approach) one another with an apparent velocity that increases linearly with increasing distance. Friedmann's models thus anticipated Hubble's law before it had been formulated on an observational basis. It was Lemaître, however, who had the good fortune of deriving the results at the time when the recession of the galaxies was being recognized as a fundamental cosmological observation. It was he who clarified the theoretical basis for the phenomenon.

The geometry of space in Friedmann's closed models is similar to that of Einstein's original model. However, there is a curvature to time as well as one to space. Unlike Einstein's model, where time runs eternally at each spatial point on an uninterrupted horizontal line that extends infinitely into the past and future, there is a beginning and end to time in Friedmann's version of a closed universe when material expands from or is recompressed to infinite densities. These instants are called the instants of the "big bang" and the "big squeeze," respectively. The global space-time diagram for the middle half of the expansion-compression phases can be depicted as a barrel lying on its side. The space axis corresponds again to any one direction in the universe, and it wraps around the barrel. Through each spatial point runs a time axis that extends along the length of the barrel on its (space-time) surface. Because the barrel is curved in both space and time, the little squares in the grid of the curved sheet of graph paper marking the space-time surface are of nonuniform size, stretching to become bigger when the barrel broadens (universe expands) and shrinking to become smaller when the barrel narrows (universe contracts).

It should be remembered that only the surface of the barrel has physical significance. The dimension off the surface toward the axle of the barrel represents the fourth spatial dimension, which is not part of the real three-dimensional world. The space axis circles the barrel and closes upon itself after traversing a circumference equal to $2\pi R$, where R, the radius of the universe (in the fourth dimension), is now a function of the time t. In a closed Friedmann model, R starts equal to zero at time $t = 0$, expands to a maximum value at time $t = t_m$ (the middle of the barrel), and recontracts to zero (not shown) at time $t = 2t_m$, with the value of t_m dependent on the total amount of mass that exists in the universe.

Imagine now that galaxies reside on equally spaced tick marks along the space axis. Each galaxy on average does not move spatially with respect to its tick mark in the spatial (ringed) direction but is carried forward horizontally by the march of time. The total number of galaxies on the spatial ring is conserved as time changes, and therefore their average spacing increases or decreases as the total circumference $2\pi R$ on the ring increases or decreases (during the expansion or contraction phases). Thus, without in a sense actually moving in the spatial direction, galaxies can be carried apart by the expansion of space itself. From this point of view, the recession of galaxies is not a "velocity" in the usual sense of the word. For example, in a closed Friedmann model, there could be galaxies that started, when R was small, very close to the Milky Way system on the opposite side of the universe. Now, 10^{10} years later, they are still on the opposite side of the universe but at a distance much greater than 10^{10} light-years away. They reached those distances without ever having had to move (relative to any local observer) at speeds faster than light—indeed, in a sense without having had to move at all. The separation rate of nearby galaxies can be thought of as a velocity without confusion in the sense of Hubble's law, if one wants, but only if the inferred velocity is much less than the speed of light.

On the other hand, if the recession of the galaxies is not viewed in terms of a velocity, then the cosmological redshift cannot be viewed as a Doppler shift. How, then, does it arise? The answer is contained in the barrel diagram when one notices that, as the universe expands, each small cell in the space-time grid also expands. Consider the propagation of electromagnetic radiation whose wavelength initially spans exactly one cell length (for simplicity of discussion), so that its head lies at a vertex and its tail at one vertex back. Suppose an elliptical galaxy emits such a wave at some time t_1. The head of the wave propagates from corner to corner on the little square grids

that look locally flat, and the tail propagates from corner to corner one vertex back. At a later time t_2, a spiral galaxy begins to intercept the head of the wave. At time t_2, the tail is still one vertex back, and therefore the wave train, still containing one wavelength, now spans one current spatial grid spacing. In other words, the wavelength has grown in direct proportion to the linear expansion factor of the universe. Since the same conclusion would have held if n wavelengths had been involved instead of one, all electromagnetic radiation from a given object will show the same cosmological redshift if the universe (or, equivalently, the average spacing between galaxies) was smaller at the epoch of transmission than at the epoch of reception. Each wavelength will have been stretched in direct proportion to the expansion of the universe in between.

A nonzero peculiar velocity for an emitting galaxy with respect to its local cosmological frame can be taken into account by Doppler-shifting the emitted photons before applying the cosmological redshift factor; the observed redshift would be a product of two factors. When the observed redshift is large, one usually assumes that the dominant contribution is of cosmological origin. When this assumption is valid, the redshift is a monotonic function of both distance and time during the expansional phase of any cosmological model. Thus, astronomers often use the redshift z as a shorthand indicator of both distance and elapsed

GEORGES LEMAÎTRE

(b. July 17, 1894, Charleroi, Belg.—d. June 20, 1966, Leuven)

Belgian astronomer and cosmologist Georges Lemaître formulated the modern big bang theory, which holds that the universe began in a cataclysmic explosion of a small, primeval "super-atom."

A civil engineer, Lemaître served as an artillery officer in the Belgian Army during World War I. After the war he entered a seminary and in 1923 was ordained a priest. He studied at the University of Cambridge's solar physics laboratory (1923–24) and then at the Massachusetts Institute of Technology, Cambridge (1925–27), where he became acquainted with the findings of the American astronomers Edwin P. Hubble and Harlow Shapley on the expanding universe. In 1927, the year he became professor of astrophysics at the Catholic University of Leuven (Louvain), he proposed his big bang theory, which explained the recession of the galaxies within the framework of Albert Einstein's theory of general relativity. Although expanding models of the universe had been considered earlier, notably by the Dutch astronomer Willem de Sitter, Lemaître's theory, as modified by George Gamow, has become the leading theory of cosmology.

Lemaître also did research on cosmic rays and on the three-body problem, which concerns the mathematical description of the motion of three mutually attracting bodies in space. His works include Discussion sur l'évolution de l'univers *(1933; "Discussion on the Evolution of the Universe") and* L'Hypothèse de l'atome primitif *(1946; "Hypothesis of the Primeval Atom").*

ALEKSANDR FRIEDMANN

(b. June 17 [June 29, New Style], 1888, St. Petersburg, Russia—d. Sept. 16, 1925, Leningrad [St. Petersburg])

Aleksandr Aleksandrovich Friedmann was a Russian mathematician and physical scientist.

After graduating from the University of St. Petersburg in 1910, Friedmann joined the Pavlovsk Aerological Observatory and, during World War I, did aerological work for the Russian army. After the war he was on the staff of the University of Perm (1918–20) and then on the staffs of the Main Physical Observatory and other institutions until his death in 1925.

In 1922–24 Friedmann used Einstein's general theory of relativity to formulate the mathematics of a dynamic (time-dependent) universe. (Einstein and Dutch mathematician Willem de Sitter had earlier studied static cosmologies.) In the Friedmann models, the average mass density is constant over all space but may change with time as the universe expands. His models, which included all three cases of positive, negative, and zero curvature, were crucial in the development of modern cosmology. Friedmann also calculated the time back to the moment when an expanding universe would have been a mere point, obtaining tens of billions of years. But it is not clear how much physical significance he attributed to this speculation. It may, however, still be considered a part of the prehistory of the big bang theory. Friedmann also considered the possibility of a cyclical universe. In his other work, he was among the founders of the science of dynamic meteorology.

time. Following from this, the statement "object X lies at $z = a$" means that "object X lies at a distance associated with redshift a." The statement "event Y occurred at redshift $z = b$" means that "event Y occurred a time ago associated with redshift b."

The open Friedmann models differ from the closed models in both spatial and temporal behaviour. In an open universe the total volume of space and the number of galaxies contained in it are infinite. The three-dimensional spatial geometry is one of uniform negative curvature in the sense that, if circles are drawn with very large lengths of string, the ratio of circumferences to lengths of string are greater than 2π. The temporal history begins again with expansion from a big bang of infinite density, but now the expansion continues indefinitely, and the average density of matter and radiation in the universe would eventually become vanishingly small. Time in such a model has a beginning but no end.

THE EINSTEIN–DE SITTER UNIVERSE

In 1932 Einstein and de Sitter proposed that the cosmological constant should be set equal to zero, and they derived a homogeneous and isotropic model that provides the separating case between the closed and open Friedmann models. Einstein and de Sitter assumed that the spatial curvature of the universe is neither positive nor negative but rather zero. The spatial geometry of the Einstein–de Sitter universe is Euclidean (infinite total volume), but space-time is not globally flat (i.e., not exactly the space-time of special relativity). Time again commences with a big bang and the galaxies recede forever, but the recession rate (Hubble's "constant") asymptotically coasts to zero as time advances to infinity. Because the geometry of space and the gross evolutionary properties are uniquely defined in the Einstein–de Sitter model, many people with a philosophical bent long considered it the most fitting candidate to describe the actual universe.

BOUND AND UNBOUND UNIVERSES AND THE CLOSURE DENSITY

The different separation behaviours of galaxies at large timescales in the Friedmann closed and open models and the Einstein–de Sitter model allow a different classification scheme than one based on the global structure of space-time. The alternative way of looking at things is in terms of gravitationally bound and unbound systems. Closed models where galaxies initially separate but later come back together again represent bound universes. Open models where galaxies continue to separate forever represent unbound universes. The Einstein–de Sitter model where galaxies separate forever but slow to a halt at infinite time represents the critical case.

The advantage of this alternative view is that it focuses attention on local quantities where it is possible to think in the simpler terms of Newtonian physics—attractive forces, for example. In this picture it is intuitively clear that the feature that should distinguish whether or not gravity is capable of bringing a given expansion rate to a halt depends on the amount of mass (per unit volume) present. This is indeed the case. The Newtonian and relativistic formalisms give the same criterion for the critical, or closure, density (in mass equivalent of matter and radiation) that separates closed or bound universes from open or unbound ones. If Hubble's constant at the present epoch is denoted as H_o, then the closure density (corresponding to an Einstein–de Sitter model) equals $3H_o^2/8\pi G$, where G is the universal gravitational constant in both Newton's and Einstein's theories of gravity. The numerical value of Hubble's constant H_o is about 22 kilometres per second per

million light-years. The closure density then equals 10^{-29} gram per cubic centimetre, the equivalent of about six hydrogen atoms on average per cubic metre of cosmic space. If the actual cosmic average is greater than this value, the universe is bound (closed) and, though currently expanding, will end in a crush of unimaginable proportion. If it is less, the universe is unbound (open) and will expand forever. The result is intuitively plausible since the smaller the mass density, the smaller the role for gravitation, so the more the universe will approach free expansion (assuming that the cosmological constant is zero).

The mass in galaxies observed directly, when averaged over cosmological distances, is estimated to be only a few percent of the amount required to close the universe. The amount contained in the radiation field (most of which is in the cosmic microwave background) contributes negligibly to the total at present. If this were all, the universe would be open and unbound. However, the dark matter that has been deduced from various dynamic arguments is about 23 percent of the universe, and dark energy supplies the remaining amount, bringing the total average mass density up to 100 percent of the closure density.

HUBBLE'S RESEARCH ON EXTRAGALACTIC SYSTEMS

The decisive piece of evidence concerning the extragalactic nature of the spirals was provided in 1923–24 by Edwin Hubble, who succeeded in resolving one field in the Andromeda Galaxy (M31) into a collection of distinct stars. Some of the stars proved to be variables of a type similar to those found by Shapley in globular clusters. Measurements of the properties of these variables yielded estimates of their distances. As it turned out, the distance to M31 put it well outside the confines of even Shapley's huge model of the Galaxy, and M31 therefore must be an independent system of stars (and gas clouds).

Hubble's findings inaugurated the era of extragalactic astronomy. He himself went on to classify the morphological types of the different galaxies he found: spirals, ellipticals, and irregulars. In 1926 he showed that, apart from a "zone of avoidance" (region characterized by an apparent absence of galaxies near the plane of the Milky Way caused by the obscuration of interstellar dust), the distribution of galaxies in space is close to uniform when averaged over sufficiently large scales, with no observable boundary or edge. The procedure was identical to that used by Kapteyn and Herschel, with galaxies replacing stars as the luminous sources. The difference was that this time the number count N was proportional to $f_o^{-3/2}$, to the limits of the original survey. Hubble's finding provided the empirical justification for the so-called cosmological principle. This term was coined by the English mathematician and astrophysicist Edward A. Milne to describe the assumption that

at any instant in time the universe is, in the large, homogeneous and isotropic—statistically the same in every place and in every direction. This represented the ultimate triumph for the Copernican revolution.

THE HUBBLE LAW

It was also Hubble who interpreted and quantified American astronomer Vesto Slipher's results on the large recessional velocities of galaxies—they correspond to a general overall expansion of the universe. On cosmological scales, galaxies (or, at least, clusters of galaxies) appear to be racing away from one another with the apparent velocity of recession being linearly proportional to the distance of the object. This relation is known as the Hubble law. Interpreted in the simplest fashion, the Hubble law implies that roughly 10^{10} years ago, all of the matter in the universe was closely packed together in an incredibly dense state and that everything then exploded in a "big bang," the signature of the explosion being written eventually in the galaxies of stars that formed out of the expanding debris of matter. Strong scientific support for this interpretation of a big bang origin of the universe comes from the detection by radio telescopes of a steady and uniform background of microwave radiation. The cosmic microwave background is believed to be a ghostly remnant of the fierce light of the primeval fireball reduced by cosmic expansion to a shadow of its former

EDWIN HUBBLE

(b. Nov. 20, 1889, Marshfield, Mo., U.S.—d. Sept. 28, 1953, San Marino, Calif.)

American astronomer Edwin Powell Hubble played a crucial role in establishing the field of extragalactic astronomy and is generally regarded as the leading observational cosmologist of the 20th century.

In 1906, Hubble won a scholarship to the University of Chicago, where he served for a year as a student laboratory assistant for physicist Robert Millikan, a future Nobel Prize winner. Hubble graduated in 1910 and was selected as a Rhodes scholar from Illinois. He spent three years at the University of Oxford and was awarded a B.A. in jurisprudence.

Upon his return to the United States later in 1913, Hubble then entered the University of Chicago and embarked on graduate studies in astronomy. Hubble conducted his observational research at the Yerkes Observatory in Williams Bay, Wis. By this time Yerkes was no longer on the cutting edge of astronomy, but Hubble did have access to a quite powerful telescope, an innovative 24-inch (61-cm) reflector.

It was Hubble's good fortune that he was completing his graduate studies just as the director of the Mount Wilson Observatory in California, George Ellery Hale, was scouting for new staff. The observatory's 100-inch (254-cm) Hooker telescope, the most powerful in the world, was nearing completion. Hubble accepted Hale's job offer, but, before he could take up the position, the United States declared war on Germany on April 6, 1917. He hastily completed his dissertation so that he could enlist in the U.S. Army. Hale held the Mount Wilson position open for him until the end of the war.

At Mount Wilson, Hubble studied the so-called spiral nebulae, objects he had investigated for his doctorate. The status of the spirals (as they were widely known) was then unclear. Were they distant star systems (galaxies in current terminology) comparable to the Milky Way Galaxy, or were they clouds of gas or sparse star clusters within, or near, the Milky Way? The theory that there are visible galaxies had fallen from favour in the second half of the 19th century but was revived early in the 20th century. At the start of the 1920s, astronomers generally reckoned that no clinching evidence was at hand to settle the debate. Such evidence, however, was soon to be provided by Hubble.

In 1923 Hubble found Cepheid variable stars in the Andromeda Nebula, a very well-known spiral. The fluctuations in light of these stars enabled Hubble to determine the nebula's distance using the relationship between the period of the Cepheid fluctuations and its luminosity. While there was no clear consensus on the size of the Milky Way, Hubble's distance estimate placed the Andromeda Nebula approximately 900,000 light-years away. If Hubble was right, the Nebula clearly lay far beyond the borders of the Milky Way Galaxy (the largest estimates of its size put its diameter at around 300,000 light-years). The Andromeda Nebula therefore had to be a galaxy and not a nebulous cloud or sparse star cluster within the Milky Way. Hubble's finds in the Andromeda Nebula and in other relatively nearby spiral nebulae swiftly convinced the great majority of astronomers that the universe in fact contains myriad galaxies. (The current distance estimate of the Andromeda Nebula—now known as the Andromeda Galaxy—is 2.48 million light-years. An improved Cepheid period-luminosity relationship accounts for much of the difference between the current estimate and Hubble's.)

Within a few years of this pathbreaking research, Hubble decided to tackle one of the outstanding puzzles about the external galaxies. Why did the vast majority seem to be moving away from Earth (if the redshifts in their spectra are interpreted as the result of Doppler shifts)? To this end, Hubble was aided by another Mount Wilson astronomer, Milton Humason. Humason measured the spectral shifts of the galaxies (and in doing so, built on the pioneering studies of the Lowell Observatory astronomer Vesto Melvin Slipher), while Hubble focused on determining their distances. In 1929, Hubble published his first paper on the relationship between redshift and distance. He tentatively concluded that there is a linear redshift-distance relationship. That is, if one galaxy is twice as far away as another, its redshift is twice as large. Two years later Hubble and Humason presented what astronomers and cosmologists widely judged to be very convincing evidence that the relationship is indeed linear, and therefore, a galaxy's redshift is directly proportional to its distance.

Starting with Albert Einstein's 1917 paper Kosmologische Betrachtungen zur Allgemeinen Relativitätstheorien ("Cosmological Considerations on the General Theory of Relativity"), a number of physicists, mathematicians, and astronomers had applied general relativity to the large-scale properties of the universe. The redshift-distance relation established by Hubble and Humason was quickly meshed by various theoreticians with the general relativity-based theory of an expanding universe. The result was that by the mid-1930s the redshift-distance relationship was generally interpreted as a velocity-distance relationship such that the spectral shifts of the galaxies were a consequence of their motions. But Hubble throughout his career resisted the definite identification of the redshifts as velocity shifts.

Edwin Hubble's study of Cepheid stars in the Andromeda Nebula revealed the existence of galaxies throughout the universe. NASA Marshall Space Flight Center

splendour but still pervading every corner of the known universe.

The simple (and most common) interpretation of the Hubble law as a recession of the galaxies over time through space, however, contains a misleading notion. In a sense, the expansion of the universe represents not so much a fundamental motion of galaxies within a framework of absolute time and absolute space, but an expansion of time and space themselves. On cosmological scales, the use of light-travel times to measure distances assumes a special significance because the lengths become so vast that even light—traveling at the fastest speed attainable by any physical entity—takes a significant fraction of the age of the universe, roughly 10^{10} years, to travel from an object to an observer. Thus, when astronomers measure objects at cosmological distances from the Local Group, they are seeing the objects as they existed during a time when the universe was much younger than it is today. Under these circumstances, Albert Einstein taught in his theory of general relativity that the gravitational field of everything in the universe so warps space and time as to require a very careful reevaluation of quantities whose seemingly elementary natures are normally taken for granted.

The Hubble law, enunciated in 1929, marked a major turning point in modern thinking about the origin and evolution of the universe. The announcement of cosmological expansion came at a time when scientists were beginning to grapple with the theoretical implications of the revolutions taking place in physics. In his theory of special relativity, formulated in 1905, Einstein had effected a union of space and time, one that fundamentally modified Newtonian perceptions of dynamics, allowing, for example, transformations between mass and energy. In his theory of general relativity, proposed in 1916, Einstein effected an even more remarkable union, one that fundamentally altered Newtonian perceptions of gravitation, allowing gravitation to be seen, not as a force, but as the dynamics of space-time. Taken together, the discoveries of Hubble and Einstein gave rise to a new worldview. The new cosmology gave empirical validation to the notion of a creation event. It assigned a numerical estimate for when the arrow of time first took flight, and it eventually led to the breathtaking idea that everything in the universe could have arisen from literally nothing.

HENRY NORRIS RUSSELL

One of the most influential astronomers during the first half of the 20th century was the American Henry Norris Russell. He played a major role in the establishment of modern theoretical astrophysics by making physics the core of astrophysical practice. Bearing his name is the Hertzsprung-Russell diagram, a graph that demonstrates the relationship between a star's intrinsic brightness and its spectral type and that represents Russell's theory of the way stars evolve.

Russell was born on Oct. 25, 1877, in Oyster Bay, N.Y. He was the first of three sons born to Alexander Gatherer Russell, a liberal Presbyterian minister, and Eliza Hoxie Norris, a proud, mathematically adept mother. Russell entered Princeton Preparatory School in 1890 and then Princeton University in 1893, from which he graduated in 1897 with highest honours. Other than his family, the primary intellectual influences on Russell were the astronomer Charles Augustus Young and the mathematician Henry B. Fine. He obtained his Ph.D. from Princeton in 1900 with a thesis—an analysis of the way that Mars perturbs the orbit of the asteroid Eros—that was very much within traditional mathematical astronomy. After a year as a special student at the University of Cambridge, Cambridgeshire, England—where he attended the lectures of the English astronomer and mathematical physicist George Darwin on orbit theory and dynamics—Russell spent almost two years at the Cambridge University Observatory, developing one of the first photographic parallax programs for determining distances to stars.

When he returned to Princeton as an instructor in 1905, Russell was already firmly convinced that the future of astronomical practice lay not in open-ended data-gathering programs, but in problem-oriented research in which theory and observation worked synergistically. He also had the good fortune at Princeton to escape the environment common at major observatories of the day, where research was largely instrument-based and defined by the interests of the observatory director. At Princeton, neither Young—who directed the university observatory until 1905—nor his successor, the mathematician E. O. Lovett, established large-scale observing programs requiring a narrowly trained labour force. Russell, therefore, was free to search out new and exciting problems and to apply his considerable mathematical talents to their solution.

Russell spent nearly his entire professional life at Princeton. He rose quickly, gaining a professorship in 1911 and becoming director of the observatory a year later. Although he maintained these administrative responsibilities until his retirement in 1947, his chief activity was always research. The details of managing the observatory, as well as much of the teaching, were left to others. Because Russell generally shunned administrative and academic responsibilities, the observatory grew little in staff and equipment during his long tenure. Among his few but notable students were Harlow Shapley, who became director of Harvard College Observatory, Cambridge, Massachusetts, in 1921; Donald Menzel, who followed Shapley to Harvard in the 1930s to establish a major training program in astrophysics; and Lyman Spitzer, Jr., who succeeded Russell as observatory director at Princeton.

Until 1920 Russell's research interests ranged widely in planetary and stellar astronomy and astrophysics. He developed quick and efficient means for the analysis of the orbits of binary stars. Most notable were his methods for calculating the masses and dimensions of eclipsing variable stars—that is, binary stars that appear to move in front of each other as they orbit about their common centre of gravity and thus show characteristic variations in brightness. He also developed statistical methods for estimating the distances, motions, and masses of groups of binary stars. Russell generally employed a heuristic, intuitive style to all his areas of interest, one that was accessible to his widening circle of astronomical colleagues—few of whom were mathematically adept. Russell's strength was in analysis, and he soon found that observational astronomers, if properly approached, were more than happy to have their hard-won data managed, and showcased, by a bright theorist.

In his stellar parallax work at Cambridge, Russell had applied his study of binary stars to what they could reveal about the lives and evolution of stars and stellar systems. After choosing stars that might test which of several competing theories of stellar evolution was correct, he used his parallax measurements to determine the intrinsic, or absolute, brightnesses of these stars. When he compared their brightness to their colours, or spectra, Russell found, as had the Danish astronomer Ejnar Hertzsprung several years earlier, that among the majority of the stars in the sky (the dwarfs), blue stars are intrinsically brighter than yellow stars and yellows are brighter than reds. Nevertheless, a few stars (the giants) did not follow this relationship. These were exceptionally bright yellow and red stars. Later, by plotting brightnesses and spectra in a diagram, Russell pictorialized the definite relationship between a star's true brightness and its spectrum. He announced his results in 1913, and the diagram, which came to be known as the Hertzsprung-Russell diagram, was published the next year.

Russell aimed to confirm a theory of stellar evolution suggested by the astronomical spectroscopist Joseph Norman Lockyer and the mathematical physicist August Ritter, and to interpret the theory in terms of the gas laws. His diagram was the best way he knew to illustrate the viability of the theory. According to Russell, stars begin their lives as vastly extended, tenuous globes of gas, condensing through gravitational contraction out of the nebulous mists. As they contract, they heat up and pass through a colour change from red to yellow to blue, eventually achieving densities that cause them to deviate from the perfect gas laws. Further contraction toward the dwarf state, therefore, is accompanied by a cooling phase, in which the stars reverse their colour change, going from blue to red, and finally become extinct. Set firmly within the context of gravitational contraction as the source of energy of the stars, this description became known as Russell's theory of stellar evolution and enjoyed considerable popularity until the mid-1920s. When the English astronomer Arthur Stanley Eddington found that all stars demonstrate the same relationship between their masses and intrinsic brightnesses and, therefore, that dwarfs were still in the perfect gas state, Russell's theory lost its theoretical underpinning. It was not replaced by a substantially different theory until the mid-1950s.

After 1920—the year in which the Indian astrophysicist Meghnad Saha announced his theory of ionization equilibrium—Russell focused much of his energies on spectrum analysis, in which he applied laboratory methods to the study of stellar conditions. Saha's theory confirmed that the spectrum of any star was governed mainly by temperature, secondarily by pressure, and in a small way by the relative abundance of the chemical elements in the star's composition. This realization, that the physical state of a star could be quantitatively analyzed through its spectrum, proved to be a major turning point in Russell's career. His shift to spectrum analysis was also influenced by his new association with George Ellery Hale, who made Russell a senior Carnegie research associate with annual residence at Mount Wilson Observatory near Pasadena, California. Russell was given the best laboratory and astronomical spectroscopic data in the world, and he eagerly exploited this to

refine and extend Saha's theory not only to the physics of stars but also to the structure of matter as studied in laboratories on Earth.

From 1921 until the early 1940s Russell spent several months each year at Mount Wilson helping Hale's solar and stellar spectroscopic staff exploit their vast stores of accumulated astrophysical data. He also formed numerous ad hoc networks of physical laboratory and observatory groups to work on term analysis—the description and evaluation of the line structure of complex spectra. Through these networks and his close association with Hale, Russell became one of the most influential astronomers of his day.

Russell extended his influence through his efforts as a promulgator and arbiter of astronomical knowledge. For 43 years, starting in 1900, Russell wrote for the lay publication *Scientific American*. Although at first a simple column that accompanied a night sky map, his writings soon became a forum on the status and progress of astronomy. Russell was a frequent commentator on astronomy for the professional journal *Science* and was constantly asked to referee papers in broad fields of spectroscopic and stellar astronomy for leading astrophysical publications. He also used his two-volume textbook, *Astronomy* (1926–27), coauthored with two Princeton colleagues, as a vehicle for the latest theories on the origin and evolution of stars, to stimulate growth in astrophysics.

Russell was a liberal Christian thinker. As a Princeton faculty member, he echoed the philosophy of James McCosh, a former president of the school (then the College of New Jersey), in his public and student lectures on a "scientific approach to Christianity." He ardently preached on the relationship of science and religion, arguing that science could strengthen religion in modern society by revealing the unity of design in nature. Russell was also a family man, marrying in 1908 and fathering four children. He died on Feb. 18, 1957, in Princeton, N.J.

SIR ARTHUR EDDINGTON

As Russell was bringing together the disciplines of astronomy and physics, the English astronomer, physicist, and mathematician Sir Arthur Stanley Eddington was doing his greatest work in astrophysics by investigating the motion, internal structure, and evolution of stars. He also was the first expositor of the theory of relativity in the English language.

Eddington was born on Dec. 28, 1882, in Kendal, Westmorland. He was the son of the headmaster of Stramongate School, an old Quaker foundation in Kendal near Lake Windermere in the northwest of England. His father, a gifted and highly educated man, died of typhoid in 1884. His mother, Sarah, took her daughter and small son to Weston-super-Mare in Somerset, where young Eddington grew up and received his schooling. He entered Owens College,

Manchester, in October 1898, and Trinity College, Cambridge, in October 1902. There he won every mathematical honour, as well as Senior Wrangler (1904), Smith's prize, and a Trinity College fellowship (1907). In 1913 he received the Plumian Professorship of Astronomy at Cambridge and in 1914 became also the director of its observatory.

From 1906 to 1913 Eddington was chief assistant at the Royal Observatory at Greenwich, where he gained practical experience in the use of astronomical instruments. He made observations on the island of Malta to establish its longitude, led an eclipse expedition to Brazil, and investigated the distribution and motions of the stars. He broke new ground with a paper on the dynamics of a globular stellar system. In *Stellar Movements and the Structure of the Universe* (1914) he summarized his mathematically elegant investigations, putting forward the thesis that the spiral nebulae—cloudy structures seen in the telescope—were galaxies like the Milky Way.

During World War I he declared himself a pacifist. This arose out of his strongly held Quaker beliefs. His religious faith also found expression in his popular writings on the philosophy of science. In *Science and the Unseen World* (1929) he declared that the world's meaning could not be discovered from science but must be sought through apprehension of spiritual reality. He expressed this belief in other philosophical books: *The Nature of the Physical World* (1928), *New*

Pathways of Science (1935), and *The Philosophy of Physical Science* (1939).

During these years, he carried on important studies in astrophysics and relativity, in addition to teaching and lecturing. In 1919 he led an expedition to Príncipe Island (West Africa) that provided the first confirmation of Einstein's theory that gravity will bend the path of light when it passes near a massive star. During the total eclipse of the sun, it was found that the positions of stars seen just beyond the eclipsed solar disk were, as the general theory of relativity had predicted, slightly displaced away from the centre of the solar disk. Eddington was the first expositor of relativity in the English language. His *Report on the Relativity Theory of Gravitation* (1918), written for the Physical Society, followed by *Space, Time and Gravitation* (1920) and his great treatise *The Mathematical Theory of Relativity* (1923)—the latter considered by Einstein the finest presentation of the subject in any language—made Eddington a leader in the field of relativity physics. His own contribution was chiefly a brilliant modification of affine (non-Euclidean) geometry, leading to a geometry of the cosmos. Later, when the Belgian astronomer Georges Lemaître produced the hypothesis of the expanding universe, Eddington pursued the subject in his own researches. These were placed before the general reader in his little book *The Expanding Universe* (1933). Another book, *Relativity Theory of Protons and Electrons* (1936), dealt with quantum theory. He gave many popular lectures on relativity, leading the English physicist Sir Joseph John Thomson to remark that Eddington had persuaded multitudes of people that they understood what relativity meant.

His philosophical ideas led him to believe that, through a unification of quantum theory and general relativity, it would be possible to calculate the values of universal constants—notably the fine-structure constant, the ratio of the mass of the proton to that of the electron, and the number of atoms in the universe. This was an attempt, never completed, at a vast synthesis of the known facts of the physical universe. It was published posthumously as *Fundamental Theory* (1946), edited by Sir Edmund Taylor Whittaker—a book that is incomprehensible to most readers and perplexing in many places to all, but which represents a continuing challenge to some.

Eddington received many honours, including honorary degrees from 12 universities. He was president of the Royal Astronomical Society (1921–23), the Physical Society (1930–32), the Mathematical Association (1932), and the International Astronomical Union (1938–44). He was knighted in 1930 and received the Order of Merit in 1938. Meetings of the Royal Astronomical Society were often enlivened by dramatic clashes between Eddington and Sir James Hopwood Jeans or Edward Arthur Milne over the validity of scientific assumptions and mathematical procedures. Eddington was an enthusiastic participant in most forms of athletics, confining himself in later years to cycling, swimming, and golf.

Eddington's greatest contributions were in the field of astrophysics, where he did pioneer work on stellar structure and radiation pressure, subatomic sources of stellar energy, stellar diameters, the dynamics of pulsating stars, the relation between stellar mass and luminosity, white dwarf stars, diffuse matter in interstellar space, and so-called forbidden spectral lines. His work in astrophysics is represented by the classic *Internal Constitution of the Stars* (1925) and in the public lectures published as *Stars and*

Atoms (1927). In his well-written popular books, he also set forth his scientific epistemology, which he called "selective subjectivism" and "structuralism"—i.e., the interplay of physical observations and geometry. He believed that a great part of physics simply reflected the interpretation that the scientist imposes on his data. The better part of his philosophy, however, was not his metaphysics but his "structure" logic. His theoretical work in physics had a stimulating effect on the thought and research of others, and many lines of scientific investigation were opened as a result of his work. He died on Nov. 22, 1944, at Cambridge.

CHAPTER 5

EXPANDING STUDY OF THE UNIVERSE

When the universe was viewed in the large in the early 20th century, a dramatic new feature, not present on small scales, emerged—namely, the cosmological expansion, as defined by the Hubble law. Hubble's original value for the constant was 150 km (93 miles) per second per 1 million light-years. Modern estimates, using measurements of the cosmic microwave background (CMB), place the value at between 21.5 and 23.4 km (13.3 and 14.5 miles) per second per 1 million light-years. The reciprocal of Hubble's constant lies between 13 billion and 14 billion years, and this cosmic timescale serves as an approximate measure of the age of the universe.

THE NATURE OF SPACE AND TIME

To speak of the expansion of space and time raises the question of what are space and time? What are their properties? Are they finite or infinite?

An issue that arises when one contemplates the universe at large is whether space and time are infinite or finite. After many centuries of thought by some of the best minds, humanity has still not arrived at conclusive answers to these questions. Aristotle's answer was that the material universe must be spatially finite, for if stars extended to infinity, they could not perform a complete rotation around Earth in 24 hours. Space must then itself also be finite because it is merely a receptacle for material bodies. On the other hand, the heavens must be temporally infinite, without beginning or end, since they are imperishable and cannot be created or destroyed.

Except for the infinity of time, these views came to be accepted religious teachings in Europe before the period of modern science. The most notable person to publicly express doubts about restricted space was the Italian philosopher-mathematician Giordano Bruno, who asked the obvious question that, if there is a boundary or edge to space, what is on the other side? For his advocacy of an infinity of suns and earths, he was burned at the stake in 1600.

In 1610 Johannes Kepler provided a profound reason for believing that the number of stars in the universe had to be finite. If there were an infinity of stars, he argued, then the sky would be completely filled with them and night would not be dark. This point was rediscussed by Edmond Halley and Jean-Philippe-Loys de Chéseaux of Switzerland in the 18th century, but it was not popularized as a paradox until Wilhelm Olbers of Germany took up the problem in the 19th century. The difficulty became potentially very real with Edwin Hubble's measurement of the enormous extent of the universe of galaxies with its large-scale homogeneity and isotropy. His discovery of the systematic recession of the galaxies provided an escape, however. At first people thought that the redshift effect alone would suffice to explain why the sky is dark at night—namely, that the light from the stars in distant galaxies would be redshifted to long wavelengths beyond the visible regime. The modern consensus is, however, that a finite age for the universe is a far more important effect. Even if the universe is spatially infinite, photons from very distant galaxies simply do not have the time to travel to Earth because of the finite speed of light. There is a spherical surface, the cosmic event horizon (roughly 10^{10} light-years in radial distance from Earth at the current epoch), beyond which nothing can be seen even in principle. The number (roughly 10^{10}) of galaxies within this cosmic horizon, the observable universe, are too few to make the night sky bright.

THE HOT BIG BANG

Given the measured radiation temperature of 2.735 K (Kelvin; roughly -270 °C, -455 °F), the energy density of the CMB can be shown to be about 1,000 times smaller than the average rest-energy density of ordinary matter in the universe. Thus, the current universe is matter-dominated. If one goes back in time to redshift z, the average number densities of particles and photons were both bigger by the same factor $(1 + z)^3$ because the universe was more compressed by this factor, and the ratio of these two numbers would have maintained its current value of about one hydrogen nucleus, or proton, for every 10^9 photons. The wavelength of each photon, however, was shorter by the

A full-sky map produced by the Wilkinson Microwave Anisotropy Probe (WMAP) showing cosmic background radiation, a very uniform glow of microwaves emitted by the infant universe more than 13 billion years ago. According to inflation theory, tiny density fluctuations in the intensity of the radiation were the "seeds" that became the galaxies. WMAP's data support the big bang and inflation models. NASA/WMAP Science Team

factor $1 + z$ in the past than it is now. Therefore, the energy density of radiation increases faster by one factor of $1 + z$ than the rest-energy density of matter. Thus, the radiation energy density becomes comparable to the energy density of ordinary matter at a redshift of about 1,000. At redshifts larger than 10,000, radiation would have dominated even over the dark matter of the universe. Between these two values radiation would have decoupled from matter when hydrogen recombined. It is not possible to use photons to observe redshifts larger than about 1,090, because the cosmic plasma at temperatures above 4,000 K (3,727 °C, 6,740 °F) is essentially opaque before recombination. One can think of the spherical surface as an inverted "photosphere" of the observable universe. This spherical surface of last scattering probably has slight ripples in it that account for the slight anisotropies observed in the cosmic microwave background today. In any case, the earliest stages of the universe's history—for example, when temperatures were 10^9 K and higher—cannot be examined by light received through any telescope. Clues must be sought by comparing the matter content with theoretical calculations.

For this purpose, fortunately, the cosmological evolution of model universes is especially simple and amenable to computation at redshifts much larger than 10,000 (or temperatures substantially above 30,000 K [29,727 °C, 53,540 °F]) because the physical properties of the dominant component, photons, then are completely known. In a radiation-dominated early universe, for example, the radiation temperature T is very precisely known as a function of the age of the universe, the time t after the big bang.

THE COSMIC MICROWAVE BACKGROUND

The CMB is electromagnetic radiation filling the universe that is a residual effect of the big bang 13.7 billion years ago. Because the expanding universe has cooled since this primordial explosion, the background radiation is in the microwave region of the electromagnetic spectrum.

Beginning in 1948, the American cosmologist George Gamow and his coworkers, Ralph Alpher and Robert Herman, investigated the idea that the chemical elements might have been synthesized by thermonuclear reactions that took place in a primeval fireball. According to their calculations, the high temperature associated with the early universe would have given rise to a thermal radiation field, which has a unique distribution of intensity with wavelength (known as Planck's radiation law), that is a function only of the temperature. As the universe expanded, the temperature would have dropped, each photon being redshifted by the cosmological expansion to longer wavelength, as the American physicist Richard C. Tolman had already shown in 1934. By the present epoch the radiation temperature would have dropped to very low values, about 5° above absolute zero (0 K [-273 °C, -460 °F]) according to the estimates of Alpher and Herman.

Interest in these calculations waned among most astronomers when it became apparent that the lion's share of the synthesis of elements heavier than helium must have occurred inside stars rather than in a hot big bang. In the early 1960s physicists at Princeton University, N.J., as well as in the Soviet Union, took up the problem again and began to build a microwave receiver that might detect, in the words of the Belgian cleric and cosmologist Georges Lemaître, "the vanished brilliance of the origin of the worlds."

The actual discovery of the relict radiation from the primeval fireball, however, occurred by accident. In experiments conducted in connection with the first Telstar communication satellite, two scientists, Arno Penzias and Robert Wilson, of the Bell Telephone Laboratories, Holmdel, N.J., measured excess radio noise that seemed to come from the sky in a completely isotropic fashion—that is, the radio noise was the same in every direction. When they consulted Bernard Burke of the Massachusetts Institute of Technology, Cambridge, about the problem, Burke realized that Penzias and Wilson had most likely found the cosmic background radiation that Robert H. Dicke, P. J. E. Peebles, and their colleagues at Princeton were planning to search for. Put in touch with one another, the two groups published simultaneously in 1965 papers detailing the prediction and discovery of a universal thermal radiation field with a temperature of about 3 K (-270 °C, -454 °F).

Precise measurements made by the Cosmic Background Explorer (COBE) satellite, launched in 1989, determined the spectrum to be exactly characteristic of a blackbody at 2.735 K (roughly -270 °C, -455 °F). The velocity of the satellite around Earth, Earth around the Sun, the Sun around the Galaxy, and the Galaxy through the universe actually makes the temperature seem slightly hotter (by about one part in 1,000) in the direction of motion rather than away from it. The magnitude of this effect—the so-called dipole anisotropy—allows astronomers to determine that the Local Group (the group of galaxies containing the Milky Way Galaxy) is moving at a speed of about 600 km per second (km/s; 400 miles per second [miles/s]) in a direction that is 45° from the direction of the Virgo cluster of galaxies. Such motion is not measured relative to the galaxies themselves (the Virgo galaxies have an average velocity of recession of about 1,000 km/s [600 miles/s] with respect to the Milky Way system) but relative to a local frame of reference in which the cosmic microwave background radiation would appear as a perfect Planck spectrum with a single radiation temperature.

The COBE satellite carried instrumentation aboard that allowed it to measure small fluctuations in intensity of the background radiation that would be the beginning of structure (galaxies and clusters of galaxies) in the universe. The satellite transmitted an intensity pattern in angular projection at a wavelength of 0.57 cm after the subtraction of a uniform background at a temperature of 2.735 K. Bright regions at the upper right and dark regions at the lower left showed the dipole asymmetry. A bright strip across the middle represented excess thermal emission from the Milky Way. To obtain the fluctuations on smaller angular scales, it was necessary to subtract both the dipole and the galactic contributions. An image was obtained showing the final product after the subtraction. Patches of light and dark represented temperature fluctuations that amount to about one part in 100,000—not much higher than the accuracy of the measurements. Nevertheless, the statistics of the distribution of angular fluctuations appeared different from random noise, and so the members of the COBE investigative team found the first evidence for the departure from exact isotropy that theoretical cosmologists long predicted must be there in order for galaxies and clusters of galaxies to condense from an otherwise structureless universe. These fluctuations correspond to distance scales on the order of 10^9 light-years across (still larger than the largest material structures seen in the universe, such as the enormous grouping of galaxies dubbed the "Great Wall").

ARNO PENZIAS

(b. April 26, 1933, Munich, Ger.)

German-American astrophysicist Arno Allan Penzias shared one-half of the 1978 Nobel Prize for Physics with Robert Woodrow Wilson for their discovery of a faint electromagnetic radiation throughout the universe. Their detection of this radiation lent strong support to the big bang model of cosmic evolution. (The other half of the Nobel Prize was awarded to the Soviet physicist Pyotr Leonidovich Kapitsa for unrelated work.)

Educated at City College of New York in New York City and Columbia University, where he received his doctorate in 1962, Penzias joined Bell Telephone Laboratories in Holmdel, N.J. In collaboration with Wilson he began monitoring radio emissions from a ring of gas encircling the Milky Way Galaxy. Unexpectedly, the two scientists detected a uniform microwave radiation that suggested a residual thermal energy throughout the universe of about 3 K (-270 °C, -454 °F). Most scientists now agree that this is the residual background radiation stemming from the primordial explosion billions of years ago from which the universe was created. In 1976 Penzias became director of the Bell Radio Research Laboratory and in 1981 vice president of research at Bell Laboratories.

Nobel Prize–winning scientists Robert Wilson (left) and Arno Penzias are shown in front of the antenna that helped them discover cosmic microwave background radiation. Ted Thai/Time & Life Pictures/Getty Images

ROBERT WOODROW WILSON

(b. Jan. 10, 1936, Houston, Texas, U.S.)

The American radio astronomer Robert Woodrow Wilson shared with Arno Penzias the 1978 Nobel Prize for Physics for a discovery that supported the big bang model of creation.

Educated at Rice University in Houston and the California Institute of Technology in Pasadena, where he received his doctorate in 1962, Wilson then worked (1963–76) at the Bell Telephone Laboratories at Holmdel, N.J. There, in collaboration with Penzias, the two scientists detected an unusual background radiation that was a remnant of the big bang.

From 1976 Wilson was head of Bell's Radio Physics Research Department. He contributed to many scientific journals on such subjects as background-temperature measurements and millimetre-wave measurements of interstellar molecules. He became a member of the U.S. National Academy of Science in 1979.

The Wilkinson Microwave Anisotropy Probe (WMAP) was launched in 1995 to observe the fluctuations seen by COBE in greater detail and with more sensitivity. The conditions at the beginning of the universe left their imprint on the size of the fluctuations. WMAP's accurate measurements showed that the early universe was 63 percent dark matter, 15 percent photons, 12 percent atoms, and 10 percent neutrinos. Today the universe is 72.6 percent dark energy, 22.8 percent dark matter, and 4.6 percent atoms. Although neutrinos are now a negligible component of the universe, they form their own cosmic background, which was discovered by WMAP. WMAP also showed that the first stars in the universe formed half a billion years after the big bang.

Apart from the small fluctuations discussed above (one part in 100,000), the observed cosmic microwave background radiation exhibits a high degree of isotropy, a zeroth order fact that presents both satisfaction and difficulty for a comprehensive theory. On the one hand, it provides a strong justification for the assumption of homogeneity and isotropy that is common to most cosmological models. On the other hand, such homogeneity and isotropy are difficult to explain because of the "light-horizon" problem. In the context of the cosmic microwave background, the problem can be expressed as follows. Consider the background radiation coming to an observer from any two opposite sides of the sky. Clearly, whatever are the ultimate sources (hot plasma) of this radiation, the photons, traveling at the speed of light since their emission by the plasma, have only had time to reach Earth now. The matter on one side of the sky could not have had time to have "communicated" with the matter on the other side (they are beyond each other's light horizon), so how is it possible (with respect to an observer in the right rest frame) that they "know" to have the same temperature to a precision approaching one part in 100,000? What accounts for the high degree of angular isotropy of the cosmic microwave background?

The isotropy, or flatness, of the cosmic microwave background has been explained by a mechanism called "inflation." In this theory, at high energies, matter is best described as a field. At the Planck era (10^{-43} second after the big bang) or at the time of grand unification (GUT era, 10^{-35} second), the lowest-energy state of such a field, or "false vacuum" would have had a negative pressure, resulting in a repulsive force that would have worked against the attractive force of gravity. The false vacuum would have contributed what was called Einstein's original theory of general relativity a cosmological constant about 10^{100} times more than that which could exist at the present time. This enormous repulsive force would have caused an exponential expansion, with the universe doubling in size every 10^{-43} or 10^{-35} second. After about 85 such doublings in size, the universe would have been 10^{26} (or 100 trillion trillion) times larger and much closer to the size it is today, and the temperature of the universe would have dropped from 10^{32} or 10^{28} K to values near absolute zero (0 K).

Inflation provides a mechanism for understanding the overall isotropy of the cosmic microwave background because the matter and radiation of the entire observable universe were in good thermal contact (within the cosmic event horizon) before inflation and therefore acquired the same thermodynamic characteristics. Rapid inflation carried different portions outside their individual event horizons. When inflation ended and the universe reheated and resumed normal expansion, these different portions, through the natural passage of time, reappeared on our horizon. Through the observed isotropy of the cosmic microwave background, they are inferred still to have the same temperatures.

PRIMORDIAL NUCLEOSYNTHESIS

According to the considerations previously outlined, at a time t less than 10^{-4} seconds, the creation of matter-antimatter pairs would have been in thermodynamic equilibrium with the ambient radiation field at a temperature T of about 10^{12} K. Nevertheless, there was a slight excess of matter particles (protons) compared to antimatter particles (antiprotons) of roughly a few parts in 10^9. This is known because, as the universe aged and expanded, the radiation temperature would have dropped and each antiproton and each antineutron would have annihilated with a proton and a neutron to yield two gamma rays. Later, each antielectron would have done the same with an electron to give two more gamma rays. After annihilation, however, the ratio of the number of remaining protons to photons would be conserved in the subsequent expansion to the present day. Since that ratio is known to be one part in 10^9, it is easy to work out that the original matter-antimatter asymmetry must have been a few parts per 10^9.

In any case, after proton-antiproton and neutron-antineutron annihilation but before electron-antielectron annihilation, it is possible to calculate that for every excess neutron there were about five excess protons in thermodynamic equilibrium with one another through neutrino and antineutrino interactions at a temperature of about 10^{10} K. When the universe reached an age of a few seconds, the temperature would have dropped significantly below 10^{10} K, and electron-antielectron annihilation would have occurred, liberating the neutrinos and antineutrinos to stream freely through the universe. With no neutrino-antineutrino reactions to replenish their supply, the neutrons would have started to decay with a half-life of 10.6 minutes to protons and electrons (and antineutrinos). However, at an age of 1.5 minutes, well before neutron decay went to completion, the temperature would have dropped to 10^9 K—low enough to allow neutrons to be captured by protons to form a nucleus of heavy hydrogen, or deuterium. (Before that time, the reaction could still have taken place, but the deuterium nucleus would immediately

have broken up under the prevailing high temperatures.) Once deuterium had formed, a very fast chain of reactions set in, quickly assembling most of the neutrons and deuterium nuclei with protons to yield helium nuclei. If the decay of neutrons is ignored, an original mix of 10 protons and two neutrons (one neutron for every five protons) would have assembled into one helium nucleus (two protons plus two neutrons), leaving more than eight protons (eight hydrogen nuclei). This amounts to a helium-mass fraction of $^4/_{12} = {}^1/_3$—i.e., 33 percent. A more sophisticated calculation that takes into account the concurrent decay of neutrons and other complications yields a helium-mass fraction in the neighbourhood of 25 percent and a hydrogen-mass fraction of 75 percent, which are close to the deduced primordial values from astronomical observations. This agreement provides one of the primary successes of hot big bang theory.

THE DEUTERIUM ABUNDANCE

Not all of the deuterium formed by the capture of neutrons by protons would be further reacted to produce helium. A small residual can be expected to remain, the exact fraction depending sensitively on the density of ordinary matter existing in the universe when the universe was a few minutes old. The problem can be turned around. Given measured values of the deuterium abundance (corrected for various effects), what density of ordinary matter needs to be present at a temperature of 10^9 K so that the nuclear reaction calculations will reproduce the measured deuterium abundance? The answer is known, and this density of ordinary matter can be expanded by simple scaling relations from a radiation temperature of 10^9 K to one of 2.735 K (-270 °C, -454 °F). This yields a predicted present density of ordinary matter and can be compared with the density inferred to exist in galaxies when averaged over large regions. The two numbers are within a factor of a few of each other. In other words, the deuterium calculation implies much of the ordinary matter in the universe has already been seen in observable galaxies. Ordinary matter cannot be the hidden mass of the universe.

THE VERY EARLY UNIVERSE

The initial conditions of the universe are of great importance, not only to the professional curiosity of astronomers but to the existence of life today. It was in those fractions of a second after the big bang that matter dominated over antimatter and the seeds of the first galaxies came into existence.

INHOMOGENEOUS NUCLEOSYNTHESIS

One possible modification to the big bang model concerns models of so-called inhomogeneous nucleosynthesis. The idea is that in the very early universe (the first microsecond), the subnuclear particles that later made up the protons and neutrons existed in a free state as a quark-gluon plasma. As the universe expanded and cooled, this quark-gluon plasma would undergo a phase transition and become confined to protons and neutrons (three quarks each). In laboratory experiments of similar phase transitions—for example, the solidification of a liquid into a solid—involving two or more substances, the final state may contain a very uneven distribution of the constituent substances, a fact exploited by industry to purify certain materials. Some astrophysicists have proposed that a similar partial separation of neutrons and protons may have occurred in the very early universe. Local pockets where protons abounded may have few neutrons and vice versa for where neutrons abounded. Nuclear reactions may then have occurred much less efficiently per proton and neutron nucleus than accounted for by standard calculations. The average density of matter may be correspondingly increased—perhaps even to the point where ordinary matter can close the present-day universe. Unfortunately, calculations carried out under the inhomogeneous hypothesis seem to indicate that conditions leading to the correct proportions of deuterium and helium-4 produce too much primordial lithium-7 to be compatible with measurements of the atmospheric compositions of the oldest stars.

THE COSMIC NEUTRINO BACKGROUND

Low-energy neutrinos that pervade the universe form the cosmic neutrino background. When the universe was one second old, it had cooled enough that neutrinos no longer interacted with ordinary matter. These neutrinos now form the cosmic neutrino background.

The theoretical basis of the cosmic neutrino background rests with the notion that a hot big bang would produce not only a primeval fireball of electromagnetic radiation but also enormous numbers of neutrinos and antineutrinos (both referred to in cosmological discussions as neutrinos for brevity's sake). Estimates suggest that every cubic metre of space in the universe contains about 108 low-energy neutrinos. This number considerably exceeds the cosmological density of atomic nuclei (mostly hydrogen) obtained by averaging the known matter in the universe over scales of hundreds of millions of light-years. The latter density amounts to less than one particle per cubic metre of space. Nevertheless, because neutrinos interact with matter only weakly (they do not, for example, emit electromagnetic radiation), they can be detected experimentally by sophisticated instruments only if they have relatively high energies (such as the neutrinos from the Sun or from supernova explosions). However, precise observations by WMAP revealed the effects of the cosmic neutrino background through its effects on the cosmic microwave background.

MATTER-ANTIMATTER ASYMMETRY

A curious number that appeared in the earlier discussion on deuterium was the few parts in 10^9 asymmetry initially between matter and antimatter (or equivalently, the ratio 10^{-9} of protons to photons in the present universe). What is the origin of such a number—so close to zero yet not exactly zero?

At one time the question posed above would have been considered beyond the ken of physics, because the net "baryon" number (for present purposes, protons and neutrons minus antiprotons and antineutrons) was thought to be a conserved quantity. Therefore, once it exists, it always exists, into the indefinite past and future.

Developments in particle physics during the 1970s, however, suggested that the net baryon number may in fact undergo alteration. It is certainly very nearly maintained at the relatively low energies accessible in terrestrial experiments, but it may not be conserved at the almost arbitrarily high energies with which particles may have been endowed in the very early universe.

An analogy can be made with the chemical elements. In the 19th century, most chemists believed the elements to be strictly conserved quantities. Although oxygen and hydrogen atoms can be combined to form water molecules, the original oxygen and hydrogen atoms can always be recovered by chemical or physical means. However, in the 20th century, with the discovery and elucidation of nuclear forces, chemists came to realize that the elements are conserved if they are subjected only to chemical forces (basically electromagnetic in origin). They can be transmuted by the introduction of nuclear forces, which enter characteristically only when much higher energies per particle are available than in chemical reactions.

In a similar manner it turns out that at very high energies new forces of nature may enter to transmute the net baryon number. One hint that such a transmutation may be possible lies in the remarkable fact that a proton and an electron seem at first sight to be completely different entities, yet they have, as far as one can tell to very high experimental precision, exactly equal but opposite electric charges. Is this a fantastic coincidence, or does it represent a deep physical connection? A connection would obviously exist if it can be shown, for example, that a proton is capable of decaying into a positron (an antielectron) plus electrically neutral particles. Should this be possible, the proton would necessarily have the same charge as the positron, for charge is exactly conserved in all reactions. In turn, the positron would necessarily have the opposite charge of the electron, as it is its antiparticle. Indeed, in some sense the proton (a baryon) can even be said to be merely the "excited" version of an anti-electron (an "antilepton").

Motivated by this line of reasoning, experimental physicists searched hard during the 1980s for evidence of proton decay. They found none and set a lower limit of 10^{32} years for the lifetime of the proton if it is unstable. This value is greater than what theoretical physicists had originally predicted on the basis of early unification schemes for the forces of nature. Later versions can accommodate the data and still allow the proton to be unstable. Despite the inconclusiveness of the proton-decay experiments, some of the apparatuses were eventually put to good astronomical use. They were converted to neutrino detectors and provided valuable information on the solar neutrino problem, as well as giving the first positive recordings of neutrinos from a supernova explosion (namely, supernova 1987A).

With respect to the cosmological problem of the matter-antimatter asymmetry, one theoretical approach is founded on the idea of a grand unified theory (GUT), which seeks to explain the electromagnetic, weak nuclear, and strong nuclear forces as a single grand force of nature. This approach suggests that an initial collection of very heavy particles, with zero baryon and lepton number, may decay into many lighter particles (baryons and leptons) with the desired average for the net baryon number (and net lepton number) of a few parts per 10^9. This event is supposed to have occurred at a time when the universe was perhaps 10^{-35} second old.

SUPERUNIFICATION AND THE PLANCK ERA

Why should a net baryon fraction initially of zero be more appealing aesthetically than 10^{-9}? The underlying motivation here is perhaps the most ambitious undertaking ever attempted in the history of science—the attempt to explain the creation of truly everything from literally nothing. In other words, is the creation of the entire universe from a vacuum possible?

The evidence for such an event lies in another remarkable fact. It can be estimated that the total number of protons in the observable universe is an integer 80 digits long. No one of course knows all 80 digits, but for the argument about to be presented, it suffices only to know that they exist. The total number of electrons in the observable universe is also an integer 80 digits long. In all likelihood these two integers are equal, digit by digit—if not exactly, then very nearly so. This inference comes from the fact that, as far as astronomers can tell, the total electric charge in the universe is zero (otherwise electrostatic forces would overwhelm gravitational forces). Is this another coincidence, or does it represent a deeper connection? The apparent coincidence becomes trivial if the entire universe was created from a vacuum since a vacuum has by definition zero electric charge. It is a truism that one cannot get something for nothing. The interesting question is whether one can get everything for nothing. Clearly, this is a very speculative topic for scientific investigation, and the ultimate answer depends on a sophisticated interpretation of what "nothing" means.

The words "nothing," "void," and "vacuum" usually suggest uninteresting empty space. To modern quantum physicists, however, the vacuum has turned out to be rich with complex and unexpected behaviour. They envisage it as a state of minimum energy where quantum fluctuations, consistent with the uncertainty principle of the German physicist Werner Heisenberg, can lead to the temporary formation of particle-antiparticle pairs. In flat space-time, destruction follows closely upon creation (the pairs are said to be virtual) because there is no source of energy to give the pair permanent existence. All the known forces of nature acting between a particle and antiparticle are attractive and will pull the pair together to annihilate one another. In the expanding space-time of the very early universe, however, particles and antiparticles may separate and become part of the observable world. In other words, sharply curved space-time can give rise to the creation of real pairs with positive mass-energy, a fact first demonstrated in the context of black holes by the English astrophysicist Stephen W. Hawking.

Yet Einstein's picture of gravitation is that the curvature of space-time itself is a consequence of mass-energy. Now, if curved space-time is needed to give birth to mass-energy, and if mass-energy is needed to give birth to curved space-time, which came first, space-time or mass-energy? The suggestion that they both rose from something still more fundamental raises a new question. What is more fundamental than space-time and mass-energy? What can give rise to both mass-energy and space-time? No one

United States Pres. Barack Obama presents the Medal of Freedom, the highest civilian honour in the country, to physicist Stephen Hawking in 2009. Chip Somodevilla/Getty Images

knows the answer to this question, and perhaps some would argue that the answer is not to be sought within the boundaries of natural science.

Hawking and the American cosmologist James B. Hartle have proposed that it may be possible to avert a beginning to time by making it go imaginary (in the sense of the mathematics of complex numbers) instead of letting it suddenly appear or disappear. Beyond a certain point in their scheme, time may acquire the characteristic of another spatial dimension, rather than refer to some sort of inner clock. Another proposal states

that, when space and time approach small enough values (the Planck values), quantum effects make it meaningless to ascribe any classical notions to their properties. The most promising approach to describe the situation comes from the theory of "superstrings."

Superstrings represent one example of a class of attempts, generically classified as superunification theory, to explain the four known forces of nature—gravitational, electromagnetic, weak, and strong—on a single unifying basis. Common to all such schemes are the postulates that quantum mechanics and special relativity underlie the theoretical framework. Another common feature is supersymmetry, the notion that particles with half-integer values of the spin angular momentum (fermions) can be transformed into particles with integer spins (bosons).

The distinguishing feature of superstring theory is the postulate that elementary particles are not mere points in space but have linear extension. The characteristic linear dimension is given as a certain combination of the three most fundamental constants of nature: (1) Planck's constant h (named after the German physicist Max Planck, the founder of quantum physics), (2) the speed of light c, and (3) the universal gravitational constant G. The combination, called the Planck length $(Gh/c^3)^{1/2}$, equals roughly 10^{-33} cm, far smaller than the distances to which elementary particles can be probed in particle accelerators on Earth.

The energies needed to smash particles to within a Planck length of each other were available to the universe at a time equal to the Planck length divided by the speed of light. This time, called the Planck time $(Gh/c^5)^{1/2}$, equals approximately 10^{-43} second. At the Planck time, the mass density of the universe is thought to approach the Planck density, c^5/hG^2, roughly 10^{93} grams per cubic centimetre. Contained within a Planck volume is a Planck mass $(hc/G)^{1/2}$, roughly 10^{-5} gram. An object of such mass would be a quantum black hole, with an event horizon close to both its own Compton length (distance over which a particle is quantum mechanically "fuzzy") and the size of the cosmic horizon at the Planck time. Under such extreme conditions, space-time cannot be treated as a classical continuum and must be given a quantum interpretation.

The latter is the goal of the superstring theory, which has as one of its features the curious notion that the four space-time dimensions (three space dimensions plus one time dimension) of the familiar world may be an illusion. Real space-time, in accordance with this picture, has 26 or 10 space-time dimensions, but all of these dimensions except the usual four are somehow compacted or curled up to a size comparable to the Planck scale. Thus the existence of these other dimensions has escaped detection. It is presumably only during the Planck era, when the usual four space-time dimensions acquire their natural Planck scales, that the existence of what is more fundamental than the usual ideas of mass-energy and space-time becomes fully revealed. Unfortunately, attempts to deduce anything more quantitative or physically illuminating from the theory have bogged down in the intractable mathematics of this difficult subject. At the present time superstring theory remains more of an enigma than a solution.

INFLATION

One of the more enduring contributions of particle physics to cosmology is the prediction of inflation by the American physicist Alan Guth and others. The basic idea is that at high energies matter is better described by fields than by classical means. The contribution of a field to the energy density (and therefore the mass density) and the pressure of the vacuum state need not have been zero in the past, even if it is today. During the time of super-unification (Planck era, 10^{-43} second) or grand unification (GUT era, 10^{-35} second), the lowest-energy state for this field may have corresponded to a "false vacuum," with a combination of mass density and negative pressure that results gravitationally in a large repulsive force. In the context of Einstein's theory of general relativity, the false vacuum may be thought of alternatively as contributing a cosmological constant about 10^{100} times larger than it can possibly be today. The corresponding repulsive force causes the universe to inflate exponentially, doubling its size roughly once every 10^{-43} or 10^{-35} second. After at least 85 doublings, the temperature, which started out at 10^{32} or 10^{28} K, would have dropped to very low values near absolute zero. At low temperatures the true vacuum state may have lower energy than the false vacuum state, in an analogous fashion to how solid ice has lower energy than liquid water. The supercooling of the universe may therefore have induced a rapid phase transition from the false vacuum state to the true vacuum state, in which the cosmological constant is essentially zero. The transition would have released the energy differential (akin to the "latent heat" released by water when it freezes), which reheats the universe to high temperatures. From this temperature bath and the gravitational energy of expansion would then have emerged the particles and antiparticles of noninflationary big bang cosmologies.

Cosmic inflation serves a number of useful purposes. First, the drastic stretching during inflation flattens any initial space curvature, and so the universe after inflation will look exceedingly like an Einstein–de Sitter universe. Second, inflation so dilutes the concentration of any magnetic monopoles appearing as "topological knots" during the GUT era that their cosmological density will drop to negligibly small and acceptable values. Finally, inflation provides a mechanism for understanding the overall isotropy of the cosmic microwave background because the matter and radiation of the entire observable universe were in good thermal contact (within the cosmic event horizon) before inflation and therefore acquired the same thermodynamic characteristics. Rapid inflation carried different portions outside their individual event horizons. When inflation ended and the universe reheated and resumed normal expansion, these different portions, through the natural passage of time, reappeared on our horizon. And through the observed isotropy of the cosmic microwave background, they are inferred still to have the same temperatures. Finally, slight anisotropies in the cosmic microwave background occurred because of quantum fluctuations in the mass density. The amplitudes of these small (adiabatic) fluctuations remained independent of comoving scale during the period of inflation. Afterward they grew gravitationally by a constant factor until the recombination era. Cosmic microwave photons seen from the last scattering surface should therefore exhibit a scale-invariant spectrum of fluctuations, which is exactly what the Cosmic Background Explorer satellite observed.

As influential as inflation has been in guiding modern cosmological thought, it has not resolved all internal difficulties. The most serious concerns the problem of a "graceful exit." Unless the effective potential describing the effects of the inflationary field during the GUT era corresponds to an extremely gently rounded hill—from whose top the universe rolls slowly in the transition from the false vacuum to the true vacuum—the exit to normal expansion will generate so much turbulence and inhomogeneity (via violent collisions of "domain walls" that separate bubbles of true vacuum from regions of false vacuum) as to make inexplicable the small observed amplitudes for the anisotropy of the cosmic microwave background radiation. Arranging a tiny enough slope for the effective potential requires a degree of fine-tuning that most cosmologists find philosophically objectionable.

STEADY STATE THEORY AND OTHER ALTERNATIVE COSMOLOGIES

Big bang cosmology, augmented by the ideas of inflation, remains the theory of choice among nearly all astronomers. However, apart from the difficulties discussed above, no consensus has been reached concerning the origin in the cosmic gas of fluctuations thought to produce the observed galaxies, clusters, and superclusters. Most astronomers would interpret these shortcomings as indications of the incompleteness of the development of the theory, but it is conceivable that major modifications are needed.

One early problem encountered by big bang theorists was an apparent large discrepancy between the Hubble time and other indicators of cosmic age. This discrepancy was resolved by revision of Hubble's original estimate for H_o, which was about an order of magnitude too large owing to confusion between Population I and II variable stars and between H II regions and bright stars. However, the apparent difficulty motivated Bondi, Hoyle, and Gold to offer the alternative theory of steady state cosmology in 1948.

By that year, of course, the universe was known to be expanding. Therefore the only way to explain a constant (steady state) matter density was to postulate the continuous creation of matter to offset the attenuation caused by the cosmic expansion. This aspect was physically very unappealing to many people, who consciously or unconsciously preferred to have all creation completed in virtually one instant in the big bang. In the steady state theory the average age of matter in the universe is one-third the

SIR FRED HOYLE

(b. June 24, 1915, Bingley, Yorkshire [now West Yorkshire], Eng.—d. Aug. 20, 2001, Bournemouth, Dorset)

British mathematician and astronomer Sir Fred Hoyle was best known as the foremost proponent and defender of the steady-state theory of the universe. This theory holds both that the universe is expanding and that matter is being continuously created to keep the mean density of matter in space constant.

Hoyle was educated at Emmanuel College and St. John's College, Cambridge, and spent six years during World War II with the British Admiralty, working on radar development. In 1945 he returned to Cambridge as a lecturer in mathematics. Three years later, in collaboration with the astronomer Thomas Gold and the mathematician Hermann Bondi, he announced the steady-state theory. Within the framework of Albert Einstein's theory of relativity, Hoyle formulated a mathematical basis for the steady-state theory, making the expansion of the universe and the creation of matter interdependent. Einstein assumed that the universe as a whole is static, i.e., its large-scale properties do not vary with time. This assumption, made before American astronomer Edwin Hubble's observational discovery of the expansion of the universe in 1927, was also natural. It was the simplest approach, as Aristotle had discovered, if one wished to avoid a discussion of a creation event. The notion that the universe on average is not only homogeneous and isotropic in space but also constant in time was philosophically attractive. Hoyle, Bondi, and Gold called it the perfect cosmological principle.

In the late 1950s and early '60s, controversy about the steady-state theory grew. New observations of distant galaxies and other phenomena, supporting the big bang theory (a phrase that Hoyle had coined in derision in the 1940s), weakened the steady-state theory, and it has since fallen out of favour with most cosmologists. Although Hoyle was forced to alter some of his conclusions, he tenaciously tried to make his theory consistent with new evidence.

Hoyle was elected to the Royal Society in 1957, a year after joining the staff of the Hale Observatories (now the Mount Wilson and Palomar observatories). In collaboration with William Fowler and others in the United States, he formulated theories about the origins of stars as well as about the origins of elements within stars. Hoyle was director of the Institute of Theoretical Astronomy at Cambridge (1967–73), an institution he was instrumental in founding. He received a knighthood in 1972.

Hoyle is known for his popular science works, including The Nature of the Universe *(1951),* Astronomy and Cosmology *(1975), and* The Origin of the Universe and the Origin of Religion *(1993). He also wrote novels, plays, short stories, and an autobiography,* The Small World of Fred Hoyle *(1986).*

Hubble time, but any given galaxy could be older or younger than this mean value. Thus, the steady state theory had the virtue of making very specific predictions, and for this reason it was vulnerable to observational disproof.

The first blow was delivered by British astronomer Martin Ryle's counts of extragalactic radio sources during the 1950s and '60s. These counts involved the same methods discussed above for the star counts by Dutch astronomer Jacobus Kapteyn and the galaxy counts by Hubble except that radio telescopes were used. Ryle found more radio galaxies at large distances from Earth than can be explained under the assumption of a uniform spatial distribution no matter which cosmological model was assumed, including that of steady state. This seemed to imply that radio galaxies must evolve over time in the sense that there were more powerful sources in the past (and therefore observable at large distances) than there are at present. Such a situation contradicts a basic tenet of the steady state theory, which holds that all large-scale properties of the universe, including the population of any subclass of objects like radio galaxies, must be constant in time.

The second blow came in 1965 with the discovery of the cosmic microwave background radiation. Though it has few adherents today, the steady state theory is credited as having been a useful idea for the development of modern cosmological thought as it stimulated much work in the field.

At various times, other alternative theories have also been offered as challenges to the prevailing view of the origin of the universe in a hot big bang. Some of these theories include the cold big bang theory (to account for galaxy formation), symmetric matter-antimatter cosmology (to avoid an asymmetry between matter and antimatter), variable G cosmology (to explain why the gravitational constant is so small), tired-light cosmology (to explain redshift), and the notion of shrinking atoms in a nonexpanding universe (to avoid the singularity of the big bang). The motivation behind these suggestions is, as indicated in the parenthetical comments, to remedy some perceived problem in the standard picture. Yet, in most cases, the cure offered is worse than the disease, and none of the mentioned alternatives has gained much of a following. The hot big bang theory has ascended to primacy because, unlike its many rivals, it attempts to address not isolated individual facts but a whole panoply of cosmological issues. And, although some sought-after results remain elusive, no glaring weakness has yet been uncovered.

DARK MATTER AND DARK ENERGY

Like the submerged part of an iceberg, much of the universe cannot be seen. There are two components, dark matter and dark energy, that, at present, are only observable through their gravitational effects.

DARK MATTER

Dark matter is a component of the universe whose presence is discerned from its gravitational attraction rather than its luminosity. Dark matter makes up 26.5 percent of the matter-energy composition of the universe. The rest is dark energy (73 percent) and "ordinary" visible matter (0.5 percent).

Originally known as the "missing mass," dark matter's existence was first inferred by Swiss American astronomer Fritz Zwicky, who in 1933 discovered that the mass of all the stars in the Coma cluster of galaxies provided only about 1 percent of the mass needed to keep the galaxies from escaping the cluster's gravitational pull. The reality of this missing mass remained in question for decades, until the 1970s when American astronomers Vera Rubin and W. Kent Ford confirmed its existence by the observation of a similar phenomenon: the mass of the stars visible within a typical galaxy is only about 10 percent of that required to keep those stars orbiting the galaxy's centre. In general, the speed with which stars orbit the centre of their galaxy is independent of their separation from the centre. Indeed, orbital velocity is either constant or increases slightly with distance rather than dropping off as expected. To account for this, the mass of the galaxy within the orbit of the stars must increase linearly with the distance of the stars from the galaxy's centre. However, no light is seen from this inner mass—hence the name "dark matter."

Since the confirmation of dark matter's existence, a preponderance of dark matter in galaxies and clusters of galaxies has been discerned through the phenomenon of gravitational lensing—matter acting as a lens by bending space and distorting the passage of background light. The presence of this missing matter in the centres of galaxies and clusters of galaxies has also been inferred from the motion and heat of gas that gives rise to observed X-rays. For example, the Chandra X-ray Observatory has observed in the Bullet cluster, which consists of two merging galaxy clusters, that the hot gas (ordinary visible matter) is slowed by the drag effect of one cluster passing through the other. The mass of the clusters, however, is not affected, indicating that most of the mass consists of dark matter.

Twenty-seven percent of the universe's matter-energy composition is matter. Only 0.5 percent is in the mass of stars and 0.03 percent of that matter is in the form of elements heavier than hydrogen. The rest is dark matter. Two varieties of dark matter have been found to exist. The first variety is about 4.5 percent of the universe and is made of the familiar baryons (protons, neutrons, and atomic nuclei), which also make up the luminous stars and galaxies. Most of this baryonic dark matter is expected to exist in the form of gas in and between the galaxies. This baryonic, or ordinary, component of dark matter has been determined by measuring the abundance of elements heavier than hydrogen, which were created in the first few minutes

Scientists hope that particle accelerators, such as the Large Hadron Collider in Geneva, Switzerland, will unlock the mysteries behind a form of dark matter known as WIMPs (weakly interacting massive particles). Fabrice Coffrini/AFP/Getty Images

after the big bang that occurred 13.7 billion years ago.

The dark matter that comprises the other 22 percent of the universe's matter is in an unfamiliar, nonbaryonic form. The rate at which galaxies and large structures composed of galaxies coalesced from density fluctuations in the early universe indicates that the nonbaryonic dark matter is relatively "cold," or "nonrelativisitic," meaning that the backbones of galaxies and clusters of galaxies are made of heavy, slow-moving particles. The absence of light from these particles also indicates

that they are electromagnetically neutral. These properties give rise to the particles' common name, weakly interacting massive particles (WIMPs). The precise nature of these particles is not currently known, and they are not predicted by the standard model of particle physics. However, a number of possible extensions to the standard model such as supersymmetric theories predict hypothetical elementary particles such as axions or neutralinos that may be the undetected WIMPs.

Extraordinary efforts are under way to detect and measure the properties of these unseen WIMPs, either by witnessing their impact in a laboratory detector or by observing their annihilations after they collide with each other. There is also some expectation that their presence and mass may be inferred from experiments at new particle accelerators, such as the Large Hadron Collider.

As an alternative to dark matter, modifications to gravity have been proposed to explain the apparent presence of "missing matter." These modifications suggest that the attractive force exerted by ordinary matter may be enhanced in conditions that occur only on galactic scales. However, most of the proposals are unsatisfactory on theoretical grounds, as they provide little or no explanation for the modification of gravity. These theories are also unable to explain the observations of dark matter physically separated from ordinary matter in the Bullet cluster. This separation demonstrates that dark matter is a physical reality and is distinguishable from ordinary matter.

DARK ENERGY

Seventy-three percent of the universe is made up of a repulsive force called dark energy. Dark energy, in contrast to both forms of matter, is relatively uniform in time and space and is gravitationally repulsive, not attractive, within the volume it occupies. The nature of dark energy is still not well understood.

A kind of cosmic repulsive force was first hypothesized by Albert Einstein in 1917. It was represented by a term, the "cosmological constant," which Einstein reluctantly introduced into his theory of general relativity in order to counteract the attractive force of gravity and account for a universe that was assumed to be static (neither expanding nor contracting). After the discovery in the 1920s by American astronomer Edwin Hubble that the universe is not static but is in fact expanding, Einstein referred to the addition of this constant as his "greatest blunder." However, the measured amount of matter in the mass-energy budget of the universe was improbably low, and therefore some unknown "missing component," much like the cosmological constant, was required to make up the deficit. Direct evidence for the existence of this component, which was dubbed dark energy, was first presented in 1998.

Dark energy is detected by its effect on the rate at which the universe expands and its effect on the rate at which large-scale structures such as galaxies and clusters of galaxies form through gravitational instabilities. The measurement of the expansion rate requires the use of telescopes to measure the distance (or light travel time) of objects seen at different size scales (or redshifts) in the history of the universe. These efforts are generally limited by the difficulty in accurately measuring astronomical distances. Since dark energy works against gravity, more dark energy accelerates the universe's expansion and retards the formation of large-scale structure. One technique for measuring the expansion rate is to observe the apparent brightness of objects of known luminosity like Type Ia supernovas. Dark energy was discovered in 1998 with this method by two international teams that included American astronomers Adam Riess and Saul Perlmutter and Australian astronomer Brian Schmidt. The two teams used eight telescopes, including those of the Keck Observatory and the MMT Observatory. Type Ia supernovas that exploded when the universe was only two-thirds of its present size were fainter and thus farther away than they would be in a universe without dark energy. This implied that the expansion rate of the universe is faster now than it was in the past, a result of the current dominance of dark energy. (Dark energy was negligible in the early universe.)

Studying the effect of dark energy on large-scale structure involves measuring subtle distortions in the shapes of galaxies arising from the bending of space by intervening matter, a phenomenon known as "weak lensing." At some point in the last few billion years, dark energy became dominant in the universe and thus prevented more galaxies and clusters of galaxies from forming. This change in the structure of the universe is revealed by weak lensing. Another measure comes from counting the number of clusters of galaxies in the universe to measure the volume of space and the rate at which that volume is increasing. The goals of most observational studies of dark energy are to measure its equation of state (the ratio of its pressure to its energy density),

variations in its properties, and the degree to which dark energy provides a complete description of gravitational physics.

In cosmological theory, dark energy is a general class of components in the stress-energy tensor of the field equations in Einstein's theory of general relativity. In this theory, there is a direct correspondence between the matter-energy of the universe (expressed in the tensor) and the shape of space-time. Both the matter (or energy) density (a positive quantity) and the internal pressure contribute to a component's gravitational field. While familiar components of the stress-energy tensor such as matter and radiation provide attractive gravity by bending space-time, dark energy causes repulsive gravity through negative internal pressure. If the ratio of the pressure to the energy density is less than -1/3, a possibility for a component with negative pressure, that component will be gravitationally self-repulsive. If such a component dominates the universe, it will accelerate the universe's expansion.

The simplest and oldest explanation for dark energy is that it is an energy density inherent to empty space, or a "vacuum energy." Mathematically, vacuum energy is equivalent to Einstein's cosmological constant. Despite the rejection of the cosmological constant by Einstein and others, the modern understanding of the vacuum, based on quantum field theory, is that vacuum energy arises naturally from the totality of quantum fluctuations (virtual particle-antiparticle pairs that come into existence and then annihilate each other shortly thereafter) in empty space. However, the observed density of the cosmological vacuum energy density is ~10^{-10} ergs per cubic centimetre. The value predicted from quantum field theory is ~10^{110} ergs per cubic centimetre. This discrepancy of 10^{120} was known even before the discovery of the far weaker dark energy. While a fundamental solution to this problem has not yet been found, probabilistic solutions have been posited, motivated by string theory and the possible existence of a large number of disconnected universes. In this paradigm the unexpectedly low value of the constant is understood as a result of an even greater number of opportunities (i.e., universes) for the occurrence of different values of the constant and the random selection of a value small enough to allow for the formation of galaxies—and thus stars and life.

Another popular theory for dark energy is that it is a transient vacuum energy resulting from the potential energy of a dynamical field. Known as "quintessence," this form of dark energy would vary in space and time, providing a possible way to distinguish it from a cosmological constant. It is also similar in mechanism (though vastly different in scale) to the scalar field energy invoked in the inflationary theory of the big bang.

Another possible explanation for dark energy is topological defects in the fabric of the universe. In the case of intrinsic defects in space-time (e.g., cosmic strings or walls), the production of new defects as the universe expands is mathematically similar to a cosmological constant, although the value of the equation of state for the defects depends on whether the defects are strings (one-dimensional) or walls (two-dimensional).

There have also been attempts to modify gravity to explain both cosmological and local observations without the need for dark energy. These attempts invoke departures from general relativity on scales of the entire observable universe.

One major challenge to understanding accelerated expansion with or without dark energy is to explain the relatively recent occurrence (in the past few billion years) of near-equality between the density of dark energy and dark matter even though they must have evolved differently. (For cosmic structures to have formed in the early universe, dark energy must have been an insignificant component.) This problem is known as the "coincidence problem" or the "fine-tuning problem."

Understanding the nature of dark energy and its many related problems is one of the most formidable challenges in modern physics. Though the challenge is formidable, astronomers have over thousands of years succeeded in explaining once-baffling facets of our universe, such as the motion of the planets and the beginning of space and time. Based on previous history, it would not be too presumptuous to expect solutions to dark energy and other, ever more difficult problems to come.

CHAPTER 6

ANCIENT AND EARLY ASTRONOMERS

Behind every belief, theory, and law pertaining to the universe lies at least one inquisitive mind and keen eye. Astronomers have been at the forefront of cosmological discovery for centuries. Many of the earliest notable astronomers hailed from Greece and the Middle East. They were philosophers and mathematicians—individuals who applied reason, logic, and precision to all pursuits, including their study of the night sky. By the 17th and 18th centuries astronomy had burgeoned as a scientific field, and astronomers throughout Europe also took up the quest to explain celestial mechanics and other heavenly phenomena.

ANCIENT TIMES

ANAXIMANDER
(b. 610 BCE, Miletus [now in Turkey]—d. 546/545)

The Greek philosopher Anaximander was the first thinker to develop a cosmology, or systematic philosophical view of the world.

Only a short fragment of Anaximander's work survives, so reconstructions of his philosophy and astronomy must be based on summaries by later Greek writers. These include the 1st- or 2nd-century CE compiler of philosophical opinions, Aëtius; the 3rd-century theologian and antipope, Hippolytus; and the 6th-century Neoplatonist philosopher Simplicius.

Anaximander is said to have been a pupil or associate of the Greek philosopher Thales of Miletus and to have written about astronomy, geography, and the nature of things. Anaximander set up a gnomon (a shadow-casting rod) at Sparta and used it to demonstrate the equinoxes and solstices and perhaps the hours of the day. He drew a map of the known world, which was later corrected by his fellow Milesian, the author Hecataeus, a well-traveled man. Anaximander may also have built a celestial globe.

In his thinking about Earth, he regarded the inhabited portion as flat, consisting of the top face of a cylinder, whose thickness is one-third its diameter. Earth is poised aloft, supported by nothing, and remains in place because it is equidistant from all other things and thus has no disposition to fly off in any one direction. He held that the Sun and the Moon are hollow rings filled with fire. Their disks are vents or holes in the rings, through which the fire can shine. The phases of the Moon, as well as eclipses of the Sun and the Moon, are due to the vents closing up.

Anaximander held an evolutionary view of living things. The first creatures originated from the moist element by evaporation. Man originated from some other kind of animal, such as fish, since man needs a long period of nurture and could not have survived if he had always been what he is now. Anaximander also discussed the causes of meteorological phenomena, such as wind, rain, and lightning.

In his cosmogony, he held that everything originated from the apeiron (the "infinite," "unlimited," or "indefinite"), rather than from a particular element, such as water (as Thales had held). Anaximander postulated eternal motion, along with the apeiron, as the originating cause of the world. This (probably rotary) motion caused opposites, such as hot and cold, to be separated from one another as the world came into being. However, the world is not eternal and will be destroyed back into the apeiron, from which new worlds will be born. Thus, all existing things must "pay penalty and retribution to one another for their injustice, according to the disposition of time," as he rather figuratively expressed it.

While Thales had already dispensed with divine explanations of the world around him, he had not written a book about his philosophy. Moreover, Anaximander went much further in trying to give a unified account of all of nature. Although Anaximander's primitive astronomy was soon superseded, his effort to provide a rational explanation of the world had a lasting influence.

ARISTARCHUS OF SAMOS
(c. 310 BCE–230)

Aristarchus of Samos was a Greek astronomer who was the first to maintain that Earth rotates and revolves around the Sun. On this ground, the Greek philosopher Cleanthes the Stoic declared in his Against Aristarchus that Aristarchus ought to be indicted for impiety "for putting into motion the hearth of the universe."

Aristarchus's work on the motion of Earth has not survived, but his ideas are known from references by the Greek mathematician Archimedes, the Greek biographer Plutarch, and the Greek philosopher Sextus Empiricus. Archimedes said in his *Sand-Reckoner* that Aristarchus had proposed a new theory which, if true, would make the universe vastly larger than was then believed. (This is because a moving Earth should produce a parallax, or annual shift, in the apparent positions of the fixed stars, unless the stars are very far away.)

In the 16th century Aristarchus was an inspiration for Polish astronomer Nicolaus Copernicus's work. In his manuscript of *Six Books Concerning the Revolutions of the Heavenly Orbs* (1543), Copernicus cited Aristarchus as an ancient authority who had espoused the motion of Earth. However, Copernicus later crossed out this reference, and Aristarchus's theory was not mentioned in the published book.

Aristarchus's only extant work is *On the Sizes and Distances of the Sun and Moon*, the oldest surviving geometric treatment of this problem. Aristarchus takes as premises that

(1) as observed during a lunar eclipse, the diameter of Earth's shadow is twice the diameter of the Moon;

(2) the Moon and Sun are each 2 degrees in angular diameter; and

(3) at the time of quarter Moon, the angular distance between the Moon and the Sun is 87 degrees.

Using premise (3), Aristarchus showed that the Sun is between 18 and 20 times farther away from Earth than the Moon is. (The actual ratio is about 390.) Using this result and premises (1) and (2) in a clever geometric construction based on lunar eclipses, he obtained values for the sizes of the Sun and Moon. He found the Moon's diameter to be between 0.32 and 0.40 times the diameter of Earth and the Sun's diameter to be between 6.3 and 7.2 times the diameter of Earth. (The diameters of the Moon and the Sun compared with that of Earth are actually 0.27 and 109, respectively.)

In Aristarchus's day the geometric method was considered more important than numerical measurements. His premise (1) is reasonably accurate. Premise (2) overestimates the Moon's angular diameter by a factor of four, which is puzzling, since this is an easy measurement to make. (In a later publication, Aristarchus gave the angular size of the Moon as half a degree, which is about right, but he apparently did not modify his earlier work.) Premise (3) was probably not based on measurement but rather on an estimate. It is equivalent to assuming that the time from first quarter Moon to third quarter Moon is one day longer than the time from third quarter to first quarter. The true angle between Sun and Moon at the time of quarter Moon is less than 90 degrees by only

9 minutes of arc—a quantity impossible to measure in antiquity.

Later Greek astronomers, especially Hipparchus and Ptolemy, refined Aristarchus's methods and arrived at very accurate values for the size and distance of the Moon. However, because the influence of premise (3), all ancient results grossly underestimated the size and distance of the Sun. Aristarchus's 19:1 ratio nevertheless remained more or less standard until the 17th century.

ERATOSTHENES OF CYRENE
(b. c. 276 BCE, Cyrene, Libya—d. c. 194, Alexandria, Egypt)

Eratosthenes of Cyrene was a Greek scientific writer, astronomer, and poet, who made the first measurement of the size of Earth for which any details are known.

At Syene (now Aswān), some 800 km (500 miles) southeast of Alexandria in Egypt, the Sun's rays fall vertically at noon at the summer solstice. Eratosthenes noted that at Alexandria, at the same date and time, sunlight fell at an angle of about 7.2° from the vertical. (Writing before the Greeks adopted the degree, a Babylonian unit of measure, he actually said "a fiftieth of a circle.") He correctly assumed the Sun's distance to be very great. Its rays, therefore, are practically parallel when they reach Earth. Given an estimate of the distance between the two cities, he was able to calculate the circumference of Earth, obtaining 250,000 stadia. Earlier estimates of the circumference of Earth had been made (for example, Aristotle

says that "some mathematicians" had obtained a value of 400,000 stadia), but no details of their methods have survived. An account of Eratosthenes' method is preserved in the Greek astronomer Cleomedes' *Meteora*. The exact length of the units (stadia) he used is doubtful, and the accuracy of his result is therefore uncertain. His measurement of Earth's circumference may have varied by 0.5 to 17 percent from the value accepted by modern astronomers, but it was certainly in the right range. He also measured the degree of obliquity of the ecliptic (in effect, the tilt of Earth's axis) and wrote a treatise on the *octaëteris*, an eight-year lunar-solar cycle. His only surviving work is *Catasterisms*, a book about the constellations, which gives a description and story for each constellation, as well as a count of the number of stars contained in it. However, attribution of this work has been doubted by some scholars. His mathematical work is known principally from the writings of the Greek geometer Pappus of Alexandria, and his geographical work from the first two books of the *Geography* of the Greek geographer Strabo.

After study in Alexandria and Athens, Eratosthenes settled in Alexandria about 255 BCE and became director of the great library there. He tried to fix the dates of literary and political events since the siege of Troy. His writings included a poem inspired by astronomy, as well as works on the theatre and on ethics. Eratosthenes was afflicted by blindness in his old age, and he is said to have committed suicide by voluntary starvation.

HERACLEIDES PONTICUS
(b. *c.* 390 BCE, Heraclea Pontica, Bithynia—d. after 322, Athens)

The Greek philosopher and astronomer Heracleides Ponticus first suggested the rotation of Earth, an idea that did not dominate astronomy until 1,800 years later. A pupil of Plato, who left the Academy temporarily in his charge, Heracleides is known to have correctly attributed the apparent motion of Mercury and Venus to their revolving around the Sun. Whether he realized that the other planets did so is uncertain. He also taught some kind of atomism. His writings, all lost except for a few fragments, include literary criticism and works on musicology. He also studied trances, cosmological visions, prophecies, portents, and cataclysms, attempting to prove the existence of gods, divine retribution, and reincarnation. He thus exemplified the supranaturalistic tendencies of Platonism and anticipated some aspects of Neoplatonism.

HIPPARCHUS
(b. Nicaea, Bithynia [now Iznik, Turkey]—d. after 127 BCE, Rhodes?)

Hipparchus was a Greek astronomer and mathematician who made fundamental contributions to the advancement of astronomy as a mathematical science and to the foundations of trigonometry. Although he is commonly ranked among the greatest scientists of antiquity, very little is known about his life, and only one of his many writings is still in existence. Knowledge of the rest of his work relies on secondhand reports, especially in the great astronomical compendium the *Almagest*, written by Ptolemy in the 2nd century CE.

LOVER OF TRUTH

As a young man in Bithynia, Hipparchus compiled records of local weather patterns throughout the year. Such weather

Hipparchus, pictured scanning the night sky at the observatory in Alexandria, Egypt. Hulton Archive/Getty Images

calendars (*parapēgmata*), which synchronized the onset of winds, rains, and storms with the astronomical seasons and the risings and settings of the constellations, were produced by many Greek astronomers from at least as early as the 4th century BCE.

Most of Hipparchus's adult life, however, seems to have been spent carrying out a program of astronomical observation and research on the island of Rhodes. Ptolemy cites more than 20 observations made there by Hipparchus on specific dates from 147 to 127, as well as three earlier observations from 162 to 158 that may be attributed to him. These must have been only a tiny fraction of Hipparchus's recorded observations. In fact, his astronomical writings were numerous enough that he published an annotated list of them.

Hipparchus also wrote critical commentaries on some of his predecessors and contemporaries. In *Tōn Aratou kai Eudoxou Phainomenōn exēgēseōs biblia tria* ("Commentary on the Phaenomena of Aratus and Eudoxus"), his only surviving book, he ruthlessly exposed errors in *Phaenomena*, a popular poem written by Aratus and based on a now-lost treatise of Eudoxus of Cnidus that named and described the constellations. Apparently his commentary *Against the Geography of Eratosthenes* was similarly unforgiving of loose and inconsistent reasoning. Ptolemy characterized him as a "lover of truth" (*philalēthēs*)—a trait that was more amiably manifested in Hipparchus's readiness to revise his own beliefs in the light of new evidence. He communicated with observers at Alexandria in Egypt, who provided him with some times of equinoxes, and probably also with astronomers at Babylon.

Solar and Lunar Theory

Hipparchus's most important astronomical work concerned the orbits of the Sun and Moon, a determination of their sizes and distances from Earth, and the study of eclipses. Like most of his predecessors—Aristarchus of Samos was an exception—Hipparchus assumed a spherical, stationary Earth at the centre of the universe (the geocentric cosmology). From this perspective, the Sun, Moon, Mercury, Venus, Mars, Jupiter, and Saturn (all of the solar system bodies visible to the naked eye), as well as the stars (whose realm was known as the celestial sphere), revolved around Earth each day.

Every year the Sun traces out a circular path in a west-to-east direction relative to the stars (this is in addition to the apparent daily east-to-west rotation of the celestial sphere around Earth). Hipparchus had good reasons for believing that the Sun's path, known as the ecliptic, is a great circle, i.e., that the plane of the ecliptic passes through Earth's centre. The two points at which the ecliptic and the equatorial plane intersect, known as the vernal and autumnal equinoxes, and the two points of the ecliptic farthest north and south from the equatorial plane, known as the summer and winter solstices, divide the ecliptic into four equal parts. However, the Sun's passage through each section of the ecliptic, or season, is not symmetrical. Hipparchus attempted to explain how the Sun could travel with uniform speed along a regular circular path and yet produce seasons of unequal length.

Hipparchus knew of two possible explanations for the Sun's apparent motion, the eccenter and the epicyclic models. These models, which assumed that the apparent irregular motion was produced by compounding two or more uniform circular motions, were probably familiar to Greek astronomers well before Hipparchus. His contribution was to discover a method of using the observed dates of two equinoxes and a solstice to calculate the size and direction of the displacement of the Sun's orbit. With Hipparchus's mathematical model one could calculate not only the Sun's orbital location on any date but also its position as seen from Earth. The history of celestial mechanics until Johannes Kepler (1571–1630) was mostly an elaboration of Hipparchus's model.

Hipparchus also tried to measure as precisely as possible the length of the tropical year—the period for the Sun to complete one passage through the ecliptic. He made observations of consecutive equinoxes and solstices, but the results were inconclusive. He could not distinguish between possible observational errors and variations in the tropical year. However, by comparing his own observations of solstices with observations made in the 5th and 3rd centuries BCE, Hipparchus succeeded in obtaining an

estimate of the tropical year, which was only 6 minutes too long.

He was then in a position to calculate equinox and solstice dates for any year. Applying this information to recorded observations from about 150 years before his time, Hipparchus made the unexpected discovery that certain stars near the ecliptic had moved about 2° relative to the equinoxes. He contemplated various explanations—for example, that these stars were actually very slowly moving planets—before he settled on the essentially correct theory that all the stars made a gradual eastward revolution relative to the equinoxes. Since Nicolaus Copernicus (1473–1543) established his heliocentric model of the universe, the stars have provided a fixed frame of reference, relative to which the plane of the Equator slowly shifts—a phenomenon referred to as the precession of the equinoxes.

Hipparchus also analyzed the more complicated motion of the Moon in order to construct a theory of eclipses. In addition to varying in apparent speed, the Moon diverges north and south of the ecliptic, and the periodicities of these phenomena are different. Hipparchus adopted values for the Moon's periodicities that were known to contemporary Babylonian astronomers, and he confirmed their accuracy by comparing recorded observations of lunar eclipses separated by intervals of several centuries. It remained, however, for Ptolemy (127–145 CE) to finish fashioning a fully predictive lunar model.

In *On Sizes and Distances* (now lost), Hipparchus reportedly measured the

Moon's orbit in relation to the size of Earth. He had two methods of doing this. One method used an observation of a solar eclipse that had been total near the Hellespont (now called the Dardanelles) but only partial at Alexandria. Hipparchus assumed that the difference could be attributed entirely to the Moon's observable parallax against the stars, which amounts to supposing that the Sun, like the stars, is indefinitely far away. (Parallax is the apparent displacement of an object when viewed from different vantage points.) Hipparchus thus calculated that the mean distance of the Moon from Earth is 77 times Earth's radius. In the second method he hypothesized that the distance from the centre of Earth to the Sun is 490 times Earth's radius—perhaps chosen because that is the shortest distance consistent with a parallax that is too small for detection by the unaided eye. Using the visually identical sizes of the solar and lunar disks, and observations of Earth's shadow during lunar eclipses, Hipparchus found a relationship between the lunar and solar distances that enabled him to calculate that the Moon's mean distance from Earth is approximately 63 times Earth's radius. (The true value is about 60 times.)

Other Scientific Work

The eccenter and epicyclic models sufficed to describe the motion of a body that has a single periodic variation in apparent speed, which so far as Hipparchus knew was the case with the Sun and Moon. According to Ptolemy, Hipparchus was aware that the movements of the planets were too complex to be accounted for by the same simple models, but he did not attempt to devise a satisfactory planetary theory.

According to Pliny the Elder (23–79 CE), Hipparchus created a star catalog that assigned names to each star along with his measurements of their positions. However, the direct evidence for this catalog is very poor and does not reveal either the number of stars that it contained or how the positions were expressed—whether in terms of a coordinate system or by location within various constellations. In the *Almagest* Ptolemy presents a catalog of 1,022 stars grouped by constellations, with apparent magnitudes (measure of brightness) and coordinates in degrees measured along the ecliptic and perpendicular to it. Although Ptolemy stated that his catalog was based on personal observations, some historians argue that it was derived in large part from Hipparchus's catalog, with a simple adjustment for the intervening precessional motion. This remains one of the most controversial topics in the study of ancient astronomy.

Hipparchus lived just before the rise of Greco-Roman astrology, but he surely knew about the Near Eastern traditions of astral divination that were already spreading in the classical world. In later astrological texts he is occasionally cited as an authority—most credibly as a source for astrological correspondences between constellations and geographical regions.

Hipparchus's principal interest in geography, as quoted from *Against the Geography of Eratosthenes* by the Greek geographer Strabo (*c.* 64 BCE–23 CE), was the accurate determination of terrestrial locations. Ancient authors preserved only a few tantalizing allusions to Hipparchus's other scientific work. For instance, *On Bodies Carried Down by Their Weight* speculated on the principles of weight and motion, and a work on optics adhered to Euclid's theory from the *Optics* that vision is produced by an emanation of rays from the eyes. Hipparchus's calculation of the exact number (103,049) of possible logical statements constructible from 10 basic assertions according to certain rules of Stoic logic is a rare surviving instance of Greek interest in combinatoric mathematics. Hipparchus's most significant contribution to mathematics may have been to develop—if not actually invent—a trigonometry based on a table of the lengths of chords in a circle of unit radius tabulated as a function of the angle subtended at the centre. Such a table would, for the first time, allow a systematic solution of general trigonometric problems, and clearly Hipparchus used it extensively for his astronomical calculations. Like so much of Hipparchus's work, his chord table has not survived.

KIDINNU
(fl. 4th or early 3rd century BCE, Babylonia)

The Babylonian astronomer and mathematician Kidinnu may have discovered the precession of the equinoxes—the slow rotation of Earth's axis that results in slight variations in the length of the year. Head of the astronomical school at Sippar, Kidinnu was probably responsible for introducing the 19-year cycle into the Babylonian calendar in 383 BCE. In this system each year had 12 lunar months, but 7 extra months were inserted at intervals during the 19-year period. The 19-year cycle of intercalations was adopted by the Jews and has remained in use.

Kidinnu also developed the more refined system (called System B) used by the Babylonians to describe more clearly the motions of the Sun and planets. This system utilized steadily increasing and decreasing values for the planetary positions, sometimes called zigzag functions. Kidinnu's calculation of the length of the synodic month (from new Moon to new Moon) yielded a value of 29.530614 days, which differs by less than one second from the true value.

PTOLEMY
(b. c. 100 CE–d. c. 170)

The Egyptian astronomer, mathematician, and geographer of Greek descent Ptolemy flourished in Alexandria during the 2nd century CE. In several fields his writings represent the culminating achievement of Greco-Roman science, particularly his geocentric (Earth-centred) model of the universe now known as the Ptolemaic system.

Virtually nothing is known about Ptolemy's life except what can be inferred from his writings. His first major astronomical work, the *Almagest*, was completed about 150 CE and contains reports of astronomical observations that Ptolemy had made over the preceding quarter of a century. The size and content of his subsequent literary production suggests that he lived until about 170 CE.

ASTRONOMER

The book that is now generally known as the *Almagest* (from a hybrid of Arabic and Greek, "the greatest") was called by Ptolemy *Hē mathēmatikē syntaxis* ("The Mathematical Collection") because he believed that its subject, the motions of the heavenly bodies, could be explained in mathematical terms. The opening chapters present empirical arguments for the basic cosmological framework within which Ptolemy worked. Earth, he argued, is a stationary sphere at the centre of a vastly larger celestial sphere that revolves at a perfectly uniform rate around Earth, carrying with it the stars, planets, Sun, and Moon—thereby causing their daily risings and settings. Through the course of a year the Sun slowly traces out a great circle, known as the ecliptic, against the rotation of the celestial sphere. (The Moon and planets similarly travel backward—hence, the planets were also known as "wandering stars"—against the "fixed stars" found in the ecliptic.) The fundamental assumption of the *Almagest* is that the apparently irregular movements of the heavenly bodies are in reality combinations of regular, uniform, circular motions.

How much of the *Almagest* is original is difficult to determine because almost all of the preceding technical astronomical literature is now lost. Ptolemy credited Hipparchus (mid-2nd century BCE) with essential elements of his solar theory, as well as parts of his lunar theory, while denying that Hipparchus constructed planetary models. Ptolemy made only a few vague and disparaging remarks regarding theoretical work over the intervening three centuries. Yet the study of the planets undoubtedly made great strides during that interval. Moreover, Ptolemy's veracity, especially as an observer, has been controversial since the time of the astronomer Tycho Brahe (1546–1601). Brahe pointed out that solar observations Ptolemy claimed to have made in 141 are definitely not genuine, and there are strong arguments for doubting that Ptolemy independently observed the more than 1,000 stars listed in his star catalog. What is not disputed, however, is the mastery of mathematical analysis that Ptolemy exhibited.

Ptolemy was preeminently responsible for the geocentric cosmology that prevailed in the Islamic world and in medieval Europe. This was not due to the *Almagest* so much as a later treatise, *Hypotheseis tōn planōmenōn* (*Planetary Hypotheses*). In this work he proposed what is now called the Ptolemaic system—a unified system in which each heavenly body is attached to its own sphere and the set of spheres nested so that it extends without gaps from Earth to the celestial sphere. The numerical tables in the *Almagest* (which enabled planetary positions and other celestial phenomena to be calculated for arbitrary dates) had a profound influence on medieval astronomy, in part through a separate, revised version of the tables that Ptolemy published as *Procheiroi kanones* ("Handy Tables"). Ptolemy taught later astronomers how to use dated, quantitative observations to revise cosmological models.

Ptolemy also attempted to place astrology on a sound basis in *Apotelesmatika* ("Astrological Influences"), later known as the *Tetrabiblos* for its four volumes. He believed that astrology is a legitimate, though inexact, science that describes the physical effects of the heavens on terrestrial life. Ptolemy accepted the basic validity of the traditional astrological doctrines, but he revised the details to reconcile the practice with an Aristotelian conception of nature, matter, and change. Of Ptolemy's writings, the *Tetrabiblos* is the most foreign to modern readers, who do not accept astral prognostication and a cosmology driven by the interplay of basic qualities such as hot, cold, wet, and dry.

MATHEMATICIAN

Ptolemy has a prominent place in the history of mathematics primarily because of the mathematical methods he applied to astronomical problems. His contributions to trigonometry are especially important. For instance, Ptolemy's table of the lengths of chords in a circle is the earliest surviving table of a trigonometric function. He also applied fundamental theorems in spherical trigonometry (apparently discovered half a century earlier by Menelaus of Alexandria) to the solution of many basic astronomical problems.

Among Ptolemy's earliest treatises, the *Harmonics* investigated musical theory while steering a middle course between an extreme empiricism and the mystical arithmetical speculations associated with Pythagoreanism. Ptolemy's discussion of the roles of reason and the

Ptolemy, c. 135 CE; engraving by George Cooke. Hulton Archive/Getty Images

senses in acquiring scientific knowledge have bearing beyond music theory.

Probably near the end of his life, Ptolemy turned to the study of visual perception in *Optica* ("Optics"), a work that only survives in a mutilated medieval Latin translation of an Arabic translation. The extent to which Ptolemy subjected visual perception to empirical analysis is remarkable when contrasted with other Greek writers on optics. For example, Hero of Alexandria (mid-1st century CE) asserted, purely for philosophical reasons, that an object and its mirror image must make equal angles to a mirror. In contrast, Ptolemy established this principle by measuring angles of incidence and reflection for planar and curved mirrors set upon a disk graduated in degrees. Ptolemy also measured how lines of sight are refracted at the boundary between materials of different density, such as air, water, and glass, although he failed to discover the exact law relating the angles of incidence and refraction.

GEOGRAPHER

Ptolemy's fame as a geographer is hardly less than his fame as an astronomer. *Geōgraphikē hyphēgēsis* (*Guide to Geography*) provided all the information and techniques required to draw maps of the portion of the world known by Ptolemy's contemporaries. By his own admission, Ptolemy did not attempt to collect and sift all the geographical data on which his maps were based. Instead, he based them on the maps and writings

of Marinus of Tyre (*c.* 100 CE), only selectively introducing more current information, chiefly concerning the Asian and African coasts of the Indian Ocean. Nothing would be known about Marinus if Ptolemy had not preserved the substance of his cartographical work.

Ptolemy's most important geographical innovation was to record longitudes and latitudes in degrees for roughly 8,000 locations on his world map, making it possible to make an exact duplicate of his map. Hence, we possess a clear and detailed image of the inhabited world as it was known to a resident of the Roman Empire at its height—a world that extended from the Shetland Islands in the north to the sources of the Nile in the south, from the Canary Islands in the west to China and Southeast Asia in the east. Ptolemy's map is seriously distorted in size and orientation compared to modern maps, a reflection of the incomplete and inaccurate descriptions of road systems and trade routes at his disposal.

Ptolemy also devised two ways of drawing a grid of lines on a flat map to represent the circles of latitude and longitude on the globe. His grid gives a visual impression of Earth's spherical surface and also, to a limited extent, preserves the proportionality of distances. The more sophisticated of these map projections, using circular arcs to represent both parallels and meridians, anticipated later area-preserving projections. Ptolemy's geographical work was almost unknown in Europe until about 1300, when Byzantine scholars began producing many manuscript copies, several of them illustrated with expert reconstructions of Ptolemy's maps. The Italian Jacopo d'Angelo translated the work into Latin in 1406. The numerous Latin manuscripts and early print editions of Ptolemy's *Guide to Geography*, most of them accompanied by maps, attest to the profound impression this work made upon its rediscovery by Renaissance humanists.

MEDIEVAL

AL-BATTĀNĪ
(b. c. 858, in or near Haran, near Urfa, Syria—d. 929, near Sāmarrā', Iraq)

The Arab astronomer and mathematician Abū 'abd Allāh Muḥammad Ibn Jābir Ibn Sinān Al-battānī Al-ḥarrānī As-ṣabi' refined existing values for the length of the year and of the seasons, for the annual precession of the equinoxes, and for the inclination of the ecliptic. He showed that the position of the Sun's apogee, or farthest point from Earth, is variable and that annular (central but incomplete) eclipses of the Sun are possible. He improved Ptolemy's astronomical calculations by replacing geometrical methods with trigonometry. From 877 he carried out many years of remarkably accurate observations at ar-Raqqah in Syria.

Al-Battānī was the best known of Arab astronomers in Europe during the Middle Ages. His principal written work, a compendium of astronomical tables, was translated into Latin in about 1116

and into Spanish in the 13th century. A printed edition, under the title *De motu stellarum* ("On Stellar Motion"), was published in 1537.

AL-BĪRŪNĪ
(b. Sept. 973, Khwārezm, Khorāsān [now in Uzbekistan]—d. 1050, Ghazna, Ghaznavid Afghanistan [now Ghaznī, Afg.])

Abū al-Rayḥān Muḥammad ibn Aḥmad al-Bīrūnī was a Persian scholar and scientist, one of the most learned men of his age, and an outstanding intellectual figure.

Possessing a profound and original mind of encyclopaedic scope, al-Bīrūnī was conversant with Turkish, Persian, Sanskrit, Hebrew, and Syriac in addition to the Arabic in which he wrote. He applied his talents in many fields of knowledge, excelling particularly in astronomy, mathematics, chronology, physics, medicine, and history. He corresponded with the great philosopher Ibn Sīnā (Avicenna). Sometime after 1017 he went to India and made a comprehensive study of its culture. Later he settled at Ghazna (now Ghaznī) in Afghanistan. He was a Shī'ite Muslim but with agnostic tendencies.

Al-Bīrūnī's most famous works are *al-Āthār al-bāqiyah* (*Chronology of Ancient Nations*); *Al-Tafhīm* ("Elements of Astrology"); *Al-Qanūn al-Mas'ūdī* ("The Mas'ūdī Canon"), a major work on astronomy, which he dedicated to Sultan Mas'ūd of Ghazna; *Tā'rīkh al-Hind* ("A

History of India"); and *Kitāb al-Ṣaydalah*, a treatise on drugs used in medicine. In his works on astronomy, he discussed with approval the theory of Earth's rotation on its axis and made accurate calculations of latitude and longitude. In works on physics, he explained natural springs by the laws of hydrostatics and determined with remarkable accuracy the specific weight of 18 precious stones and metals. In geography, he advanced the daring view that the valley of the Indus had once been a sea basin.

RENAISSANCE

GEORG RHETICUS
(b. Feb. 16, 1514, Feldkirch, Austria—d. Dec. 5, 1576, Kassa, Hung.)

The Austrian-born astronomer and mathematician Georg Joachim Rheticus was among the first to adopt and spread the heliocentric theory of Nicolaus Copernicus.

In 1536 Rheticus was appointed to a chair of mathematics and astronomy at the University of Wittenberg. Intrigued by the news of the Copernican theory that Earth revolves around the Sun, he went to Frauenburg (now Frombork, Pol.) in 1539, where he studied for two years with Copernicus. Rheticus published the first account of the new views in his *De libris revolutionum . . . Nic. Copernici . . . narratio prima . . .* (1540; "The First Account of the Book on the Revolutions by Nicolaus Copernicus"). He encouraged Copernicus to complete his great

work and took it to Nürnberg for publication, though in 1542 he moved to Leipzig to take up a new appointment before it was actually printed.

From his stay at Wittenberg until his death, Rheticus also worked on his great treatise, which was completed and published after his death by his pupil Valentin Otto as *Opus Palatinum de triangulis* (1596; "The Palatine Work on Triangles"). The treatise contains tables of values for the trigonometric functions (of an arc or angle) computed in intervals of 10 seconds of arc and calculated to 10 decimal places.

17TH CENTURY

JOHANN BAYER
(b. 1572, Rain, Bavaria [Ger.]—d. March 7, 1625, Augsburg [Ger.])

Johann Bayer was a German astronomer whose book *Uranometria* (1603) promulgated a system of identifying all stars visible to the naked eye.

Bayer entered Ingolstadt University in 1592 to study philosophy and later moved to Augsburg. He became a lawyer by profession but, like many of his time, took a curious interest in the new advances in astronomy, leading to his publication of *Uranometria*, a popular guide to the constellations. In 1612 he was appointed legal adviser to the city council of Augsburg.

Before Bayer's work, star charts were based on Ptolemy's star catalog, which was incomplete and ambiguous. Bayer updated Ptolemy's list of 48 constella-tions, adding 12 constellations newly recognized in the Southern Hemisphere. Based upon Tycho Brahe's determina-tions of stellar positions and magnitudes, Bayer assigned each visible star in a con-stellation one of the 24 Greek letters. For constellations with more than 24 visible stars, Bayer completed his listing with Latin letters. The nomenclature that Bayer developed is still used today and has been extended to apply to about 1,300 stars.

GIAN DOMENICO CASSINI
(b. June 8, 1625, Perinaldo, Republic of Genoa—d. Sept. 14, 1712, Paris)

The Italian-born French astronomer Gian Domenico Cassini was one of the discov-erers of the Cassini Division, the dark gap between the rings A and B of Saturn. He also discovered four of Saturn's moons. In addition, he was the first to record obser-vations of the zodiacal light.

Cassini's early studies were princi-pally observations of the Sun, but after he obtained more powerful telescopes, he turned his attention to the planets. He was the first to observe the shadows of Jupiter's satellites as they passed between that planet and the Sun. His observation of spots on the surface of the planet allowed him to measure Jupiter's rotational period. In 1666, after similar observations of Mars, he found the value of 24 hours, 40 minutes for Mars's rotational period. It is now given as 24 hours, 37 minutes, and 22.66

seconds. Two years later he compiled a table of the positions of Jupiter's satel-lites that was used in 1675 by the Danish astronomer Ole Rømer to establish that the speed of light is finite. In addition, he wrote several memoirs on flood con-trol, and he experimented extensively in applied hydraulics.

Hearing of Cassini's discoveries and work, King Louis XIV of France invited him to Paris in 1669 to join the recently formed Académie des Sciences. Cassini assumed the directorship of the Observatoire de Paris after it was com-pleted in 1671, and two years later he became a French citizen.

Continuing the studies begun in Italy, Cassini discovered the Saturnian satellites Iapetus (1671), Rhea (1672), Tethys (1684), and Dione (1684). He also discovered the flattening of Jupiter at its poles (a consequence of its rotation on its axis). In 1672, as part of a concerted effort to determine the size of the solar system more accurately, Cassini sent his colleague, Jean Richer, to South America so that roughly simultaneous measure-ments of the position of Mars could be made at Paris and Cayenne, French Guiana. This led to a better value for the Martian parallax and, indirectly, for the distance of the Sun. Between 1671 and 1679 Cassini made observations of the Moon, compiling a large map, which he presented to the Académie. In 1675 he discovered the Cassini Division and expressed the opinion that Saturn's rings were swarms of tiny moonlets too small to be seen individually—an opinion that has been substantiated. In 1683, after a careful study of the zodiacal light, he concluded that it was of cosmic origin and not a meteorological phenomenon, as some proposed.

In 1683 Cassini began the measurement of the arc of the meridian (longitude line) through Paris. From the results, he concluded that Earth is somewhat elongated (it is actually somewhat flattened at the poles). A traditionalist, he accepted the solar theory of Nicolaus Copernicus within limits, but he rejected the theory of Johannes Kepler that planets travel in ellipses. He proposed that their paths were certain curved ovals, which came to be known as Cassinians, or ovals of Cassini. Although Cassini resisted new theories and ideas, his discoveries and observations unquestionably place him among the most important astronomers of the 17th and 18th centuries.

He was the first of four successive generations of Cassinis to direct the Paris Observatory.

John Flamsteed
(b. Aug. 19, 1646, Denby, near Derby, Derbyshire, Eng.—d. Dec. 31, 1719, Greenwich, London)

John Flamsteed was the founder of the Greenwich Observatory and the first astronomer royal of England.

Poor health forced Flamsteed to leave school in 1662. He studied astronomy on his own and later (1670–74) continued his education at the University of Cambridge. In 1677 he became a member of the Royal Society. Ordained a clergyman in 1675, Flamsteed in 1684 received the income of the living of Burstow, Surrey. His report to the Royal Society on the need for a new observatory resulted in the founding (1675) of the Royal Greenwich Observatory, of which he was the first director (and hence astronomer royal). He found that he himself had to supply all the instruments at Greenwich, apart from a few gifts. He was forced to take private pupils to augment his income. A small inheritance from his father, who died in 1688, provided the means to construct a mural arc, a wall-mounted instrument for measuring the altitudes of stars as they passed the meridian.

The latter part of Flamsteed's life passed in controversy over the publication of his excellent stellar observations. He struggled to withhold them until completed, but they were urgently needed by Isaac Newton and Edmond Halley, among others. Newton, through the Royal Society, led the movement for their immediate publication. In 1704 Prince George of Denmark undertook the cost of publication. Despite the prince's death in 1708 and Flamsteed's objections, the incomplete observations were edited by Halley, and 400 copies were printed in 1712. Flamsteed later managed to burn 300 of them. His own star catalog, *Historia Coelestis Britannica* (1725), listed more stars (3,000) and gave their positions much more accurately than did any other previous work. Some stars, such as 61 Cygni, are still known by their numbers in his system.

JOHANNES HEVELIUS
(b. Jan. 28, 1611, Gdańsk, Pol.—d. Jan. 28, 1687, Gdańsk)

Johannes Hevelius compiled an atlas of the Moon (*Selenographia*, published 1647) containing one of the earliest detailed maps of its surface as well as names for many of its features. A few of his names for lunar mountains (e.g., the Alps) are still in use, and a lunar crater is named for him. Hevelius also made a catalog of 1,564 stars, the most comprehensive of its time, and a celestial atlas in which several constellations, now accepted, were shown for the first time. After his death, the catalog and the atlas were published together (*Prodromus Astronomiae*, 1690) by his wife, Elisabetha, who had collaborated with him in his observations.

A member of a noble family of Gdańsk, Hevelius was a city councillor and a brewer. After studying at the University of Leiden in the Netherlands, he returned to Gdańsk and built an observatory atop his house and equipped it with fine instruments of his own making. Although he built and used telescopes, he preferred to measure celestial positions without the aid of lenses. In 1679 the English astronomer Edmond Halley visited Hevelius and

Johannes Hevelius. © Photos.com/ Jupiterimages

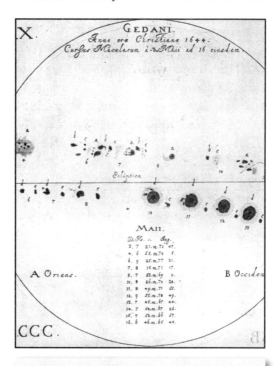

Diagram of sunspot observations made by Johannes Hevelius, 1647. © Photos.com/Jupiterimages

compared the use of a sextant having telescopic sights with Hevelius's sextant with open sights. Hevelius showed that he could determine stellar positions about as accurately without a telescope as Halley could with one.

Jeremiah Horrocks
(b. c. 1617, Toxteth Park, near Liverpool [now in Merseyside], Eng.—d. Jan. 3, 1641, Toxteth Park)

Jeremiah Horrocks was a British astronomer and clergyman who applied Johannes Kepler's laws of planetary motion to the Moon and whose observations of a transit of Venus (1639) are the first recorded.

Horrocks studied at the University of Cambridge from 1632 to 1635. He then became a tutor at Toxteth and studied astronomy in his spare time. He was ordained to the curacy of Hoole, Lancashire, in 1639. The transit of Venus—which had been overlooked in Kepler's tables but which Horrocks had predicted—took place on Sunday, November 24 (Old Style), and he observed it between church services.

He showed the Moon's orbit to be approximately elliptical, thus making a partial basis for Sir Isaac Newton's later work. Horrocks also studied tides and the mutual perturbation of Jupiter and Saturn. He calculated an improved value of 14 minutes for the solar parallax, a measure of Earth's mean distance from the Sun, and suggested correctly that the Sun had a perturbing effect on the Moon's orbit.

Simon Marius
(b. Jan. 10, 1573, Gunzenhausen, Bavaria [Ger.]—d. Dec. 26, 1624, Anspach)

German astronomer Simon Marius named the four largest moons of Jupiter: Io, Europa, Ganymede, and Callisto. All four are named after mythological figures with whom Jupiter fell in love. He and Italian astronomer Galileo Galilei both claimed to have discovered them, about 1610, and it is likely both did so independently. A dispute over priority resulted in unwarranted obloquy for Marius. The two were antagonists for the rest of their lives, and on several occasions Galileo attacked Marius in print and accused him of plagiarizing his work.

Marius studied briefly with Tycho Brahe and later became one of the first astronomers to use a telescope. He was the first to publish, in 1611, the telescopic observation of the Andromeda galaxy, describing the sight as "like a candle seen at night through a horn" (referring to horn lanterns, then common). He was also among the first to observe sunspots.

Nicolas-Claude Fabri de Peiresc
(b. Dec. 1, 1580, Belgentier, France—d. June 24, 1637, Aix-en-Provence)

French antiquary, humanist, and influential patron of learning Nicolas-Claude Fabri de Peiresc discovered the Orion Nebula (1610) and was among the first to emphasize the study of coins for historical research.

Travels in Italy (1599–1602), studies at Padua, and acquaintance there with Galileo stimulated Peiresc's antiquarian and astronomical interests. A senator at the Parlement of Aix from 1605, he corresponded with the Flemish painter Peter Paul Rubens and many of the noted scholars of the day. Peiresc was first to verify William Harvey's discovery of the circulation of blood, and Sir Isaac Newton made use of his work on optics. He encouraged the legal studies of the Dutch jurist Hugo Grotius, on whose writings much of international law is based, and was largely responsible for the publication of a well-known political satire of the time, *Argenis,* by the Scottish poet John Barclay (1621). No published works by Peiresc are known, but the records of his correspondence indicate the catholicity of his interests.

JEAN PICARD
(b. July 21, 1620, La Flèche, France—d. July 12, 1682, Paris)

French astronomer Jean Picard first accurately measured the length of a degree of a meridian (longitude line) and from that computed the size of Earth.

Picard became a professor of astronomy at the Collège de France, Paris, in 1655. His measurement of Earth was used by Sir Isaac Newton to verify his theory of gravitation. In 1671 Picard went to the observatory of astronomer Tycho Brahe at Hven Island, Sweden, to determine its exact location so that Brahe's observations could be more precisely compared with those made elsewhere. He brought back copies of the originals of Brahe's principal work.

Picard is also credited with the introduction of telescopic sights and the use of pendulum clocks as contributions to greater precision in astronomical observations. In 1675 he made the first recorded observation of barometric light, the light that appears in the vacuum above the mercury in a barometer when the barometer is moved around. In 1679 he founded and became editor of *La Connaissance des temps ou des mouvements célestes* ("Knowledge of Time or the Celestial Motions"), the first national astronomical ephemeris, or collection of tables giving the positions of celestial bodies at regular intervals.

JEAN RICHER
(b. 1630—d. 1696, Paris, France)

Jean Richer was a French astronomer whose observations of the planet Mars from Cayenne, French Guiana, in 1671–73 contributed to both astronomy and geodesy. The French government sent Richer to Cayenne to investigate atmospheric refraction at a site near the Equator, to observe the Sun in order to get a better value for the obliquity of the ecliptic, and especially to measure the parallax of Mars at its opposition. Comparison of Richer's Mars observations with those made elsewhere made it possible to determine the distances of Mars and the Sun from Earth, leading to the first reasonably accurate calculation of the dimensions of the solar system and showing the system to be much larger than previously believed.

Richer's observations also led to a discovery about Earth's shape. Through experimentation, Richer discovered that the beat of a pendulum is slower at Cayenne than at Paris, which is at a different latitude. This meant that gravity must be weaker at Cayenne than at Paris. Sir Isaac Newton and Dutch mathematician Christiaan Huygens used this discovery to prove that Earth is not a sphere but is actually flattened at the poles (an oblate spheroid). Thus, Cayenne is farther than Paris from Earth's centre.

OLE RØMER
(b. Sept. 25, 1644, Århus, Jutland, Den.—d. Sept. 23, 1710, Copenhagen)

The Danish astronomer Ole Christensen Rømer demonstrated conclusively that light travels at a finite speed.

Rømer went to Paris in 1672, where he spent nine years working at the Royal Observatory. The observatory's director, Italian-born French astronomer Gian Domenico Cassini, was engaged with a problem that had been studied long before by Galileo: how to use the periodic eclipses of the moons of Jupiter as a universal clock that would be an aid to navigation. (As a satellite goes behind Jupiter, it passes into the shadow of the planet and disappears.) Cassini and his coworkers discovered that the times between successive eclipses of the same satellite (e.g., Io) show an irregularity that is connected with the location of Earth on

its own orbit. The time elapsed between successive eclipses of Io becomes shorter as Earth moves closer to Jupiter and becomes longer as Earth and Jupiter draw farther apart. Cassini had considered, but then rejected, the idea that this might be due to a finite propagation speed for light.

In 1676, Rømer announced that the eclipse of Io scheduled for November 9 would be 10 minutes later than the time deduced on the basis of earlier eclipses of the same satellite. When events transpired as he had predicted, Rømer explained that the speed of light was such that it takes light 22 minutes to cross the diameter of Earth's orbit. (Seventeen minutes would be more accurate.) Dutch mathematician Christiaan Huygens, in his *Traité de la lumière* (1690; "Treatise on Light"), used Rømer's ideas to give an actual numerical value for the speed of light that was reasonably close to the value accepted today—though somewhat inaccurate due to an overestimate of the time delay and some error in the then-accepted figure for the diameter of Earth's orbit.

In 1679 Rømer went on a scientific mission to England, where he met Sir Isaac Newton and the astronomers John Flamsteed and Edmond Halley. Upon his return to Denmark in 1681, he was appointed royal mathematician and professor of astronomy at the University of Copenhagen. At the university observatory he set up an instrument with altitude and azimuth circles and a telescope, which accurately measured the position of celestial objects. He also held several public offices, including that of mayor of Copenhagen in 1705.

18TH CENTURY

JEAN-SYLVAIN BAILLY
(b. Sept. 15, 1736, Paris, France—d. Nov. 12, 1793, Paris)

French astronomer Jean-Sylvain Bailly was noted for his computation of an orbit for Halley's Comet (1759) and for his studies of the four satellites of Jupiter then known. He was also a statesman who took part in the revolutionary events of his age.

Bailly began his study of Halley's Comet in 1759. One year later he established an observatory where he could undertake observations of Jupiter's satellites. He was elected to the Académie des Sciences in 1763. His major works include *Essai sur la théorie des satellites de Jupiter* (1766; "Essay on the Theory of Jupiter's Satellites") and *Mémoires sur les inégalités de la lumière des satellites de Jupiter* (1771; "Memoirs on the Uneven Illumination of Jupiter's Satellites").

Later in his career Bailly wrote widely read histories of astronomy: *Histoire de l'astronomie ancienne depuis son origine jusqu'à l'établissement de l'école d'Alexandrie* (1775; "History of Ancient Astronomy from Its Origin to the Establishment of the School of Alexandria") and *Histoire de l'astronomie moderne depuis la fondation de l'école d'Alexandrie, jusqu'à l'époque de M.D.CC.XXX* (1779;

"History of Modern Astronomy from the Foundation of the School of Alexandria to the Epoch 1730"). However, these were soon superceded by the more scholarly histories of French astronomer Jean-Baptiste-Joseph Delambre. Bailly's *Traité de l'astronomie indienne et orientale* (1787; "Treatise on Indian and Oriental Astronomy") was part of a wave of 18th-century interest in the history and methods of non-Western astronomy. In 1784 Bailly was a member of a royal commission appointed to investigate the claims of animal magnetism made by German physician Franz Mesmer. He was also the author of the report concluding that Mesmer's magnetic fluid probably did not exist and that the effects on his human subjects were likely due to imagination and imitation.

The French Revolution interrupted his studies. Elected deputy from Paris to the Estates-General, he was chosen president of the third estate on May 5, 1789, and led the famous proceedings in the Tennis Court on June 20. He was proclaimed the first mayor of Paris on July 15, 1789. He was reelected mayor in August 1790 but lost popularity—particularly after his order to the national guard to disperse a riotous crowd led to the massacre of the Champ de Mars on July 17, 1791. Bailly retired on Nov. 16, 1791, and went to Nantes in July 1792, where he composed *Mémoires d'un témoin de la Révolution* ("Memoirs of a Witness of the Revolution"), an incomplete narrative of the extraordinary events of his public life. Late in 1793 Bailly went to Melun to join his friend, scientist Pierre-Simon Laplace, but was recognized, arrested, and taken before the revolutionary tribunal at Paris on November 10. He was subsequently guillotined.

JEAN-BAPTISTE-GASPARD BOCHART DE SARON
(b. Jan. 16, 1730, Paris, France—d. April 20, 1794, Paris)

Jean-Baptiste-Gaspard Bochart de Saron was a French lawyer and natural scientist who became especially known for his contributions to astronomy.

After studies at the Collège Louis-le-Grand, a part of the University of Paris, Saron became legal counselor to the Parlement of Paris in 1748, master of requests in 1750, advocate general in 1753, a judicial president in 1755, and president of the Parlement of Paris in 1789—a few months prior to the outbreak of the French Revolution.

Well-to-do, he became a patron of the sciences, financing the publication of the marquis de Laplace's *Theory of the Movement and Elliptic Figure of the Planets* (1784) and developing one of Europe's largest and finest collections of reflecting telescopes and other astronomical instruments for his own use and the use of his scientific friends. Saron's own studies included calculation of the orbits of comets, using data contributed by his long-time collaborator Charles Messier. In 1779 Saron was received into the Academy of Sciences as an honorary member.

Saron was one of several astronomers who tried to fit orbits to British astronomer William Herschel's new "comet" of 1781. He was the first to argue that the object must be at a great distance and tried to fit it with a circular orbit with a radius equal to 12 times the distance from Earth to the Sun. This was a step in the right direction and helped establish the "comet" Uranus as a planet.

Saron protested the dissolution of the Parlement and was guillotined during the Reign of Terror.

JOHANN BODE
(b. Jan. 19, 1747, Hamburg [Ger.]—d. Nov. 23, 1826, Berlin)

German astronomer Johann Elert Bode was best known for his popularization of Bode's law, or the Titius-Bode rule, an empirical mathematical expression for the relative mean distances between the Sun and its planets.

In 1774 Bode founded the well-known *Astronomisches Jahrbuch* ("Astronomic Yearbook"), 51 yearly volumes of which he compiled and issued. He became director of the Berlin Observatory in 1786 and withdrew from official life in 1825. Among his other publications was *Uranographia* (1801), a collection of 20 star maps accompanied by a catalog of 17,240 stars and nebulae. In 1776 he propounded a theory of the solar constitution similar to that developed in 1795 by Sir William Herschel. He gave currency to the empirical rule known as Bode's law, which was actually announced by Johann

Daniel Titius of Wittenberg in 1766. This law was an important factor in the discovery of the minor planets, most of which are located between Mars and Jupiter.

PIERRE BOUGUER
(b. Feb. 16, 1698, Le Croisic, France—d. Aug. 15, 1758, Paris)

The versatile French scientist Pierre Bouguer was best remembered as one of the founders of photometry, the measurement of light intensities.

Bouguer was a prodigy trained by his father, Jean Bouguer, in hydrography and mathematics. Upon his father's death, Pierre—at age 15—succeeded the elder Bouguer as royal professor of hydrography. During the 1720s he made some of the earliest measurements in astronomical photometry, comparing the apparent brightness of celestial objects to that of a standard candle flame. In 1735 he set off on an expedition with C. M. de la Condamine to measure an arc of the meridian near the Equator in Peru. He used the results obtained to make a new determination of Earth's shape. He gave a full account of his researches in *La Figure de la terre* (1749; "The Shape of the Earth"). Bouguer measured gravity by pendulum at different altitudes and was the first to attempt to measure the horizontal gravitational pull of mountains. He observed the deviation of the force of gravity, measured on a high plateau, from that calculated on the basis of the elevation, and correctly ascribed the effect to the mass of matter between his station and mean sea level. He made tables of atmospheric refraction, investigated the absorption of light in the atmosphere, and formulated Bouguer's law (sometimes called Lambert's law), regarding the attenuation of a light beam in a transparent medium. This law and his photometric work he published in his *Essai d'optique sur la gradation de la lumière* (1729; *Optical Treatise on the Gradation of Light*).

Bouguer devoted much of his life to the study of nautical problems. He wrote on naval maneuvers and navigation and, in ship design, derived a formula for calculating the metacentric radius, a measure of ship stability.

JACQUES CASSINI
(b. Feb. 18, 1677, Paris, France—d. April 15/16, 1756, Thury)

French astronomer Jacques Cassini compiled the first tables of the orbital motions of Saturn's satellites.

He succeeded his father, the astronomer Gian Domenico Cassini, as head of the Paris Observatory in 1712 and in 1718 he completed the measurement of the arc of the meridian (longitude line) between Dunkirk and Perpignan. In his *De la grandeur et de la figure de la terre* (1720; "Concerning the Size and Shape of the Earth"), he supported the theory that Earth is an elongated sphere, rather than flattened.

Cassini's astronomical studies are found principally in *Éléments d'astronomie* (1740; "Elements of Astronomy") and

Tables astronomiques du soleil, de la lune, des planètes, des étoiles fixes et des satellites de Jupiter et de Saturne (1740; "Astronomical Tables of the Sun, Moon, Planets, Fixed Stars, and Satellites of Jupiter and Saturn"). An ardent opponent of Sir Isaac Newton's gravitational theory, he continually defended his father's work. However, he was unable to reconcile his observations with his father's theories.

JEAN-BAPTISTE-JOSEPH DELAMBRE
(b. Sept. 19, 1749, Amiens, France—d. Aug. 19, 1822, Paris)

French astronomer Jean-Baptiste-Joseph Delambre prepared tables that plot the location of Uranus.

In 1771 Delambre became tutor to the son of M. d'Assy, receiver general of finances. In 1788 d'Assy built an observatory for Delambre's use. There he observed and computed almost uninterruptedly and in 1792 published *Tables du Soleil, de Jupiter, de Saturne, d'Uranus et des satellites de Jupiter* ("Tables of the Sun, Jupiter, Saturn, Uranus, and Jupiter's Satellites"). He was admitted to the Institut de France upon its organization in 1795 and became, in 1803, perpetual secretary to its mathematical section. He served from 1795 on the bureau of longitudes. From 1792 to 1799 he was occupied with the measurement of the arc of the meridian extending from Dunkirk, France, to Barcelona, and published a detailed account of the operations in *Base du*

système métrique (3 vol., 1806, 1807, 1810; "Basis of the Metric System"). In 1807 he became professor of astronomy at the Collège de France in Paris and was treasurer to the Imperial University from 1808 until its suppression in 1815. Delambre also wrote histories of ancient, medieval, and modern astronomy. His *Tables écliptiques des satellites de Jupiter* ("Ecliptic Tables of Jupiter's Satellites") was republished by the bureau of longitudes in 1817. A large crater on the Moon is named in his honour.

JOSEPH-NICOLAS DELISLE
(b. April 4, 1688, Paris, France—d. Sept. 11, 1768, Paris)

Joseph-Nicolas Delisle was a French astronomer who proposed that the series of coloured rings sometimes observed around the Sun is caused by diffraction of sunlight through water droplets in a cloud. He also worked to find the distance of the Sun from Earth by observing transits of Venus and Mercury across the face of the Sun.

In 1725 Delisle went to St. Petersburg to establish an astronomical institute. Intending to be there only 4 years, he stayed for 22 and trained the first generation of Russian astronomers. His *Mémoires pour servir à l'histoire et au progrès de l'astronomie* (1738; "Memoirs Recounting the History and Progress of Astronomy") gave the first method for determining the heliocentric (Sun-centred) coordinates of sunspots. He returned to Paris in 1747, was appointed geographic astronomer to the naval department, and installed an observatory in the Hôtel Cluny. In 1753 he organized a worldwide study of a transit of Venus (1761), the first such systematic study to be made.

JOHN GOODRICKE
(b. Sept. 17, 1764, Groningen, Neth.—d. April 20, 1786, York, Yorkshire, Eng.)

English astronomer John Goodricke was the first to notice that some variable stars (stars whose observed light varies noticeably in intensity) were periodic. He also gave the first accurate explanation for one type of periodic variable.

Goodricke was deaf and mute, probably because of a serious illness he had contracted in childhood. He nevertheless proved to be a bright student. In 1778 he entered Warrington Academy, where he excelled in mathematics and his interest in astronomy was awakened. After leaving the academy in 1781 he started making his own astronomical observations. In November 1782 he was regularly observing the star known as Algol and soon realized that its brightness varies regularly over a period of a few days. By further observations he confirmed these periodic variations and accurately estimated the period at a bit less than 2 days and 21 hours. Variations in brightness of Algol, Mira, and other stars had been noted by earlier astronomers, but Goodricke was the first to establish that some variables are truly periodic in nature. Goodricke reported his findings to the Royal Society, and the society awarded him a Copley Medal in 1783.

In the remainder of his short life Goodricke discovered the variability of two other stars that are visible with the naked eye. More importantly, he suggested that the variability of Algol was due to its being periodically eclipsed by a darker companion body. This theory was eventually confirmed for Algol, which belongs to the class of stars known as eclipsing variables. Goodricke died at age 21, as a consequence, his contemporaries believed, of his exposure to cold night air while making his observations. Goodricke worked in collaboration and competition with Edward Pigott, another amateur astronomer, who discovered his own variable stars and who carried on the work after Goodricke's death.

NICOLAS DE LACAILLE
(b. May 15, 1713, Rumigny, France—d. March 21, 1762, Paris)

French astronomer Nicolas Louis de Lacaille mapped the constellations visible from the Southern Hemisphere and named many of them.

In 1739 Lacaille was appointed professor of mathematics in the Mazarin College, Paris, and in 1741 was admitted to the Academy of Sciences. He led an expedition (1750–54) to the Cape of Good Hope, where he determined in only two years' time the positions of nearly 10,000 stars—many still referred to by his catalog numbers. His observations from South Africa of the Moon, Venus, and Mars, in conjunction with similar observations already made in the Northern

Hemisphere, led to the calculation of more accurate values for the distances of these bodies.

Before leaving the Cape, Lacaille measured the first arc of a meridian in South Africa. After his return to France in 1754, he laboured alone in compiling his data, and overwork apparently hastened his death. His *Coelum Australe Stelliferum* ("Star Catalog of the Southern Sky") was published in 1763.

JÉRÔME LALANDE
(b. July 11, 1732, Bourg-en-Bresse, France—d. April 4, 1807, Paris)

The tables of planetary positions of French astronomer Joseph-Jérôme Lefrançais de Lalande were considered the best available until the end of the 18th century.

A law student in Paris, Lalande became interested in astronomy while he was lodging at the Hôtel de Cluny, where the noted astronomer Joseph-Nicolas Delisle had his observatory. In 1751 Lalande went to Berlin to make lunar observations in concert with the work of Nicolas Louis de Lacaille at the Cape of Good Hope. The success of this task and the subsequent calculation of the Moon's distance secured for Lalande—before he reached the age of 21—admission to the Academy of Berlin and the post of adjunct astronomer to the Academy of Paris.

Lalande then devoted himself to the improvement of planetary theory, publishing in 1759 a corrected edition of the tables of Halley's Comet. He helped organize international collaboration in observing the transits of Venus in 1761 and 1769. The data obtained made possible the accurate calculation of the distance between Earth and the Sun. In 1762 Lalande was appointed to the chair of astronomy in the Collège de France, Paris—a position that he held for 46 years. A popularizer of astronomy, he instituted the Lalande Prize in 1802 for the chief astronomical contribution of each year.

Among his voluminous works are *Traité d'astronomie* (1764; "Treatise on Astronomy"), *Histoire céleste française* (1801; "French Celestial History"), and *Bibliographie astronomique* (1803; "Astronomical Bibliography"), which is still a valuable resource for historians of 18th-century astronomy.

JOHANN MAYER
(b. Feb. 17, 1723, Marbach, Württemberg [Ger.]—d. Feb. 20, 1762, Göttingen)

German astronomer Johann Tobias Mayer developed lunar tables that greatly assisted navigators in determining longitude at sea. Mayer also discovered the libration (or apparent wobbling) of the Moon.

A self-taught mathematician, Mayer had already published two original geometrical works when, in 1746, he entered the employ of a cartographic establishment in Nürnberg. Mayer published his calculations of the Moon's libration and equatorial inclination in the transactions of the Nürnberg Cosmographic Society. This gained him a scientific reputation that led to his appointment to the chair of economy and mathematics at the

University of Göttingen in 1751. He became superintendent of the university observatory in 1754.

Mayer began calculating lunar and solar tables in 1753. Two years later he submitted to the British government an amended body of tables, which were found to be sufficiently accurate to determine longitude at sea within about half a degree. A London edition of the tables (1770) also contained Mayer's method of determining longitude by lunar distances (the angular separation between the Moon and another celestial object), as well as a formula for correcting errors in longitude caused by atmospheric refraction.

CHARLES MESSIER
(b. June 26, 1730, Badonviller, France—d. April 12, 1817, Paris)

French astronomer Charles Messier was the first to compile a systematic catalog of nebulae and star clusters. In Messier's time, *nebula* was a term used to denote any blurry celestial light source.

In 1751 Messier became a draftsman and recorder of astronomical observations for the noted French astronomer Joseph-Nicolas Delisle. Messier was the first in France to observe the anticipated return of Halley's Comet in 1758–59, and from that time he became an ardent searcher for new comets. Called the comet ferret by King Louis XV, Messier independently discovered 13 of them and observed many more.

In 1760 he began compiling a list of nebulae so that he could distinguish better between nebulae and comets, which look alike when viewed with a small telescope such as was available to Messier. Many of these nebulae, including some of the most prominent, are still known by his catalog numbers. Messier was elected a foreign member of the Royal Society of London in 1764 and obtained a seat in the Paris Academy of Sciences in 1770.

DAVID RITTENHOUSE
(b. April 8, 1732, Germantown, Pa., U.S.—d. June 26, 1796, Philadelphia, Pa.)

David Rittenhouse was an American astronomer and inventor who was an early observer of the atmosphere of Venus.

A clockmaker by trade, Rittenhouse built mathematical instruments and, it is believed, the first telescope in the United States. He also introduced the use of natural spider webbing to form the reticle (system of crosshairs) in telescope transits and other position-measuring instruments. Rittenhouse was highly esteemed as a surveyor; he supervised the establishment of the boundaries between Pennsylvania and Maryland, New Jersey, New York, and the Northwest Territory, and parts of those between New York and New Jersey and between New York and Massachusetts.

Rittenhouse was elected to the American Philosophical Society in 1768, and in 1769 he observed the transit of Venus across the face of the Sun. During this transit he observed that Venus has an atmosphere. His findings were similar to those of the Russian scientist Mikhail Vasilyevich Lomonosov, who had identified Venus's atmosphere during a transit in 1761. Though both had written about their observations, neither report was published nor publicized for more than a century.

Rittenhouse was the treasurer of the state of Pennsylvania from 1777 to 1789. In 1792 Pres. George Washington appointed him the first director of the U.S. Mint in Philadelphia, a position he held for three years. He was elected a fellow of the Royal Society of London in 1795 and served as president of the American Philosophical Society from 1791 until his death.

JOHANN TITIUS
(b. Jan. 2, 1729, Konitz, Prussia [now Chojnice, Pol.]—d. Dec. 11, 1796, Wittenberg, Saxony [Ger.])

Johann Daniel Titius was a Prussian astronomer, physicist, and biologist whose law (1766) expressing the distances between the planets and the Sun was popularized by German astronomer Johann Elert Bode in 1772.

Having received a degree from the University of Leipzig (1752), Titius joined the faculty of the University of Wittenberg in 1756. Titius proposed his law of planetary distances in an unsigned interpolation in his German translation of Swiss philosopher Charles Bonnet's *Contemplation de la nature* ("Contemplation of Nature"). Titius fixed the scale by assigning 100 to the distance of Saturn from the Sun. On this scale, Mercury's distance from the Sun is approximately 4. Titius therefore proposed that the sequence of planetary distances (starting from Mercury and moving outward) has the form

$$4, 4 + 3, 4 + 6, 4 + 12, 4 + 24, 4 + 48, 4 + 96, \ldots$$

There was an empty place at distance 28, or 4 + 24 (between Mars and Jupiter), which, Bode asserted, the Founder of the Universe surely had not left unoccupied. Titius's sequence stopped with Saturn, the most distant planet then known. His law was reprinted, without credit, by Bode in the second edition of his *Deutliche Anleitung zur Kenntniss des gestirnten Himmels* (1772; "Clear Guide to Knowledge of the Starry Heaven"). In later editions, Bode did credit Titius, but this mostly escaped notice. During the 19th century the law was usually associated with Bode's name.

The Titius-Bode law (also called Bode's law) proved to be accurate in accounting for the average distance between the Sun and the first asteroids (discovered in 1801), which were found in the gap at distance 28 and also for the distance between the Sun and Uranus (discovered in 1781). It did not, however, accurately predict the distance of Neptune. Although best known for his law, Titius was also active in physics, concentrating on thermometry, and in biology, classifying plants, animals, and minerals.

CHAPTER 7

NOTABLE ASTRONOMERS OF THE 19TH CENTURY

The 1800s saw several advances to telescopes and other observational technology, which enabled astronomers to expand upon existing knowledge of the universe and make new, previously unimaginable discoveries of their own. Theories were both proven and disproven at an astonishing rate, and many astronomical laws were established over the course of the 19th century.

JOHN COUCH ADAMS

(b. June 5, 1819, Laneast, Cornwall, Eng.—d. Jan. 21, 1892, Cambridge, Cambridgeshire)

British mathematician and astronomer John Couch Adams was one of two people who independently discovered the planet Neptune. On July 3, 1841, Adams had entered in his journal: "Formed a design in the beginning of this week of investigating, as soon as possible after taking my degree, the irregularities in the motion of Uranus . . . in order to find out whether they may be attributed to the action of an undiscovered planet beyond it . . ." In September 1845 he gave James Challis, director of the Cambridge Observatory, accurate information on where the new planet, as yet unobserved, could be found. Unfortunately the planet was not recognized at Cambridge until much later, after its discovery at the Berlin Observatory on Sept. 23, 1846.

Adams also showed (1866) that the Leonid meteor shower had an orbit closely matching that of a comet (1866 I). He described the Moon's motion more exactly than had Pierre-Simon Laplace and studied terrestrial magnetism.

After being made professor of mathematics at the University of St. Andrews (Fife) in 1858 and Lowndean professor of astronomy and geometry at Cambridge in 1859, he became director of Cambridge Observatory in 1861.

SIR GEORGE AIRY

(b. July 27, 1801, Alnwick, Northumberland, Eng.—d. Jan. 2, 1892, Greenwich, London)

English scientist Sir George Biddell Airy was astronomer royal from 1835 to 1881.

Airy graduated from Trinity College, Cambridge, in 1823. He became Lucasian professor of mathematics at Cambridge in 1826 and Plumian professor of astronomy and director of the Cambridge observatory in 1828. In 1835 he was appointed the seventh astronomer royal—director of the Royal Greenwich Observatory—a post he would hold for more than 45 years.

Airy completely reorganized the Greenwich observatory, installing new apparatus and rescuing thousands of lunar observations from oblivion. Most importantly, he modernized the observatory's system for making extremely precise observations of stellar positions. He wielded great power within the British scientific community, and he opposed government support of pure science, arguing that original research was best left to private individuals and institutions.

Airy was severely criticized for his part in the failure of British astronomers to search for a new planet (Neptune) whose existence and probable location were predicted in 1845 by British astronomer John Couch Adams, on the basis of irregularities in the motion of Uranus. A similar calculation was made in the next year by the French astronomer Urbain-Jean-Joseph Le Verrier, which led almost immediately to the discovery of Neptune by German astronomer Johann Gottfried Galle and his student Heinrich Louis d'Arrest at the Berlin observatory. Modern scholars differ on how much blame to give Airy, and from today's perspective the one-year delay in the discovery of Neptune does not seem very important. However, at the time, it produced a stormy episode in British-French scientific relations.

Airy in 1827 made the first successful attempt to correct astigmatism in the human eye (his own) by use of a cylindrical eyeglass lens. He also contributed to the study of interference fringes, and the Airy disk—the central spot of light in the diffraction pattern of a point light source—is named for him. In 1854 he used a new method to determine the mean density of Earth. This involved swinging the same pendulum at the top and bottom of a deep mine to measure the change in the strength of gravity between the top and bottom of the mine. Airy was also the first to propose (c. 1855) the theory that mountain ranges must have root structures of lower density, proportional to their height, in order to maintain isostatic equilibrium. He was knighted in 1872.

FRIEDRICH ARGELANDER
(b. March 22, 1799, Memel, East Prussia—d. Feb. 17, 1875, Bonn)

German astronomer Friedrich Wilhelm August Argelander established the study of variable stars as an independent branch of astronomy and is renowned for his great catalog listing the positions and magnitudes of 324,188 stars. He studied at the University of Königsberg, Prussia, where he was a pupil and later the successor of German astronomer Friedrich Wilhelm Bessel. Argelander was appointed director of the Åbo (Turku) Observatory in Finland in 1823 and of the Helsinki Observatory in 1832. In 1837 he published a major investigation of the Sun's motion through space, improving on the methods of British astronomer William Herschel. His investigation, however, did not substantially modify Herschel's result that the solar system is moving in the direction of the constellation Hercules. In the same year he was appointed director of the new observatory in Bonn. In 1844 Argelander began studies of variable stars.

His greatest achievement was the publication of the *Bonner Durchmusterung* (1859–62; "Bonn Survey"), which cataloged stars from the north celestial pole to 2° south of the celestial equator. The result of 25 years' labour, the catalog included all stars down to about the ninth magnitude. This work was reissued in 1950.

Argelander founded the Astronomische Gesellschaft (Astronomical Society), which in collaboration with many observatories

Friedrich Argelander, c. 1860. Hulton Archive/Getty Images

expanded his work to produce the AG catalogs.

EDWARD EMERSON BARNARD
(b. Dec. 16, 1857, Nashville, Tenn., U.S.—d. Feb. 6, 1923, Williams Bay, Wis.)

Edward Emerson Barnard was an American astronomer who pioneered in celestial photography and who was the leading observational astronomer of his time.

In 1889 he began to photograph the Milky Way with large-aperture lenses, revealing much new detail. He discovered 16 comets and Jupiter's fifth satellite (1892). In 1916 he discovered the star (Barnard's star) that has the greatest known proper motion (motion of an individual star relative to the other stars). He published a catalog of dark nebulae in 1919.

From 1883 to 1887 he studied at Vanderbilt University, Nashville, and was in charge of the observatory there. In 1887 he was appointed astronomer at Lick Observatory, Mt. Hamilton, California. From 1895 until his death he was professor of practical astronomy at the University of Chicago and astronomer at Yerkes Observatory in Williams Bay, Wis. His eyesight was renowned. He observed Mars in a position that was not directly opposite the Sun, when detail is revealed through shadowing, and also observed Martian craters in the 1890s. He made neither of those observations public at the time.

WILLIAM CRANCH BOND
(b. Sept. 9, 1789, Falmouth, District of Maine, Mass. [now Portland, Maine], U.S.—d. Jan. 29, 1859, Cambridge, Mass.)

American astronomer William Cranch Bond, with his son George Phillips Bond (1825–65), discovered Hyperion, the eighth satellite of Saturn, and an inner ring called Ring C, or the Crepe Ring. They also took some of the first recognizable photographs of celestial objects.

Largely self-educated, Bond was a watchmaker who became interested in astronomy after observing the solar eclipse of 1806. He built a home observatory that was one of the finest in the United States at that time. Bond independently discovered many comets, and in recognition of his efforts, he was appointed the first astronomical observer at Harvard College in 1839. He became the first director of the Harvard Observatory in 1847 and was elected an associate of Britain's Royal Astronomical Society two years later—the first American so honoured.

In 1848 Bond undertook extensive studies of the Orion Nebula and Saturn, and that year he discovered Hyperion in collaboration with his son. (The English astronomer William Lassell independently discovered Hyperion the same night as did the Bonds.) The Bonds made the first recognizable daguerreotype of the Moon and of a star (Vega) in 1850. That same year, they discovered the dark inner ring of Saturn (the Crepe Ring), which Lassell discovered independently only a few nights later. The Bonds made the first recognizable photographic print of the Moon in 1857. After William died in 1859, his son George Phillips succeeded him as director of the Harvard Observatory.

LEWIS BOSS
(b. Oct. 26, 1846, Providence, R.I., U.S.—d. Oct. 5, 1912, Albany, N.Y.)

Lewis Boss was an American astronomer best known for his compilation of star catalogs.

Boss worked for the U.S. government at Washington, D.C., and on a survey of the U.S.-Canadian border. In 1876 he became director of the Dudley Observatory at Albany, and in 1882 he led an expedition to Chile to observe a transit of Venus. About 1895 Boss began to plan a general catalog of stars, giving their positions and motions. The project was supported by the Carnegie Institution, Washington, D.C., after 1906. With an enlarged staff he observed the northern stars from Albany and the southern stars from Argentina. With the new data, he corrected catalogs that had been compiled in the past, and in 1910 he published the *Preliminary General Catalogue of 6,188 Stars for the Epoch 1900*. Though he died leaving his work unfinished, his son Benjamin completed it in 1937 (*General Catalogue of 33,342 Stars for the Epoch 1950*, 5 vol.).

WILLIAM WALLACE CAMPBELL
(b. April 11, 1862, Hancock county, Ohio, U.S.—d. June 14, 1938, San Francisco, Calif.)

American astronomer William Wallace Campbell was known particularly for his spectrographic determinations of the radial velocities of stars—i.e., their motions toward Earth or away from it. In addition, he discovered many spectroscopic binary stars, and in 1924 he published a catalog listing more than 1,000 of them.

To include measurements of radial velocities of stars visible only from the Southern Hemisphere, Campbell sent a 36-inch telescope, equipped with spectrograph, to Santiago, Chile. Combining data from Lick Observatory, Mt. Hamilton, California, and from Santiago, he determined the direction and speed of the Sun's motion in the Galaxy as well as the average random velocities of stars of various spectral types. He led seven solar eclipse expeditions from Lick and brought back a wealth of material on the Sun's corona and flash spectrum.

Campbell joined the staff at Lick Observatory in 1890, after two years as an instructor in astronomy at the University of Michigan, Ann Arbor. He became director of Lick in 1901. From 1923 to 1930 he was president of the University of California. He was president of the National Academy of Sciences from 1931 to 1935.

JAMES CHALLIS

(b. Dec. 12, 1803, Braintree, Essex,
Eng.—d. Dec. 3, 1882, Cambridge,
Cambridgeshire)

British clergyman and astronomer James Challis is famous in the history of astronomy for his failure to discover the planet Neptune.

Elected a fellow of Trinity College, Cambridge, in 1826 and ordained in 1830, Challis became Plumian professor of astronomy and director of the Cambridge Observatory in 1836. He contributed 225 mathematical, physical, and astronomical papers to scientific journals and published, in 12 volumes, *Astronomical Observations Made at the Observatory of Cambridge* (1832–64), the chief results of his work.

In September 1845 John Couch Adams, another Cambridge astronomer who had been making calculations of perturbations of the orbit of Uranus, asked Challis to look for an unknown planet in a specific position. Challis procrastinated but on further urging finally began making observations in July 1846. On September 23 the Berlin Observatory announced the discovery of Neptune, very close to where Adams's calculations had predicted it would be. On checking his observations, Challis found that he had actually observed the planet one night in August but, because he failed to compare his observations of that night with those of his previous night of search, had not realized it.

This failure did not appreciably interfere with his career. Although he was succeeded at the observatory by Adams in 1861, he retained the Plumian chair until his death.

HEINRICH D'ARREST

(b. July 13, 1822, Berlin,
Prussia [Ger.]—d. June 14, 1875,
Copenhagen, Den.)

German astronomer Heinrich Louis d'Arrest, while a student at the Berlin Observatory, hastened the discovery of Neptune by suggesting comparison of the sky, in the region indicated by Urbain Le Verrier's calculations, with a recently prepared star chart. The planet was found the same night.

In 1851 while associated with the Leipzig Observatory, d'Arrest discovered a periodic comet that was subsequently named for him. In that same year he published a book on the 13 asteroids known at that time and began his studies of the nebulae for which he received the Gold Medal of the Royal Astronomical Society in 1875.

SIR GEORGE DARWIN

(b. July 9, 1845, Downe, Kent, Eng.—d.
Dec. 7, 1912, Cambridge,
Cambridgeshire)

English astronomer Sir George Howard Darwin championed the theory that the Moon was once part of Earth, until it was pulled free to form a satellite.

The second son of the eminent naturalist Charles Darwin, he became Plumian professor of astronomy and experimental philosophy at Cambridge University in

1883. His monumental analysis of tides, published in 1884, was based on the methods developed by Pierre-Simon Laplace and Lord Kelvin. In *The Tides and Kindred Phenomena in the Solar System* (1898), he discussed the effects of tidal friction on the Earth–Moon system and theorized that the Moon was formed from matter pulled away from the still-molten Earth by solar tides, a hypothesis now considered unlikely to be true. His great achievement was that he was the first to develop a theory of evolution for the Sun–Earth–Moon system based on mathematical analysis in geophysical theory.

Darwin made extensive studies of the orbits of three rotating bodies, such as the Sun–Earth–Moon system; he computed where each would be at a specific time. As part of his investigation of the origin of the Moon, he studied the shapes at which rotating masses of fluid become stable. His conclusion that a pear-shaped rotating fluid body is stable is now considered incorrect. Darwin became president of the Royal Astronomical Society in 1899 and of the British Association six years later. He was made Knight Commander of the Bath in 1905.

WILLIAM RUTTER DAWES
(b. March 19, 1799, London—d. Feb. 15, 1868, Haddenham, Buckinghamshire, Eng.)

English astronomer William Rutter Dawes was known for his extensive measurements of double stars and for his meticulous planetary observations.

Trained as a physician, Dawes practiced at Haddenham and (from 1826) Liverpool; subsequently he became a Nonconformist clergyman. In 1829 he set up a private observatory at Ormskirk, Lancashire, where he measured more than 200 double stars before taking charge of George Bishop's Observatory at South Villa, Regent's Park, London, in 1839. He later set up private observatories at Cranbrook, Kent (1844); Wateringbury, Kent (1850); and Haddenham (1857). He was one of several independent discoverers of the "crepe ring" of Saturn (1850). He observed Jupiter's Great Red Spot (1857) several years before its existence was generally recognized, and he prepared exceptionally accurate drawings of Mars in 1864. Dawes received the Gold Medal of the Royal Astronomical Society in 1855 and was elected a fellow of the Royal Society in 1865. A crater on the Moon is named after him.

CHARLES-EUGÈNE DELAUNAY
(b. April 9, 1816, Lusigny-sur-Barse, France—d. Aug. 5, 1872, near Cherbourg)

Charles-Eugène Delaunay was a French mathematician and astronomer whose theory of lunar motion advanced the development of planetary-motion theories.

Delaunay was educated as an engineer at the École des Mines from 1836, becoming an engineer in 1843 and chief engineer in 1858. He studied mathematics and astronomy with Jean-Baptiste Biot at the Sorbonne (1841–48). He taught mechanics at the École Polytechnique from 1850 and also later taught at the École des Mines. He was made a member of the Académie des Sciences in 1855. In 1870 he succeeded U.-J.-J. Le Verrier as director of the Paris Observatory.

He wrote *Cours élémentaire de mécanique* (1850; 8th ed., 1874; "Elementary Course of Mechanics"), *Cours élémentaire d'astronomie* (1853; 5th ed., 1870; "Elementary Course of Astronomy"), *La Théorie du mouvement de la lune,* 2 vol. (1860–67; "The Theory of Lunar Motion"), *Traité de mécanique rationnelle* (1856; 4th ed., 1873; "Treatise of Theoretical Mechanics"), *Ralentissement de la rotation de la terre* (1866; "Slowing of the Rotation of the Earth"), and *Rapport sur les progrès de l'astronomie* (1867; "Report on the Progress of Astronomy").

JOHAN DREYER
(b. Feb. 13, 1852, Copenhagen, Den.—d. Sept. 14, 1926, Oxford, Eng.)

Danish astronomer Johan Ludvig Emil Dreyer compiled the *New General Catalogue of Nebulae and Clusters of Stars*, published in 1888, and its supplements, published in 1895 and 1908. This work, together with the supplements, was republished in 1953. It still remains one of the standard reference catalogs.

In 1874 Dreyer was appointed assistant at Lord Rosse's observatory in Parsonstown (now Birr), County Offaly, Ire. Four years later he moved to Dunsink Observatory in Dublin. In 1882 he became director of the observatory at Armagh, Ire. He retired

from this post in 1916. That same year he was awarded the Gold Medal of the Royal Astronomical Society. He later served as the society's president (1923–24).

In addition to his catalog of nebulae and star clusters, Dreyer published a number of other astronomical works. He wrote a biography of his illustrious countryman, *Tycho Brahe* (1890), and collected and edited all of Tycho's works and correspondence in 15 volumes (published between 1913 and 1929). His *History of the Planetary Systems from Thales to Kepler* (1906), reprinted under the title *A History of Astronomy from Thales to Kepler* (1953), is a still useful study.

JOHANN FRANZ ENCKE
(b. Sept. 23, 1791, Hamburg [Ger.]—d. Aug. 26, 1865, Spandau, Ger.)

In 1819 German astronomer Johann Franz Encke established the period of the comet now known by his name.

Encke was educated at Hamburg and the University of Göttingen, where he worked under the direction of Carl Friedrich Gauss. In 1816 Encke became assistant at the Seeberg Observatory near Gotha, Ger., where he was made vice director in 1820 and director in 1822. In 1825 he was appointed professor of astronomy and director of the observatory of the University of Berlin. There he planned and supervised the construction of a new observatory, completed in 1835.

Besides the comet that bears his name, Encke is also known for his discovery of Encke's Division, in the outermost ring of Saturn. From observations of the transits of Venus recorded in 1761 and 1769, he derived a value for the solar parallax (in effect, for the Sun's distance from Earth) that, at 8″.57, is close to the presently accepted figure. He also established methods for calculating the orbits of minor planets and orbits of double stars.

WILLIAMINA PATON STEVENS FLEMING
(b. May 15, 1857, Dundee, Tayside [now in Dundee], Scot.—d. May 21, 1911, Boston, Mass., U.S.)

American astronomer Williamina Paton Stevens Fleming was a pioneer in the classification of stellar spectra.

Mina Stevens was educated in public schools and from age 14 was a teacher as well as a student. In May 1877 she married James O. Fleming, with whom she immigrated to the United States and settled in Boston the next year. The failure of her marriage in 1879 forced her to seek employment, and she soon became housekeeper for Edward C. Pickering, professor of astronomy and director of the Harvard College Observatory. Before the year was out Pickering had asked her to work at the observatory as a temporary employee and in 1881 she became a permanent member of the research staff. For the next 30 years she collaborated on the analysis of stellar spectrum photography. In 1898 she was appointed curator of astronomical photographs at Harvard.

Fleming is best known for her work on the classification of stellar spectra—the pattern of lines caused by the dispersion of a star's light through a prism placed before a telescope lens. Using a technique that came to be known as the Pickering-Fleming system, she studied the tens of thousands of celestial photographs taken for the Draper Memorial—a project dedicated to the amateur astronomer Henry Draper of New York. In the course of her work she discovered 10 novae, 52 nebulae, and hundreds of variable stars. She also established the first photographic standards of magnitude used to measure the variable brightness of stars.

Fleming's most important works include the *Draper Catalogue of Stellar Spectra* (1890), "A Photographic Study of Variable Stars" (1907), and "Stars Having Peculiar Spectra" (1912). In 1906 she became the first American woman elected to the Royal Astronomical Society. Her work provided the foundation for the future contributions of Annie Jump Cannon.

JOSEPH VON FRAUNHOFER
(b. March 6, 1787, Straubing, Bavaria [Ger.]—d. June 7, 1826, Munich)

German physicist Joseph von Fraunhofer first studied the dark lines of the Sun's spectrum, now known as Fraunhofer lines. He also was the first to use extensively the diffraction grating, a device that disperses light more effectively than a prism does. His work set the stage for the development of spectroscopy.

Fraunhofer worked as an optician at the Untzschneider Optical Institute at

Benedictbeuern, near Munich, of which he became manager in 1818. While measuring the light-bending properties of various kinds of glass, he noticed dark lines in the light spectrum of a sodium flame, and he continued looking for such lines in the spectra of other elements. Fraunhofer plotted hundreds of spectral lines, and by measuring their wavelengths he found that the relative positions of the lines in the spectra of elements are constant—whether the spectra are produced by the direct rays of the Sun or by the reflected light of the Moon and planets, by a gas, or by a heated metal in the laboratory.

JOHANN GALLE
(b. June 9, 1812, near Gräfenhainichen, Prussian Saxony—d. July 10, 1910, Potsdam, Ger.)

German astronomer Johann Gottfried Galle on Sept. 23, 1846, was the first to observe the planet Neptune.

Galle joined the staff of the Berlin Observatory, where he served as assistant director under J. F. Encke from 1835 until 1851. He studied the rings of Saturn and suggested a method, later successful, of measuring the scale of the solar system by observing the parallax of asteroids. He looked for Neptune at the request of the French astronomer U.-J.-J. Le Verrier, who had computed the planet's probable position before it was seen. From 1851 until 1897 Galle was director of the Breslau Observatory.

SIR DAVID GILL
(b. June 12, 1843, Aberdeen, Aberdeenshire, Scot.—d. Jan. 24, 1914, London, Eng.)

Scottish astronomer Sir David Gill was known for his measurements of solar and stellar parallax, showing the distances of the Sun and other stars from Earth, and for his early use of photography in mapping the heavens. To determine the parallaxes, he perfected the use of the heliometer, a telescope that uses a split image to measure the angular separation of celestial bodies.

Gill was educated at the University of Aberdeen, and in 1872 he became director of James Ludovic Lindsay's private observatory near Aberdeen. From there he undertook expeditions to Mauritius in 1874, to observe the transit of Venus, and to Ascension Island in 1877, when Mars was in opposition. His measurements of Mars's position as it neared Earth enabled him to roughly calculate the solar parallax. In 1888–89 he carried out, with the cooperation of many astronomers, a program of intensive observation of selected minor planets with the heliometer. This led to the first determination (1901) of the solar parallax with modern accuracy.

As royal astronomer at the Cape of Good Hope from 1879 to 1907, he photographed the sky within 19° of the south celestial pole in great detail. From these pictures, J. C. Kapteyn compiled the *Cape Photographic Durchmusterung*, a catalog of nearly 500,000 stars. Gill was knighted in 1900.

JAMES GILLISS

(b. Sept. 6, 1811, Georgetown, Md.,
U.S.—d. Feb. 9, 1865, Washington, D.C.)

James Melville Gilliss was a U.S. naval officer and astronomer who founded the Naval Observatory in Washington, D.C., the first U.S. observatory devoted entirely to research.

Gilliss entered the U.S. Navy in 1827 and 10 years later was put in charge of the navy's Depot of Charts and Instruments, in Washington, D.C. His responsibilities included making astronomical observations necessary for longitude determinations of newly explored land. At his recommendation, funds were provided by Congress in 1842 for founding the Naval Observatory, and he supervised its construction (1843–44).

Gilliss undertook an astronomical expedition, constructing a station (later a permanent observatory) in Santiago, Chile, to observe Mars and Venus (1847–52). During this expedition he also charted more than 23,000 stars and made many other observations. He later led expeditions to Peru (1858) and Washington Territory (1860). From 1861 he served as director of the Naval Observatory.

BENJAMIN GOULD

(b. Sept. 27, 1824, Boston, Mass., U.S.—d.
Nov. 26, 1896, Cambridge, Mass.)

American astronomer Benjamin Apthorp Gould's star catalogs helped fix the list of constellations of the Southern Hemisphere.

A child prodigy who could read aloud at age three and compose poems in Latin at age five, Gould studied mathematics and the physical sciences under Benjamin Peirce at Harvard University. In 1845 he went to Germany to study astronomy and was the first American to earn a doctorate in this field, at the University of Göttingen in 1848. Returning to the United States, Gould was anxious to raise American astronomy to the European level. In 1849 he founded *The Astronomical Journal*, which was modeled on the German journal *Astronomische Nachrichten* and was the first journal of professional astronomical research published in the United States. Publication lapsed in 1861 because of financial difficulties and the outbreak of the Civil War. After a 25-year hiatus, Gould restarted *The Astronomical Journal* in 1886, and it continues to the present day.

From 1852 until 1867 Gould was in charge of the longitude department of the U.S. Coast Survey. In 1859 he published a treatise on the positions and proper motions of the circumpolar stars that were used as standards by the U.S. Coast Survey. Gould was one of the first to use the telegraph to determine longitudes. This he did by simultaneously finding the Sun's direction at two sites, one for which the longitude was known, and comparing the findings to compute the unknown longitude. In 1866 he made use of the Atlantic cable to establish the difference of longitude between the observatories at Greenwich, Eng., and Washington, D.C.

Because Gould was temperamental and difficult to work with and made many personal enemies, he had an unhappy career in the United States and was unable to secure a permanent position as an astronomer. But he was invited by the government of Argentina to found and direct the National Observatory at Córdoba in 1868. Two years later he began his observations and in 1874 completed his *Uranometria Argentina* (1879; "An Argentine Uranometry"). In 1884 he published a zone catalog, covering 73,160 stars in a particular portion of the sky, and one year later a general catalog of 32,448 stars in the Southern Hemisphere. He returned to Massachusetts in 1885.

JOHANN HAGEN
(b. March 6, 1847, Bregenz, Austria—d. Sept. 5, 1930, Rome, Italy)

Jesuit priest and astronomer Johann Georg Hagen is noted for his discovery and study of dark clouds of tenuous, interstellar matter sometimes known as Hagen's clouds.

Hagen served as director of the Georgetown College Observatory, Washington, D.C., from 1888 to 1906, when Pope Pius X appointed him director of the Vatican Observatory. In 1893, while compiling a general catalog of bright and dark nebulae, Hagen began an intensive study of dark nebulae. Over a period of several decades, he became convinced that he sometimes observed dark interstellar matter through the telescope, although he failed to detect

it photographically, presumably because of its faint luminosity. Modern astronomers tend to discount the existence of Hagen's clouds and attribute his observations to other causes, such as inconsistencies in the reaction of the human eye.

Hagen is also noted for his work on variable stars (stars whose intensity changes cyclically). His studies on variable stars appear in *Atlas Stellarum Variabilium* (1890–1908; "Atlas of Variable Stars"), and his observations of Hagen's clouds are summarized in a paper that appeared in *Specola Astronomica Vaticana 14* (1931; "Vatican Astronomical Observatory").

GEORGE HILL
(b. March 3, 1838, New York, N.Y., U.S.—d. April 16, 1914, West Nyack, N.Y.)

U.S. mathematical astronomer George William Hill was considered by many of his peers to be the greatest master of celestial mechanics of his time. After receiving a B.A. from Rutgers College (1859), Hill joined the Nautical Almanac Office in 1861. Among his many accomplishments, Hill was the first to use infinite determinants to analyze the motion of the Moon's perigee (1877). He also developed a theory of the motion of Jupiter and Saturn. His most significant theory, dealing with the effects of the planets on the Moon's motion, is considered fundamental in the development of celestial mechanics.

For his research on the motions of the Moon, Hill received the Gold Medal of the Royal Astronomical Society in 1887, the Damoiscan Prize from the Académie des Sciences in 1898, and the Royal Society's Copley Medal in 1909. He was elected to the U.S. National Academy of Sciences (1874) and the Royal Society (1902). From 1894 to 1896 he served as president of the American Mathematical Society. Many of his papers were republished by the Carnegie Institution in *The Collected Mathematical Works of George William Hall.*

SIR WILLIAM HUGGINS
(b. Feb. 7, 1824, Stoke Newington, London, Eng.—d. May 12, 1910, London)

English astronomer Sir William Huggins revolutionized observational astronomy by applying spectroscopic methods to the determination of the chemical constituents of stars and other celestial objects.

Huggins built a private observatory at Tulse Hill, London, in 1856. From 1859 he was one of a number of astronomers who began to apply Robert Wilhelm Bunsen's and Gustav Robert Kirchhoff's discoveries in spectrum analysis to astronomy. Huggins's first spectroscopic observations, published in 1863, showed that stars are composed of the same elements that occur on the Sun and Earth. In 1864 the spectra he obtained of various nebulae established that they are composed mainly of incandescent gas (rather than aggregations of stars), thus settling a long debate over their composition. Soon afterward he obtained the spectra of several comets and was able to identify

the presence of hydrocarbons in them. Huggins's most important innovation in the use of spectroscopy came in 1868, when he became the first to measure the radial velocity of a star by the Doppler shift of its spectral lines. This particular technical innovation would later assume profound importance in studies of the structure and evolution of the universe.

After 1875 Huggins worked mainly in collaboration with his wife, Margaret Huggins. He was knighted in 1897.

PIERRE JANSSEN
(b. Feb. 22, 1824, Paris, France—d. Dec. 23, 1907, Meudon)

In 1868 French astronomer Pierre-Jules-César Janssen discovered how to observe solar prominences without an eclipse. His work was independent of that of the Englishman Joseph Norman Lockyer, who made the same discovery at about the same time.

Janssen was permanently lamed by an accident in early childhood. He studied at the University of Paris, and in 1865 he became professor of general science in the school of architecture. He was an enthusiastic observer of eclipses. In 1868 Janssen discovered how to use a spectroscope to observe solar prominences in daylight. This enabled many more such observations to be made than previously, when such phenomena had been observable only for the few minutes' duration of solar eclipses. In 1870, when Paris was besieged during the Franco-German War, Janssen fled the surrounded city in a balloon so that he could reach the path of totality of a solar eclipse in Africa. (His effort went for nothing, for the eclipse was obscured by clouds.) In 1876 he was appointed the first director of the Meudon Observatory, near Paris. In 1893, using observations from the meteorological observatory he had established on Mont Blanc, he proved that strong oxygen lines appearing in the solar spectrum were caused by oxygen in Earth's atmosphere. He was the first to regularly use photographs to study the Sun. In 1904 Janssen published his great *Atlas des photographies solaires,* containing more than 6,000 solar pictures. A crater on the Moon is named for him.

JAMES KEELER
(b. Sept. 10, 1857, La Salle, Ill., U.S.—d. Aug. 12, 1900, San Francisco, Calif.)

James Edward Keeler was an American astronomer who confirmed that Saturn's ring system is not a solid unit but is composed of a vast swarm of tiny particles.

Interested in astronomy from an early age, Keeler became assistant to the noted astronomer Samuel P. Langley at the Allegheny Observatory, Pittsburgh, Pa., in 1881. From 1886 to 1891 he was on the staff of the Lick Observatory, Mount Hamilton, Calif., where he headed the spectroscopic program. Among the outstanding results that he achieved was the measurement of the rate of expansion of the Orion Nebula together with proof that it is located within the Milky Way Galaxy.

In 1891 Keeler became director of the Allegheny Observatory, where he performed his studies of Saturn's rings. Returning to the Lick Observatory as director in 1898, he undertook photographic observations of 120,000 galaxies with the recently acquired Crossley 36-inch (91-centimetre) reflecting telescope. This work established the reflecting telescope as the supreme instrument for photographing faint celestial objects and demonstrated that a spiral galaxy is the most common type of galaxy in the observable universe.

JOHANN VON LAMONT
(b. Dec. 13, 1805, Braemar, Aberdeenshire, Scot.—d. Aug. 6, 1879, Munich, Ger.)

Scottish-born German astronomer Johann von Lamont discovered that the magnetic field of Earth fluctuates with a period somewhat in excess of 10 years.

In 1827 Lamont began working at the Royal Observatory, Bogenhausen, near Munich. He adopted German nationality and worked at Bogenhausen for the rest of his life, as director of the observatory from 1835 and also as professor of astronomy at the University of Munich from 1852. In addition to his other work, he determined the orbits of Saturn's satellites Enceladus and Tethys, the periods of Uranus's satellites Ariel and Titan, and the mass of Uranus. He also cataloged more than 34,000 stars. He established a magnetic observatory at Bogenhausen in 1840 and 10 years later discovered the variation in Earth's magnetic field. In 1862 he discovered the existence of large-scale surges of electrical charge within Earth's crust that are associated with ionospheric disturbances. Lamont's most noteworthy work is *Handbuch des Erdmagnetismus* (1849; "Handbook of Terrestrial Magnetism"). He was elected a foreign member of the Royal Society of London in 1852.

JONATHAN LANE

(b. Aug. 9, 1819, Geneseo, N.Y., U.S.—d. May 3, 1880, Washington, D.C.)

U.S. astrophysicist Jonathan Homer Lane was the first to investigate mathematically the Sun as a gaseous body. His work demonstrated the interrelationships of pressure, temperature, and density inside the Sun and was fundamental to the emergence of modern theories of stellar evolution.

Lane became an assistant examiner in the U.S. Patent Office in 1848 and three years later became principal examiner. From 1857 he worked as an expert counsellor in patent cases. His solar studies culminated in Lane's law, which states that as a gaseous body contracts (under the influence of gravity, for example), the contraction generates heat. He used this law to explain how the Sun built up its intense heat over the eons. His most important publication was *On the Theoretical Temperature of the Sun* (1870).

Lane also studied electricity and worked on a machine for calculating mathematical roots. In addition, he devised an electromechanical governor, a "visual telegraph," and an air pump. He also experimented with mechanical refrigeration.

WILLIAM LASSELL

(b. June 18, 1799, Bolton, Lancashire, Eng.—d. Oct. 5, 1880, Maidenhead, Berkshire)

William Lassell was an amateur English astronomer who discovered Ariel and Umbriel, satellites of Uranus, and Triton, a satellite of Neptune. He also discovered a satellite of Saturn, Hyperion (also discovered independently by William Bond and George Bond).

Lassell started a brewery business about 1825, after a seven-year apprenticeship. He became interested in astronomy and, in 1844, began construction of a 24-inch reflecting telescope, using a machine of his own design for polishing the mirror. With this telescope, the first of its size to be set in an equatorial mounting, he discovered Triton on Oct. 10, 1846, only 17 days after Neptune itself had been discovered. In 1848 he discovered Hyperion (on the night that the Bonds made the same discovery). Two years later Lassell made his first sighting of the dark inner ring of Saturn (called the Crepe Ring). He spent the entire night verifying the discovery only to find in his morning newspaper an article announcing Bond's discovery of the same phenomenon.

Lassell discovered Ariel and Umbriel in 1851–52 while at Malta, and there in 1861 he erected a 48-inch reflector—which he used to observe and catalog hundreds of new nebulae. He was elected a fellow of the Royal Society of London in 1849 and was president of the Royal Astronomical Society from 1870 to 1872.

URBAIN-JEAN-JOSEPH LE VERRIER

(b. March 11, 1811, Saint-Lô, France—d. Sept. 23, 1877, Paris)

French astronomer Urbain-Jean-Joseph Le Verrier predicted by mathematical means the existence of the planet Neptune.

Appointed a teacher of astronomy at the École Polytechnique (Polytechnic School), Paris, in 1837, Le Verrier first undertook an extensive study of the theory of the planet Mercury's orbit and compiled greatly improved tables of the motion of that planet.

In 1845 he turned his attention to the irregular orbit of Uranus, which he explained by assuming the presence of a previously unknown planet. Independently of the English astronomer John C. Adams, he calculated the size and position of the unknown body and asked the German astronomer Johann G. Galle to look for it. On Sept. 23, 1846, after only an hour of searching, Galle found Neptune within one degree of the position that had been computed by Le Verrier. As a result of this achievement Le Verrier received, among other awards, the Copley Medal from the Royal Society of London and was named an officer in the Legion of Honour. A chair of astronomy was created for him at the University of Paris.

In 1854 Le Verrier became director of the Observatory of Paris. He reestablished the efficiency of this institution, but some of the uncompromising measures taken raised a storm of protest that was appeased only by his removal in 1870. On the death of his successor in 1873 he was reinstated, but with his authority restricted by the supervision of an observatory council.

During his difficulties as director of the observatory, he carried out a complete revision of the planetary theories and compared them with the best observations then available. In particular, in 1855 he took up the problem of explaining an unusual characteristic of the motion of Mercury. He postulated a second asteroid belt inside Mercury's orbit, and, when an amateur astronomer reported finding an inner planet, Le Verrier assumed it was one of the larger of his asteroids and named it Vulcan. Further observations failed to confirm the find, however. The unusual orbital motion of Mercury, which includes an advance of its perihelion, was completely explained in 1915 by Albert Einstein's general theory of relativity.

SIR JOSEPH LOCKYER

(b. May 17, 1836, Rugby, Warwickshire, Eng.—d. Aug. 16, 1920, Salcombe Regis, Devon)

Sir Joseph Norman Lockyer was a British astronomer who in 1868 discovered in the Sun's atmosphere a previously unknown element, which he named helium after

Hēlios, the Greek name for the Sun and the Sun god.

Lockyer became a clerk in the War Office in 1857, but his interest in astronomy eventually led to a career in that field. He initiated in 1866 the spectroscopic observation of sunspots, and in 1868 he found that solar prominences are upheavals in a layer that he named the chromosphere. Also in 1868, he and French astronomer Pierre Janssen, working independently, discovered a spectroscopic method of observing solar prominences without the aid of an eclipse to block out the glare of the Sun. Lockyer identified the element helium in the solar spectrum 27 years before that element was found on Earth.

Between 1870 and 1905, Lockyer conducted eight expeditions to observe solar eclipses. He also built a private observatory at Sidmouth and theorized on stellar evolution. A prolific writer, he founded the science periodical *Nature* in 1869 and edited it until a few months before his death. He was knighted in 1897.

PERCIVAL LOWELL
(b. March 13, 1855, Boston, Mass., U.S.—d. Nov. 12, 1916, Flagstaff, Ariz.)

American astronomer Percival Lowell predicted the existence of a planet beyond the orbit of Neptune and initiated the search that ended in the discovery of Pluto.

A member of the distinguished Lowell family of Massachusetts (he was brother to A. Lawrence Lowell and Amy Lowell), he devoted himself (1883–93) to literature and travel, much of the time in the Far East. He described his travels in *Chosön* (1886), *The Soul of the Far East* (1888), *Noto* (1891), and *Occult Japan* (1895). During part of this time he was counselor and foreign secretary to the Korean Special Mission to the United States.

In the 1890s, inspired by Giovanni Schiaparelli's discovery of "canals" on Mars, Lowell decided to devote his fortune and energy to the study of Mars. After careful consideration of desirable sites, he built a private observatory at Flagstaff, Ariz. Lowell championed the now-abandoned theory that intelligent inhabitants of a dying Mars constructed

Percival Lowell, c. 1905. Kean Collection/ Hulton Archive/Getty Images

a planet-wide system of irrigation, utilizing water from the polar ice caps, which melt annually. He thought the canals were bands of cultivated vegetation dependent on this irrigation. Among his many books on this subject is *Mars and Its Canals* (1906). Lowell's theory, long vigorously opposed, was finally put to rest by information received from the U.S. spacecraft Mariner 4 when it flew past Mars in July 1965.

Early in the 20th century Lowell made an elaborate mathematical study of the orbit of Uranus. He attributed certain irregularities to the action of an unseen planet beyond Neptune and calculated its probable position. In 1905 he organized a systematic search for the planet by the staff of his observatory, and in 1915 he published his "Memoir on a Trans-Neptunian Planet." Fourteen years after his death the search culminated in the discovery of Pluto.

JOHANN VON MÄDLER

(b. May 29, 1794, Berlin, Prussia [Ger.]—d. March 14, 1874, Hanover, Ger.)

German astronomer Johann Heinrich von Mädler (with Wilhelm Beer) published the most complete map of the Moon of the time, *Mappa Selenographica,* 4 vol. (1834–36). It was the first lunar map to be divided into quadrants, and it remained unsurpassed in its detail until J. F. Julius Schmidt's map of 1878. The *Mappa Selenographica* was accompanied in 1837 by a volume providing micrometric measurements of the diameters of 148 craters

and the elevations of 830 mountains on the Moon's surface. Beer and Mädler also collaborated in publishing in 1830 the first systematic chart of the surface features of the planet Mars.

Graduating from a Gymnasium in 1817, Mädler taught in a seminary in Berlin. There he befriended Beer (1797–1850), a banker and amateur astronomer who owned a private observatory. In 1840, after the publication of the *Mappa Selenographica*, Mädler ended his partnership with Beer and accepted the directorship of the Dorpat Observatory. There, besides studying double stars, he turned to educating the public about astronomy through popular lectures, articles in newspapers and journals, and his *Populäre Astronomie* (1841), which went through several editions.

MARIA MITCHELL

(b. Aug. 1, 1818, Nantucket, Mass., U.S.—d. June 28, 1889, Lynn, Mass.)

Maria Mitchell was the first professional woman astronomer in the United States.

Mitchell was educated in schools on her native Nantucket, Massachusetts, including the one conducted by her father. Her interest in astronomy was stimulated by her father, who let her assist in his work of rating chronometers for the Nantucket whaling fleet and who encouraged her independent use of his telescope. From 1836 to 1856 she worked as a librarian in the Nantucket Atheneum during the day (often acting as an informal teacher) and became a regular observer of the skies at night.

In October 1847 Mitchell succeeded in establishing the orbit of a new comet. The discovery gained her immediate recognition in scientific circles. The following year she became the first woman elected to the American Academy of Arts and Sciences. In 1849 she was appointed a computer for the *American Ephemeris and Nautical Almanac*, and the next year she was elected to the American Association for the Advancement of Science. A gift of a large equatorial telescope was arranged by a group of prominent American women led by Elizabeth Peabody in 1858. Mitchell's accomplishments were subsequently kept in the public eye by feminists, and from 1857 to 1858 she traveled in Europe, meeting many leading scientists. In 1861 she moved with her widowed father to Lynn, Massachusetts.

Reluctantly, but encouraged by her father, Mitchell accepted an appointment in 1865 to Vassar Female College, which opened that year in Poughkeepsie, New York. As director of the observatory and professor of astronomy there, she was, in those early days, the most prominent member of the faculty. Several of her students, who included Christine Ladd-Franklin and Ellen Swallow (Richards), later testified to the great influence she had as a teacher and as an example.

Mitchell pioneered in the daily photography of sunspots. She was the first to find that they were whirling vertical cavities rather than clouds, as had been earlier believed. She also studied comets, nebulae, double stars, solar eclipses, and the satellites of Saturn and Jupiter. Elected

Maria Mitchell, c. 1860. Hulton Archive/ Getty Images

to the American Philosophical Society in 1869, she helped found the Association for the Advancement of Women (1873) and served as its president (1875–76). Mitchell retired from Vassar in failing health in 1888 and died the next year.

WILHELM OLBERS
(b. Oct. 11, 1758, Arbergen, near Bremen, Ger.—d. March 2, 1840, Bremen)

German astronomer and physician Heinrich Wilhelm Matthäus Olbers discovered the asteroids Pallas and Vesta, as well as five comets.

In 1779 Olbers devised a new method of calculating the orbits of comets. Two years later he opened his medical practice in Bremen, where he equipped the upper portion of his house for use as an observatory and devoted the greater part of each night to astronomy.

He took a leading role in the search for a planet between Mars and Jupiter. In March 1802 he discovered Pallas, the second asteroid to be identified. Because Bode's law (which gave the sequence of planetary distances in terms of a numerological formula) implied that there should be a planet between Mars and Jupiter, Olbers proposed that asteroids are the broken-up remnants of a medium-sized planet that once orbited in the asteroid belt region.

In 1811 Olbers formed the theory that the tail of a comet always points away from the Sun because of pressure from the Sun's radiation. (In the 20th century, radiation pressure from light was demonstrated in the laboratory.) Four years later he discovered the object now known as Olbers's Comet. In 1832 he predicted from observations of Biela's Comet that Earth would pass through its tail. The prediction caused much tumult in Europe, but no catastrophic effects were noticed during the passage.

Olbers also proposed what is known as Olbers's paradox, which relates to the problem of why the sky is dark at night. If the universe is endless and uniformly populated with luminous stars, then every line of sight must eventually terminate at the surface of a star. Hence, contrary to observation, this argument implies that the night sky should everywhere be bright, with no dark spaces between the stars.

EDWARD PICKERING
(b. July 19, 1846, Boston, Mass., U.S.—d. Feb. 3, 1919, Cambridge, Mass.)

U.S. physicist and astronomer Edward Charles Pickering introduced the use of the meridian photometer to measure the magnitude of stars and established the *Harvard Photometry* (1884), the first great photometric catalog.

In 1867 Pickering became professor of physics at the Massachusetts Institute of Technology, Cambridge, where he established the first U.S. laboratory in which students were required to use laboratory instruments to make measurements. In 1876 he was appointed professor of astronomy and director of the Harvard College Observatory.

He invented the meridian photometer, which utilized a calcite prism to juxtapose the image of a star with one of a designated group of north polar stars to compare their brightnesses, and used it to compile his catalog. After the Arequipa Observatory was established in Peru in 1891, it became possible to include measurements of the southern stars within the scope of the work of the Harvard College Observatory. Under Pickering this work included photometry, a scale of photographic magnitudes, a system of classification of variable stars, and a system of stellar spectroscopy that was for many years universally adopted.

WILLIAM PICKERING

(b. Feb. 15, 1858, Boston, Mass., U.S.—d.
Jan. 17, 1938, Mandeville, Jam.)

U.S. astronomer William Henry Pickering discovered Phoebe, the ninth satellite of Saturn.

In 1891 Pickering joined his brother Edward in establishing the Boyden station of the Harvard Observatory at Arequipa, Peru. He returned to the United States in 1893 and the next year erected the observatory and telescope at Flagstaff, Ariz., for the noted U.S. astronomer Percival Lowell. In 1900 he established a station for the Harvard Observatory at Mandeville.

He discovered Phoebe in 1899 and noted that it revolves around Saturn in the opposite direction (retrograde) from that of Saturn's other satellites. His announcement in 1905 of a 10th satellite, which he named Themis, is generally discounted, for it was never observed again. The 10th satellite (Janus), which was discovered in 1967, is probably not the same one, for its orbit is the innermost of all Saturn's moons, whereas Pickering's Themis was supposed to lie between Titan and Hyperion. In 1919 Pickering also predicted the existence of, and gave a position for, an object orbiting beyond Neptune. This work contributed to the discovery of Pluto.

LEWIS RUTHERFURD

(b. Nov. 25, 1816, Morrisania, N.Y.,
U.S.—d. May 30, 1892, Tranquility, N.J.)

American astrophysicist Lewis Morris Rutherfurd made the first telescopes designed for celestial photography.

Although trained as a scientist during his studies at Williams College (Williamstown, Mass.), Rutherfurd later became a lawyer. He gave up his practice in 1849 and traveled to Europe because of his wife's health. He had maintained an interest in science and in Europe met the Italian astronomer Giovanni Amici, who was working on achromatism in microscopes. In 1856 he set up a small observatory at his home in New York City and obtained his first photographs of the Moon two years later. Not satisfied with taking pictures through a regular telescope, he devised a lens system that converted it into a photographic telescope (essentially a camera using a telescope as a lens). He successfully tested his invention in 1860, photographing a solar eclipse from Labrador.

Rutherfurd's interest turned to spectroscopy, and in 1863 he published the first attempt to classify stellar spectra. His classification agrees in essence with the one later published by Angelo Secchi of Italy.

Rutherfurd began systematically photographing the heavens and devised a machine for measuring stellar positions on photographic plates. Convinced that the value of a photographic record of stellar positions depended on stable negatives, he found a method of treating film to increase its stability. He also constructed a machine to rule diffraction gratings (devices for breaking light down to its component colours) with up to 6,700 lines per cm (17,000 lines per inch).

A trustee of Columbia College (later Columbia University), Rutherfurd helped establish the department of geodesy and practical astronomy (1881) and gave the college all his equipment and records of his investigations (1883).

SIR EDWARD SABINE

(b. Oct. 14, 1788, Dublin, Ire.—d. June 26, 1883, East Sheen, Surrey, Eng.)

Sir Edward Sabine was an English astronomer and geodesist noted for his experiments in determining the shape of Earth and for his studies of Earth's magnetic field.

He served in the Royal Artillery and was appointed astronomer to the Arctic expeditions of Sir John Ross (1818) and Sir William Parry (1819) in search of the Northwest Passage. In 1821 he began experiments on the coasts of Africa and North America and in the Arctic to determine Earth's shape more precisely by observing the motion of a pendulum. He published the first results of his work in 1825 and three years later continued his research in Paris and London.

Sabine superintended the establishment of magnetic observatories throughout the world. In 1852 he discovered that the periodic variation of sunspots correlates with certain changes in magnetic disturbances on Earth and thus was able to show a relation between these two phenomena. Sabine was president of the Royal Society of London from 1861 to 1871

and was made Knight Commander of the Order of the Bath in 1869.

GIOVANNI SCHIAPARELLI

(b. March 14, 1835, Savigliano, Italy—d. July 4, 1910, Milan)

Giovanni Virginio Schiaparelli was an Italian astronomer and senator whose reports of groups of straight lines on Mars touched off much controversy on the possible existence of life on that planet.

Schiaparelli went to Berlin in 1854 to study astronomy under Johann F. Encke. Two years later he was appointed assistant observer at the Pulkovo Observatory, Russia, a post he resigned in 1860 for a similar one at the Brera Observatory, Milan. He remained there until his retirement in 1900. He became director in 1862.

In 1861 Schiaparelli discovered the asteroid Hesperia. Five years later he demonstrated that meteor swarms have orbits similar to certain comets and concluded that the swarms are the remnants of comets. In particular, he calculated that the Perseid meteors are remnants of Comet 1862 III and the Leonids of Comet 1866 I. He also observed double stars and made extensive studies of Mercury, Venus, and Mars.

Schiaparelli called the peculiar markings he observed on Mars in 1877 *canali*. The word, erroneously translated into English as "canals" instead of "channels," led to widespread speculation over whether the "canals" were constructed by intelligent beings. From his observations of Mercury and Venus, Schiaparelli concluded that those planets rotate on their axes at the same rate at which they revolve about the Sun, thus always keeping one side facing the Sun. This view was generally accepted until the late 1960s, when advanced radar techniques and space probes gave different values. On his retirement Schiaparelli studied the astronomy of the ancient Hebrews and Babylonians and wrote *L'astronomia nell'antico testamento* (1903; *Astronomy in the Old Testament*, 1905).

ANGELO SECCHI
(b. June 29, 1818, Reggio nell'Emilia, duchy of Modena [now in Italy]—d. Feb. 26, 1878, Rome, Italy)

Italian Jesuit priest and astrophysicist Pietro Angelo Secchi made the first survey of the spectra of stars and suggested that stars be classified according to their spectral type.

Secchi entered the Society of Jesus in 1833 and became lecturer in physics and mathematics at the Jesuit College in Loreto, Italy, in 1839. He returned to Rome in 1844, where he completed his theological studies and lectured at the Roman College.

When the Jesuits were expelled from Rome in 1848, Secchi went to Stonyhurst College, Clitheroe, Lancashire, Eng., and then to Georgetown University, Washington, D.C. Because of his reputation as an astronomer, he was allowed to return to Rome in 1849, where he became professor of astronomy and director of the

observatory at the Roman College. He erected a new observatory in which he carried out his research in stellar spectroscopy, terrestrial magnetism, and meteorology.

From his survey of stellar spectra, Secchi concluded that stars could be arranged in four classes according to the type of spectra they display. These divisions were later expanded into the Harvard classification system, which is based on a simple temperature sequence. Secchi proved that prominences seen during a solar eclipse are features on the Sun itself, and he discovered many aspects of their behaviour and of the finer prominence-like jets of gases now known as spicules.

FRIEDRICH VON STRUVE
(b. April 15, 1793, Altona, Den. [now in Germany]—d. Nov. 23, 1864, St. Petersburg, Russia)

Friedrich Georg Wilhelm von Struve was one of the greatest 19th-century astronomers and the first in a line of four generations of distinguished astronomers, who founded the modern study of binary stars.

To avoid conscription by the Napoleonic armies, Struve left Germany in 1808 and went first to Denmark and then to Russia. In 1813 he became professor of astronomy and mathematics at the University of Dorpat (now Tartu, Estonia), and four years later he was appointed director of the Dorpat Observatory. In 1824 he obtained a refracting telescope with an aperture of 24 cm (9.6 inches), at that time the finest ever built, and used it in a binary-star survey of unprecedented scope. In his survey of 120,000 stars from the north celestial pole to 15° S declination, he measured 3,112 binaries, more than 75 percent of which were previously unknown. He published his findings in the catalog *Stellarum Duplicium Mensurae Micrometricae* (1837; "Micrometric Measurement of Double Stars"), one of the classics of binary-star astronomy.

In 1835, at the request of Tsar Nicholas I of Russia, Struve went to Pulkovo to supervise the construction of a new observatory. He became director of the Pulkovo Observatory in 1839 but continued his binary-star studies.

It was in 1835 that Struve began efforts to measure the parallax of Vega, a star he had selected for its brightness and large proper motion, which suggested that it might be near Earth. Parallax is the apparent shift in position of a nearby star, such as Vega, with respect to more distant stars as Earth moves from one part of its orbit to another. Astronomers had known since the time of Copernicus that stellar parallax must exist and had been trying seriously to measure it since the 1670s, but the instruments and techniques had not been good enough to measure such small angular shifts. In 1837 Struve announced a parallax for Vega of one-eighth of a second of arc, which is close to the modern value. Later, after continued measurement, he increased his estimate, but not for the better. Much more accurate parallaxes for other stars were announced in quick succession by German astronomer Friedrich Wilhelm Bessel in 1838 and by Scottish astronomer Thomas Henderson in 1839.

HERMANN VOGEL
(b. April 3, 1842, Leipzig, Ger.—d. Aug. 13, 1907, Potsdam)

German astronomer Hermann Karl Vogel discovered spectroscopic binaries—double-star systems that are too close for the individual stars to be discerned by any telescope but, through the analysis of their light, have been found to be two individual stars rapidly revolving around one another.

An assistant at the Leipzig Observatory from 1867, Vogel became director of a private observatory at Bothkamp, Ger., in 1870. His early work centred on the study of planetary spectra (the characteristic wavelengths of the light from the planets) to obtain data on the planetary atmospheres. It was published in his *Spectra der Planeten* (1874; "Spectra of the Planets"). In 1874 he joined the staff of the new Astrophysical Observatory at Potsdam and in 1882 became its director.

In 1887 Vogel began a program of spectroscopic measurement of the radial motions of the stars and introduced the use of photography in stellar spectroscopy. In the course of his work he proved that the star Algol is accompanied by a dark companion (about the size of the Sun) that periodically eclipses it, thus accounting for Algol's periodic and regular variations in brightness. (This explanation of the regular variability of Algol had been conjectured a hundred years earlier by British astronomer John Goodricke.) Vogel is also noted for his work in stellar classification. First proposed in 1874 and revised in 1895, the Vogel system is based on the previous work of the Italian astronomer Pietro Angelo Secchi.

MAX WOLF
(b. June 21, 1863, Heidelberg, Baden [Ger.]—d. Oct. 3, 1932, Heidelberg)

German astronomer Maximillian Franz Joseph Cornelius Wolf applied photography to the search for asteroids and discovered 228 of them.

Wolf showed an early interest in astronomy. He was only 21 years old when he discovered a comet, now named for him. In 1890 he was appointed *Privatdozent* (unsalaried lecturer) at the University of Heidelberg. One year later he adapted a camera to a motor-driven telescope to seek out asteroids. (All previous discoveries had been made one by one by direct observation.) Using a time exposure of the heavens, Wolf demonstrated that the asteroids, because of their orbital motion, would show up in the photograph as a short line rather than a point of light, which denoted a star.

In 1893 Wolf became director of the new Königstuhl Observatory and was appointed to an extraordinary professorship in astrophysics at Heidelberg. Nine years later he was elected to the chair of astronomy at Heidelberg. Through his photographic studies he established the presence of dark clouds of interstellar matter in the Milky Way Galaxy, and he was the first to use the stereocomparator (a type of stereoscopic viewer), which greatly helps in the discovery and identification of variable or moving objects in celestial photographs. In 1906 he discovered Achilles, the first of the Trojan planets, two groups of asteroids that move around the Sun in Jupiter's orbit— one group 60° ahead of Jupiter, the other 60° behind.

RUDOLF WOLF
(b. July 7, 1816, Fällenden, near Zürich, Switz.—d. Dec. 6, 1893, Zürich)

Johann Rudolf Wolf was a Swiss astronomer and astronomical historian.

Wolf studied at the universities of Zürich, Vienna, and Berlin and in 1839 went to the University of Bern as a teacher of mathematics and physics. He became professor of astronomy there in 1844. In 1855 he accepted a professorship of astronomy at both the University of Zürich and the Federal Institute of Technology in Zürich. At his instigation an observatory was opened at Zürich in 1864.

Wolf confirmed S. H. Schwabe's discovery of a cycle in sunspot activity and by use of earlier records defined the cycle's length more accurately, at an average of 11.1 years. Wolf also correlated this solar cycle with the observations of Earth's magnetism made by Johann von Lamont. In 1849 he devised a system, still in use, of gauging solar activity by counting sunspots and sunspot groups, which are known as Wolf's sunspot numbers.

CHAPTER 8

20TH-CENTURY ASTRONOMERS

In addition to traditional observation and theoretical contemplation, contemporary astronomy has expanded to include physical and chemical research into the nature of celestial objects. The modern fields of astrophysics and cosmology have led modern astronomers to many revelations concerning the nature of the universe.

CHARLES ABBOT

(b. May 31, 1872, Wilton, N.H., U.S.—d. Dec. 17, 1973, Riverdale, Md.)

As director of the Smithsonian Astrophysical Observatory in Washington, D.C., for almost four decades, American astrophysicist Charles Greeley Abbot engaged in a career-long campaign to demonstrate that the Sun's energy output varies and has a measurable effect on Earth's weather.

The youngest of four children of a New Hampshire farming family, Abbot received an M.Sc. degree from the Massachusetts Institute of Technology in 1895 and was immediately hired as assistant to Samuel Pierpont Langley, the first director of the Smithsonian observatory. Abbot helped Langley map the infrared spectrum of the Sun and measure the total solar radiation energy received by Earth over a given area and time—a value called the solar constant.

Assuming acting directorship of the observatory after Langley's death in 1906 and directorship the next year, Abbot created a synoptic monitoring program to search for possible variations in the solar constant. Abbot soon persuaded himself that sizeable variations had been detected by his staff and that they correlated with variations in Earth's weather. In the belief that he had found an important key to weather prediction, he spent much of the next half century trying to convince the world of its reality. The cyclic variations that Abbot observed in the solar constant, amounting to as much as 3–5 percent, were actually due to changing weather conditions and incomplete analysis of his data—as subsequently shown by satellite observations above the atmosphere and computer analysis of the data.

Abbot's most important scientific legacies are the establishment of the modern value of the solar constant—previous estimates of which had ranged widely—at 1.93 calories per square centimetre per minute on a theoretical surface outside the atmosphere and his emphasis on the question of its variation. Modern reanalyses of Abbot's data do show evidence for minute variations in the solar constant, confirmed by satellite observations, that are caused by changes in the number and intensity of sunspots and faculae on the solar surface.

Abbot served as secretary of the Smithsonian Institution from 1928 until his retirement from both the institution and the observatory posts in 1944. To popularize the importance of solar energy, he designed solar heaters and cookers to use for lectures and demonstrations. Abbot

continued to pursue his analysis of solar data in retirement, convinced of the correctness of the variations he had found.

VIKTOR AMBARTSUMIAN
(b. Sept. 5 [Sept. 18, New Style], 1908, Tbilisi, Georgia, Russian Empire—d. Aug. 12, 1996, Byurakan Observatory, near Yerevan, Arm.)

Soviet astronomer and astrophysicist Viktor Amazaspovich Ambartsumian was best known for his theories concerning the origin and evolution of stars and stellar systems. He was also the founder of the school of theoretical astrophysics in the Soviet Union.

Ambartsumian was born of Armenian parents. His father, a prominent philologist, encouraged the development of his aptitude for mathematics and physics. In 1925 he entered the University of Leningrad (now Saint Petersburg State University) with the intention of devoting his life to research in astrophysics. In the following year he published a paper on solar activity, the first of 10 papers he published while an undergraduate. After graduating in 1928, Ambartsumian became a graduate student in astrophysics under the direction of A. A. Belopolskii at Pulkovo Observatory near Leningrad (now St. Petersburg).

From 1931 to 1943 he lectured at the University of Leningrad, where he headed the Astrophysical Department. In 1932 he advanced his theory of the interaction of ultraviolet radiation from hot stars with the surrounding gas, a theory that led to a series of papers on the physics of gaseous clouds. His statistical analysis of stellar systems in 1934–36, in which for the first time their physical properties were taken into account, was found to be applicable to many related problems, such as the evolution of double stars and star clusters. He was elected a corresponding member of the Academy of Sciences of the U.S.S.R. in 1939 and was appointed a deputy rector of the University of Leningrad in 1941–43. His theory of the behaviour of light in a scattering medium of cosmic space, put forward in 1941–43, became an important tool in geophysics, space research, and particularly astrophysics, such as in studies of interstellar matter.

In 1943 Ambartsumian joined the Armenian Academy of Sciences in Yerevan, the capital of Armenia, and began teaching at Yerevan State University. In 1946 he organized the construction near Yerevan of the Byurakan Astronomical Observatory, where he began another successful period of activity as the observatory's director. In 1947 he discovered a new type of comparatively recent stellar system, which he named stellar association. The most important result of his study is the conclusion that the process of star formation in the Milky Way Galaxy that contains the Sun and its planetary system still continues and, specifically, that most stars have their origin in changing systems of groups of stars.

Later, Ambartsumian studied the phenomena in the atmosphere of stars that are changing in physical characteristics, such as luminosity, mass, or density. He saw these changes as being connected with the direct release of interstellar energy in the outer layers of the stars. He also investigated nonstationary processes in galaxies. These investigations are of great importance, both for the problem of the evolution of galaxies and for the study of still-unknown properties of matter.

His textbook *Theoretical Astrophysics* (1958) went through many editions and translations. It contains examples of his unique and fruitful approaches to stubborn astronomical problems. In addition, he studied radio signals coming from outside the Milky Way Galaxy. He was led to conclude that these radio signals represent not colliding systems of stars, as according to a widely accepted interpretation, but the subatomic process of fission within galaxies. Therefore, according to his view, "radio galaxies" may represent systems of stars, interacting in close proximity, that were formed from superdense formations of stellar material. In support of this view, he pointed out the presence of jets, condensations, and streamers that are bluish in colour. Found around certain galaxies, these are characteristics of an early stage in stellar development. Ambartsumian's later works include *Problemy sovremennoi kosmogonii* (1969; "Problems of Modern Cosmogony") and *Filosofskie voprosy nauki o Vselennoi* (1973; "Philosophical Problems of the Study of the Universe").

Ambartsumian's thought-provoking manner of presentation drew large audiences to his lectures at international symposia, where he enlivened even his most abstrusely mathematical lectures with quotations from classic and contemporary poets.

The Soviet government presented many decorations and awards to Ambartsumian. In 1947 he was elected president of the Armenian S.S.R. Academy of Sciences and a member of the Parliament of Soviet Armenia. From 1950 he served in the Supreme Soviet of the U.S.S.R. In 1953 he was elected to full membership in the Academy of Sciences of the U.S.S.R. In 1948–56 he was vice president, and in 1961–63 president, of the International Astronomical Union. In 1968 he became president of the International Council of Scientific Unions, and he participated in activities of many foreign academies and scientific societies. He was awarded two Stalin prizes and five Orders of Lenin, among many other honours. He continued to head the Byurakan Observatory until 1988.

HALTON ARP
(b. March 21, 1927, New York, N.Y., U.S.)

American astronomer Halton Christian Arp is noted for challenging the theory that redshifts of quasars indicate their great distance.

Arp received a bachelor's degree from Harvard University in 1949 and a Ph.D. from the California Institute of Technology in 1953. He subsequently accepted a research fellowship to conduct postdoctoral studies at the nearby Hale Observatories (now the Mt. Wilson

and Palomar Observatories). After he worked as a research associate at Indiana University from 1955 to 1957, Arp returned to Mt. Wilson, securing a post as an assistant astronomer on the observatory staff. He was appointed astronomer there in 1965.

Arp became skeptical about the distance of quasars when he noticed that some of the galaxies that he had included in his *Atlas of Peculiar Galaxies* (1966) seemed to lie near quasars. Using photographic evidence, Arp tried to prove that the low-red-shift galaxies and the high-red-shift quasars not only appear close together but are actually connected by gaseous bridges. Arp theorized that the nuclei of galaxies may explode, ejecting quasars with a velocity great enough to account for their redshifts. His theory was later rejected when it could not account for galaxies and quasars that were at the same distance.

PATRICK BLACKETT
(b. Nov. 18, 1897, London, Eng.—d. July 13, 1974, London)

Patrick Maynard Stuart Blackett, Baron Blackett of Chelsea, won the Nobel Prize for Physics in 1948 for his discoveries in the field of cosmic radiation. He accomplished this primarily with cloud-chamber photographs that revealed the way in which a stable atomic nucleus can be disintegrated by bombarding it with alpha particles (helium nuclei). Although such nuclear disintegration had been observed previously, his data explained this phenomenon for the first time and were useful in explaining disintegration by other means.

After graduating from Cambridge University in 1921, Blackett spent 10 years as a research worker in the Cavendish Laboratory. There he began to develop the Wilson cloud chamber—a device that detects the path of ionizing particles—into an automatic instrument for the study of cosmic radiation. He received the Nobel Prize for his interpretation of the data he obtained from this device.

Blackett became professor of physics at the University of London in 1933 and Langworthy professor of physics at the University of Manchester in 1937. He established a school of cosmic-ray research and stimulated the development of other research interests, which led to the creation of the first chair of radio astronomy, at the University of Manchester, and to the building of the Jodrell Bank Experimental Station for Radio Astronomy. In 1953 he was appointed professor and head of the physics department of the Imperial College of Science and Technology in London, where he became senior research fellow in 1965. That year he was named president of the Royal Society. He was created a life peer in 1969.

BART BOK

(b. April 28, 1906, Hoorn, Neth.—d. Aug. 7, 1983, Tucson, Ariz., U.S.)

Dutch-born American astronomer Bart Jan Bok was known for his work on the structure and evolution of the Milky Way Galaxy and for his study of "Bok globules," small dark clouds observable against the background of bright nebulae. Bok suggested that these globules may be condensed clouds of interstellar gas and dust in the process of contracting into stars.

Bok studied at the universities of Leiden and Groningen (Ph.D. 1932). He then pursued an academic career of research and teaching at Harvard University (1929–57), the Australian National University (1957–66), and the University of Arizona (1966–74). He remained at Arizona as professor emeritus, having become a U.S. citizen in 1938. He served as director of the Mount Stromlo Observatory (1957–66) in Australia and as director of the Steward Observatory (1966–70) in Arizona. With his wife, Priscilla F. Bok, he wrote the classic work *The Milky Way* (1941; 5th ed., 1981). Bok served as vice president of the International Astronomical Union (1970–76) and as president of the American Astronomical Society (1972–74).

SIR HERMANN BONDI

(b. Nov. 1, 1919, Vienna, Austria—d. Sept. 10, 2005, Cambridge, Eng.)

Sir Hermann Bondi was an Austrian-born British mathematician and cosmologist who, with Fred Hoyle and Thomas Gold, formulated the steady-state theory of the universe.

Bondi received an M.A. from Trinity College, Cambridge. During World War II he worked in the British Admiralty (1942–45). He then taught mathematics at Cambridge (1945–54) and at King's College in London (1954–85; emeritus 1985). He served as master of Churchill College, Cambridge, from 1983 to 1990. Bondi combined his academic career with active involvement in public service. He was director general of the European Space Research Organization (1967–71), chief scientific adviser to the British Ministry of Defence (1971–77), chief scientist of the Department of Energy (1977–80), and chairman of the Natural Environment Research Council (1980–84).

In 1948, after three-way discussions about cosmology, Bondi and Gold published a paper and Hoyle published another, which, although based on different approaches, jointly established a steady-state theory of the universe. According to the theory, the universe is the same everywhere and for all time. This means that as the universe expands, new matter would have to be created to balance this expansion. The theory of an eternal, steady-state universe, with no origin in time, has fallen into disrepute since the discovery in 1963 of the cosmic microwave background (i.e., a faint glow of radio radiation emanating from all directions in space). The theory strongly suggests that the universe began at some definable moment in the big bang, a violent explosion of an extremely dense and intensely hot mass of material.

Works by Bondi include *Cosmology* (1952; reissued 1960), *The Universe at Large* (1960), *Relativity and Commonsense* (1964), and *Assumption and Myth in Physical Theory* (1967). He was made a fellow of the Royal Society in 1959 and was knighted in 1973. His autobiography, *Science, Churchill, and Me*, was published in 1990.

I. S. BOWEN
(b. Dec. 21, 1898, Seneca Falls, N.Y., U.S.—d. Feb. 6, 1973, Los Angeles, Calif.)

Ira Sprague Bowen was an American astrophysicist whose explanation of the strong green emission from nebulae (clouds of rarefied gas) led to major advances in the study of celestial composition. This emission, which was unlike that characteristic of any known element, had previously been attributed to a hypothetical element, "nebulium." Bowen showed, however, that the emission was identical with that calculated to be produced by ionized oxygen and nitrogen under extremely low pressure.

Bowen in 1926 joined the faculty of the California Institute of Technology, Pasadena, where he became a full professor in 1931. In 1946 he became director of the Mount Wilson Observatory and served as director of the Hale Observatories—which comprised Mt. Wilson and Palomar observatories—from 1948 until 1964. In 1938 Bowen invented the image slicer, a device that improves the efficiency of the slit spectrograph, which is used to break up light into its component colours for study. Bowen retired as observatory director in 1964, becoming a distinguished-service staff member.

DIRK BROUWER

(b. Sept. 1, 1902, Rotterdam, Neth.—d.
Jan. 31, 1966, New Haven, Conn., U.S.)

Dutch-born U.S. astronomer and geophysicist Dirk Brouwer was known for his achievements in celestial mechanics, especially for his pioneering application of high-speed digital computers.

After leaving the University of Leiden, Brouwer served as a faculty member at Yale University from 1928 until his death, becoming both professor of astronomy and director of the Yale Observatory in 1941. At Yale he first studied changes in Earth's rotation, later tackling orbital problems. Along with W. J. Eckert, he developed a method of calculating orbit corrections (1937) that has been widely accepted. With Eckert and G. M. Clemence (1951), Brouwer was the first to use a computer to calculate planetary positions accurately. Among his other notable contributions, Brouwer formulated the term *ephemeris time* to describe time measurement unaffected by variation in the rate of Earth's rotation.

Brouwer was elected to the U.S. National Academy of Sciences in 1951, and for his contributions to celestial mechanics he was awarded the Gold Medal of the Royal Astronomical Society in 1955.

MARGARET BURBIDGE

(b. Aug. 12, 1919, Davenport,
Cheshire, Eng.)

English-born American astronomer Eleanor Margaret Burbidge was the first woman to be appointed director of the Royal Greenwich Observatory. She made notable contributions to the theory of quasars (quasi-stellar sources), to measurements of the rotation and masses of galaxies, and to the understanding of how chemical elements are formed in the depths of stars through nuclear fusion. Burbidge also championed the fight for opportunities for women in science.

Burbidge served as assistant director (1948–50) and acting director (1950–51) of the Observatory of the University of London. In 1955 her husband, theoretical astrophysicist Geoffrey Burbidge, obtained a Carnegie fellowship for astronomical research at the Mount Wilson Observatory, near Pasadena, California, U.S. Because women were then ineligible for such an appointment, she chose to accept a minor research post at the California Institute of Technology, Pasadena. In 1957 she became Shirley Farr fellow and, later, associate professor at Yerkes Observatory, Williams Bay, Wisconsin. She served as research astronomer (1962–64) and thereafter as professor of astronomy at the University of California, San Diego (UCSD). She took a leave of absence from this post to serve as director of the Royal Greenwich Observatory from 1972–73. Her Greenwich duties did not come with the traditional honorary title of Astronomer Royal, which instead was given to a male astronomer. Burbidge saw this as another instance of discrimination against women in the astronomical community. In 1972 she refused the Annie J. Cannon Prize from the American Astronomical Society

Input

—

(AAS) because, as it was an award for women only, it represented for her another facet of the same discrimination. Her action led to the formation of a standing AAS committee for the status of women in astronomy. Burbidge later became a naturalized American citizen. From 1979 to 1988 Burbidge directed the UCSD's Center for Astrophysics and Space Sciences, where she helped develop some of the Hubble Space Telescope's original instruments. She became a professor emeritus of the university in 1990.

In the 1950s Burbidge carried out stellar-spectra research that served as the foundation of the B^2FH theory named for the formulators: the Burbidges, William A. Fowler of the United States, and Sir Fred Hoyle of Great Britain. This theory, published in 1957, provided a revolutionary explanation of the origin in stars of all the elements in the periodic table from helium to iron, starting with the lightest element, hydrogen. Her publications include *Quasi-Stellar Objects* (1967), with Geoffrey Burbidge. She was elected a fellow of the Royal Society of London in 1964. She served as president of the AAS (1976–78) and of the American Association for the Advancement of Science (1983).

ANNIE JUMP CANNON

(b. Dec. 11, 1863, Dover, Del., U.S.—d. April 13, 1941, Cambridge, Mass.)

American astronomer Annie Jump Cannon specialized in the classification of stellar spectra.

Cannon was the oldest daughter of Wilson Cannon, a Delaware state senator, and Mary Jump. She studied physics and astronomy at Wellesley College, graduating in 1884. For several years thereafter she traveled and dabbled in photography and music. In 1894 she returned to Wellesley for a year of advanced study in astronomy, and in 1895 she enrolled at Radcliffe in order to continue her studies under Edward C. Pickering—who

Annie Jump Cannon, c. 1900. Hulton Archive/Getty Images

was director of the Harvard College Observatory. In 1896 she was named an assistant at the Harvard Observatory, becoming one of a group known as "Pickering's Women." There, joining Williamina P. S. Fleming, Cannon devoted her energies to Pickering's ambitious project, begun in 1885, of recording, classifying, and cataloging the spectra of all stars down to those of the ninth magnitude. The scheme of spectral classification by surface temperature used for the project and later (1910) universally adopted was largely work that Cannon had developed from earlier systems. She eventually obtained and classified spectra for more than 225,000 stars. Her work was published in nine volumes as the *Henry Draper Catalogue* (1918–24).

In 1911 Cannon succeeded Fleming as curator of astronomical photographs at the observatory, and in 1938 she was named William Cranch Bond Professor of Astronomy. After 1924 she extended her work, cataloging tens of thousands of additional stars down to the 11th magnitude for the two-volume *Henry Draper Extension* (1925, 1949). The work was an invaluable contribution to astronomy, bearing strongly on countless other problems and areas of research and exerting major influence on the evolution of the science of astronomy from one of mere observation to one of great theoretical and philosophical content. In the course of her work Cannon also discovered some 300 variable stars and 5 novae.

Among the numerous honours and awards accorded her were the first honorary doctorate from the University of Oxford to be awarded to a woman (1925) and the Henry Draper Medal of the National Academy of Sciences in 1931. She was also the first woman to become an officer in the American Astronomical Society. In 1933 she established that organization's Annie J. Cannon Prize, which is given to a North American female astronomer (within five years of receiving a doctorate) for her distinguished contribution to astronomy. Cannon officially retired from the observatory in 1940 but carried on research until her death the next year.

SUBRAHMANYAN CHANDRASEKHAR

(b. Oct. 19, 1910, Lahore, India [now in Pakistan]—d. Aug. 21, 1995, Chicago, Ill., U.S.)

Subrahmanyan Chandrasekhar was an Indian-born American astrophysicist who, with William A. Fowler, won the 1983 Nobel Prize for Physics for key discoveries that led to the currently accepted theory on the later evolutionary stages of massive stars.

Chandrasekhar was the nephew of Sir Chandrasekhara Venkata Raman, who won the Nobel Prize for Physics in 1930. Chandrasekhar was educated at Presidency College, at the University of Madras, and at Trinity College, Cambridge. From 1933 to 1936 he held a position at Trinity.

By the early 1930s, scientists had concluded that, after converting all of their hydrogen to helium, stars lose energy and contract under the influence of their own gravity. These stars, known as white dwarf stars, contract to about the size of Earth, and the electrons and nuclei of their constituent atoms are compressed to a state of extremely high density. Chandrasekhar determined what is known as the Chandrasekhar limit—that a star having a mass more than 1.44 times that of the Sun does not form a white dwarf but instead continues to collapse, blows off its gaseous envelope in a supernova explosion, and becomes a neutron star. An even more massive star continues to collapse and becomes a black hole. These calculations contributed to the eventual understanding of supernovas, neutron stars, and black holes.

Chandrasekhar joined the staff of the University of Chicago, rising from assistant professor of astrophysics (1938) to Morton D. Hull distinguished service professor of astrophysics (1952), and became a U.S. citizen in 1953. He did important work on energy transfer by radiation in stellar atmospheres and convection on the solar surface. He also attempted to develop the mathematical theory of black holes, describing his work in *The Mathematical Theory of Black Holes* (1983).

Chandrasekhar was awarded the Gold Medal of the Royal Astronomical Society in 1953 and the Royal Medal of the Royal Society in 1962. His other books include *An Introduction to the Study of Stellar Structure* (1939), *Principles of Stellar Dynamics* (1942), *Radiative Transfer* (1950), *Hydrodynamic and Hydromagnetic Stability* (1961),

and *Truth and Beauty: Aesthetics and Motivations in Science* (1987).

ROBERT DICKE
(b. May 6, 1916, St. Louis, Mo., U.S.—d. March 4, 1997, Princeton, N.J.)

American physicist Robert Henry Dicke was noted for his theoretical work in cosmology and investigations centring on the general theory of relativity. He also made a number of significant contributions to radar technology and to the field of atomic physics.

Dicke received a bachelor's degree from Princeton University (1939) and a doctorate from the University of Rochester (1941). In 1941, he became a staff scientist at the radiation laboratory of MIT. Dicke joined the Princeton faculty in 1946. In 1975 he was appointed Albert Einstein professor of science, becoming emeritus professor in 1984.

During the early 1940s Dicke and other researchers at the Massachusetts Institute of Technology (MIT) played a key role in the development of microwave radar. He himself invented various microwave-circuit devices and radar systems, including mono-pulse radar and coherent pulse radar. In 1944 he developed a microwave radiometer that has become an integral component of most modern radio telescopes. For the next 10 years or so, Dicke devoted much attention to microwave atomic spectroscopy, conducting extensive research on fundamental radiation processes. His work led him to formulate what is often considered the first quantum theory of the emission of coherent radiation. (This type of radiation consists of electromagnetic waves, such as those in a beam of laser light, that are in phase.)

By the 1960s Dicke had become actively interested in gravitation. He carried out a series of studies on the subject, the most notable of which was an experiment testing the principle of equivalence (i.e., that the gravitational mass of a body is equal to its inertial mass) that forms the cornerstone of Einstein's concept of gravitation—the general theory of relativity. High-precision experiments with this objective had first been performed by the Hungarian physicist Roland von Eötvös, who confirmed the principle to an accuracy of one part in 10^8. Dicke improved upon Eötvös's accuracy by another factor of 1,000. Together with Carl Brans he investigated the idea of a changing gravitational constant, which had first been proposed in 1937 by Paul Dirac. Dicke and Brans developed a theory of gravitation in which, as a result of the expansion of the universe, the gravitational constant is not actually a constant but decreases at a rate of two parts in 10^{11} per year.

In 1964 Dicke and several colleagues hypothesized that the entire universe is pervaded by a background radiation of microwave wavelengths—the remnant of the intense thermal radiation associated with the apparent explosive origin of the cosmos. They were unaware that the existence of such residual radiation of the primordial fireball had been postulated some 16 years earlier by George Gamow,

Ralph Alpher, and Robert Herman. Before Dicke attempted any observational work, Arno Penzias and Robert Wilson of Bell Telephone Laboratories discovered a faint glow of microwave radiation closely matching that predicted by theory.

SIR FRANK DYSON

(b. Jan. 8, 1868, Measham, near Ashby-de-la-Zouch, Leicestershire, Eng.—d. May 25, 1939, at sea, en route from Australia to England)

In 1919 British astronomer Sir Frank Watson Dyson organized observations of stars seen near the Sun during a solar eclipse, which provided evidence supporting Einstein's prediction in the theory of general relativity of the bending of light in a gravitational field.

In 1894 Dyson became chief assistant at the Royal Greenwich Observatory and was a member of eclipse expeditions to Portugal (1900), Sumatra (1901), and Tunisia (1905). His observations of the corona and chromosphere of the Sun were published in *Determination of Wave-Lengths from Spectra Obtained at the Total Solar Eclipses of 1900, 1901, and 1905* (1906). Dyson was elected a fellow of the Royal Society of London in 1901, and in 1905 he was appointed Astronomer Royal for Scotland. He returned to Greenwich in 1910 to become the ninth astronomer royal of England, and five years later he was knighted. In 1921 he was honoured for his investigations of the distribution and movements of stars and the relationship of these to the structure of the Galaxy.

Dyson's *Eclipses of the Sun and Moon* (1937) was written with British astronomer Richard van der Riet Woolley.

WILLIAM FOWLER
(b. Aug. 9, 1911, Pittsburgh, Pa., U.S.—d. March 14, 1995, Pasadena, Calif.)

William Alfred Fowler was an American nuclear astrophysicist who, with Subrahmanyan Chandrasekhar, won the Nobel Prize for Physics in 1983 for his role in formulating a widely accepted theory of element generation.

Fowler studied at Ohio State University (B.S., 1933) and at the California Institute of Technology (Ph.D., 1936), where he became a professor in 1939. His theory of element generation, which he developed with Sir Fred Hoyle, Margaret Burbidge, and Geoffrey Burbidge in the 1950s, suggests that in stellar evolution elements are synthesized progressively from light elements to heavy ones, in nuclear reactions that also produce light and heat. With the collapse of more massive stars, the explosive rebound known as supernova occurs. According to theory, this phase makes possible the synthesis of the heaviest elements.

Fowler also worked in radio astronomy, proposing with Hoyle that the cores of radio galaxies are collapsed "superstars" emitting strong radio waves and that quasars are larger versions of these collapsed superstars.

Fowler received the National Medal of Science (1974) and the Legion of Honour (1989).

VITALY GINZBURG
(b. Oct. 4 [Sept. 21, Old Style], 1916, Moscow, Russia)

Russian physicist and astrophysicist Vitaly Lazarevich Ginzburg won the Nobel Prize for Physics in 2003 for his pioneering work on superconductivity. He shared the award with Alexey A. Abrikosov of Russia and Anthony J. Leggett of Great Britain. Ginzburg was also noted for his work on theories of radio-wave propagation, radio astronomy, and the origin of cosmic rays.

After graduating from Moscow State University (1938), Ginzburg was appointed to the P. N. Lebedev Physical Institute of the U.S.S.R. Academy of Sciences in 1940, and from 1971 to 1988 he headed the institute's theory group. He also taught at Gorky University (1945–68) and from 1968 at the Moscow Technical Institute of Physics. Ginzburg received the State Prize of the Soviet Union in 1953 and the Lenin Prize in 1966.

Ginzburg conducted his prizewinning research on superconductivity in the 1950s. First identified in 1911, superconductivity is the disappearance of electrical resistance in various solids when they are cooled below a characteristic temperature, which is typically very low. Scientists formulated various theories on why the phenomenon occurred in certain metals, termed type I superconductors. Ginzburg also developed such a theory, and it proved so comprehensive that Abrikosov later used it to build a theoretical explanation for type II superconductors. Ginzburg's achievement also enabled other scientists to create and test new superconducting materials and build more powerful electromagnets.

Another significant theory developed by Ginzburg was that cosmic radiation in interstellar space is produced not by thermal radiation but by the acceleration of high-energy electrons in magnetic fields, a process known as synchrotron radiation. In 1955 Ginzburg (with I. S. Shklovsky) discovered the first quantitative proof that the cosmic rays observed near Earth originated in supernovae. Upon the 1969 discovery of pulsars (believed to be neutron stars formed in supernova explosions), he expanded his theory to include pulsars as a related source of cosmic rays.

THOMAS GOLD

(b. May 22, 1920, Vienna, Austria—d. June 22, 2004, Ithaca, N.Y., U.S.)

Austrian-born British astronomer Thomas Gold promulgated the steady-state theory of the universe, holding that, although the universe is expanding, a continuous creation of matter in intergalactic space is gradually forming new galaxies, so that the average number of galaxies in any part of the universe remains approximately the same. Many of Gold's theories were unconventional, and they often generated much controversy.

Gold studied at Trinity College, Cambridge (B.A., 1942; M.Sc., 1946), and during World War II served in the British Admiralty. He was elected a fellow of Trinity College in 1947 and became university demonstrator in physics in 1949 at the Cavendish Laboratory, Cambridge. During the late 1940s, in collaboration with Hermann Bondi and Fred Hoyle, Gold formulated the steady-state theory, of which Hoyle became the leading proponent. Later evidence, however, contradicted this theory and instead supported the big bang model.

In 1952 Gold joined the staff of the Royal Greenwich Observatory, London. Five years later he became professor of astronomy at Harvard University. There he worked on the maser (microwave amplification by stimulated emission of radiation) amplifier for use with radio telescopes. In 1959 he joined the faculty of Cornell University in Ithaca, New York, as professor of astronomy. He served as director of the Center for Radiophysics and Space Research from 1959 to 1981. An early supporter of space exploration, Gold contributed significant theories and conjectures on the structure of the Moon, on the effect of solar flares and storms on Earth's atmosphere, and on the origin of the solar system and of life. He served as a consultant to the National Aeronautics and Space Administration and in the 1960s advised on the organization's Apollo program. In the 1970s Gold began concentrating on the world's energy supply. He generated much criticism with his theory that oil and natural gas are continually being formed through geologic processes and are not, as is commonly believed, created by decaying natural matter. The theory, which he outlined in *The Deep Hot Biosphere* (1999), remains unproven.

STEPHEN W. HAWKING
(b. Jan. 8, 1942, Oxford, Oxfordshire, Eng.)

English theoretical physicist Stephen William Hawking's theory of exploding black holes drew upon both relativity theory and quantum mechanics. He also worked with space-time singularities.

Hawking studied mathematics and physics at University College, Oxford (B.A., 1962), and Trinity Hall, Cambridge (Ph.D., 1966). He was elected a research fellow at Gonville and Caius College at Cambridge. In the early 1960s Hawking contracted amyotrophic lateral sclerosis, an incurable degenerative neuromuscular disease. He continued to

Stephen W. Hawking (left) receiving the Copley Medal of the Royal Society, 2006. The Royal Society/NASA

work despite the disease's progressively disabling effects.

Hawking worked primarily in the field of general relativity and particularly on the physics of black holes. In 1971 he suggested the formation, following the big bang, of numerous objects containing as much as 1,000,000,000 tons of mass but occupying only the space of a proton. These objects, called mini black holes, are unique in that their immense mass and gravity require that they be ruled by the laws of relativity, while their minute size requires that the laws of quantum mechanics apply to them also. In 1974 Hawking proposed that, in accordance with the predictions of quantum theory, black holes emit subatomic particles until they exhaust their energy and finally explode. Hawking's work greatly spurred efforts to theoretically delineate the properties of black holes, objects about which it was previously thought that nothing could be known. His work was also important because it showed these properties' relationship to the laws of classical thermodynamics and quantum mechanics.

Hawking's contributions to physics earned him many exceptional honours. In 1974 the Royal Society elected him one of its youngest fellows. He became professor of gravitational physics at Cambridge in 1977, and in 1979 he was appointed to Cambridge's Lucasian professorship of mathematics, a post once held by Isaac Newton. Hawking was made a Commander of the British Empire (CBE) in 1982 and a Companion of Honour in 1989. He received the Copley Medal from the Royal Society in 2006. In 2008 he accepted a visiting research chair at the Perimeter Institute for Theoretical Physics in Waterloo, Ont.

His publications include *The Large Scale Structure of Space-Time* (1973; coauthored with G. F. R. Ellis), *Superspace and Supergravity* (1981), *The Very Early Universe* (1983), and the best sellers *A Brief History of Time: From the Big Bang to Black Holes* (1988), *The Universe in a Nutshell* (2001), and *A Briefer History of Time* (2005).

OTTO HECKMANN

(b. June 23, 1901, Opladen, Ger.—d. May 13, 1983, Regensburg)

German astronomer Otto Hermann Leopold Heckmann was noted for his work in measuring stellar positions and for his studies of relativity and cosmology. He also made notable contributions to statistical mechanics.

After obtaining his Ph.D. (1925) at the University of Bonn, Heckmann became assistant astronomer at its observatory (1925–27) and at the University Observatory in Göttingen (1927–35). He became lecturer in astronomy at the University of Göttingen in 1929 and assistant professor in 1935. From 1941 to 1962 he was director of the Hamburg Observatory and head of the department of astronomy at Hamburg University.

Heckmann organized an international program to photograph and chart the positions of the stars in the Northern Hemisphere. This monumental task, involving observatories in England, France, West Germany, East Germany, the Soviet Union, Canada, and the United States, led to the 1975 publication of the third German Astronomical Society catalog, *Astronomische Gesellschaft Katalog,* commonly known as the *AGK3.*

In 1931 Heckmann proved that, under the assumptions that matter is homogeneously distributed throughout the universe and is isotropic (having identical properties in every direction), the theory of general relativity could result in an open, or Euclidean, universe as readily as a closed one.

During the 1950s, in collaboration with Engelbert Schücking, Heckmann found that an expanding universe might have an absolute rotation, which would have extraordinary influence upon the choice of an evolutionary cosmological model. The mathematical analysis of these models is so complex, however, that definite results have not yet been found.

From 1967 to 1970, Heckmann was president of the International Astronomical Union. Among his many honours, he received the Watson Medal of the U.S. National Academy of Sciences (1961) and the Bruce Medal of the Astronomical Society of the Pacific (1964).

EJNAR HERTZSPRUNG
(b. Oct. 8, 1873, Frederiksberg, near Copenhagen, Den.—d. Oct. 21, 1967, Roskilde, Den.)

Danish astronomer Ejnar Hertzsprung classified types of stars by relating their colour to their absolute brightness—an accomplishment of fundamental importance to modern astronomy. The Hertzsprung–Russell diagram of stellar types was named (in part) for him. In 1913 he established the luminosity scale of Cepheid variable stars, a tool for measurement of intergalactic distances.

He had no formal education in astronomy but studied in technological colleges in Denmark and became a chemical engineer. Keenly interested in the chemistry of photography, he turned to astronomy in 1902, working in small Danish observatories, where he applied photography to the measurement of starlight. In two papers, published in 1905 and 1907, he showed that a relationship exists between the colours of the stars and their true brightness and that giant and dwarf stars must exist. The correlation of colour with true brightness became the basis of a widely used method of deducing the so-called spectroscopic parallaxes of stars (estimates of their distances from Earth). Because the spectrum of a star is a reliable index of its absolute magnitude, its distance can be inferred from the known relationship between the apparent and absolute magnitudes. This work so impressed Karl Schwarzschild, director of the observatory at Potsdam, that he found a place for Hertzsprung on the staff at Göttingen Observatory (1909) and later the same year as a senior astronomer at Potsdam. Hertzsprung was appointed assistant director of the university observatory at Leiden, the Netherlands, in 1919 and became director in 1935. He retired in 1945 and returned to Denmark.

VICTOR FRANCIS HESS
(b. June 24, 1883, Waldstein, Styria, Austria—d. Dec. 17, 1964, Mount Vernon, N.Y., U.S.)

Austrian-born physicist Victor Francis Hess was a joint recipient, with Carl D. Anderson of the United States, of the Nobel Prize for Physics in 1936 for his discovery of cosmic rays—high-energy radiation originating in outer space.

Educated at the University of Graz, Hess received his Ph.D. from the University of Vienna in 1906. His research dealt chiefly with radioactivity and atmospheric electricity. For many years scientists had been unable to explain the source of an ionizing background radiation in the atmosphere that penetrated electroscopes sent aloft in balloons. It was assumed that the radiation must have its source on Earth, but preliminary findings suggesting that the radiation increased when measured at higher points above Earth's surface cast doubt upon this hypothesis. In a series of balloon ascents in 1911–13, Hess found that the radiation increased rapidly with altitude, and suggested it had extraterrestrial origins. In 1925, Hess's theory was confirmed by Robert Andrews Millikan, who gave the radiation the name of cosmic rays. Cosmic-ray research soon emerged as an important branch of physics and led to the discovery of several new fundamental particles—including the positron, discovered by Anderson in

1932—as well as advances in astrophysics and cosmology.

Hess taught and conducted research at the universities of Vienna (1910–20), Graz (1920–31), and Innsbruck (1931–37). He left Austria in 1937 to escape the Nazis and settled in the United States, where he taught at Fordham University in New York City until 1956.

ANTONY HEWISH
(b. May 11, 1924, Fowey, Cornwall, Eng.)

British astrophysicist Antony Hewish won the Nobel Prize for Physics in 1974 for his discovery of pulsars (cosmic objects that emit extremely regular pulses of radio waves).

Hewish was educated at the University of Cambridge and in 1946 joined the radio astronomy group there led by Sir Martin Ryle. While directing a research project at the Mullard Radio Astronomy Observatory at Cambridge in 1967, Hewish recognized the significance of an observation made by a graduate assistant, Jocelyn Bell. He determined that the regularly patterned radio signals, or pulses, that Bell had detected were not caused by earthly interference or, as some speculated, by intelligent life forms trying to communicate with distant planets but rather were energy emissions from certain stars. For this work in identifying pulsars as a new class of stars, he was awarded jointly with Ryle the Nobel Prize for Physics in 1974, the first time the prize had been given for observational astronomy.

Hewish was professor of radio astronomy at the Cavendish Laboratory, Cambridge, from 1971 to 1989.

RUSSELL HULSE
(b. Nov. 28, 1950, New York, N.Y., U.S.)

In 1983 American physicist Russell Alan Hulse shared the Nobel Prize for Physics with his former teacher, the astrophysicist Joseph H. Taylor, Jr., for their joint discovery of the first binary pulsar.

Hulse studied at Cooper Union College in New York City (B.S., 1970) and earned a Ph.D. degree in physics (1975) from the University of Massachusetts at Amherst, where he was a graduate student under Taylor. Using the large radio telescope at Arecibo, Puerto Rico, they discovered dozens of pulsars, which are rapidly spinning neutron stars that emit rapid, regular bursts of radio waves. Irregularities in the radio emissions of the pulsar PSR 1913 + 16 led them to deduce that the pulsar had a companion neutron star with which it was locked in a tight orbit. This discovery was made by Taylor and Hulse in 1974.

PSR 1913 + 16 proved doubly important because it provided the first means of detecting gravity waves. The two stars' enormous interacting gravitational fields were affecting the regularity of the radio pulses, and by timing these and analyzing their variations, Taylor and Hulse found that the stars were rotating ever faster around each other in an increasingly tight orbit. This orbital decay is presumed to occur because the system is losing energy in the form of gravity waves. This finding, as reported by Taylor and Hulse in 1978, afforded the first experimental evidence for the existence of the gravitational waves predicted by Albert Einstein in his general theory of relativity.

In 1977 Hulse changed fields from astrophysics to plasma physics and joined the Plasma Physics Laboratory at Princeton University. There he conducted research associated with the Tokamak Fusion Test Reactor, an experimental nuclear-fusion facility.

SIR JAMES JEANS
(b. Sept. 11, 1877, London, Eng.—d. Sept. 16, 1946, Dorking, Surrey)

English physicist and mathematician Sir James Hopwood Jeans was the first to propose that matter is continuously created throughout the universe. He made other innovations in astronomical theory but is perhaps best known as a writer of popular books about astronomy.

Jeans taught at the University of Cambridge (1904–05, 1910–12) and at Princeton University (1905–09). In 1923 he became a research associate at Mt. Wilson Observatory, Pasadena, Calif., where he remained until 1944. In 1928, the year he was knighted, he proposed his continuous-creation theory.

His work included investigations of spiral nebulae, the source of stellar energy, binary and multiple star systems, and giant and dwarf stars. He also analyzed the breakup of rapidly spinning bodies under the stress of centrifugal force and concluded that the nebular hypothesis of Laplace, which stated that the planets and Sun condensed from a single gaseous cloud, was invalid. He proposed instead the catastrophic or tidal theory, first suggested by the American geologist Thomas C. Chamberlin. According to this theory, a star narrowly missed colliding with the Sun and, in its passing, drew away from the Sun stellar debris that condensed to form the planets.

Jeans applied mathematics to problems in thermodynamics and radiant heat

Sir James Hopwood Jeans. Popperfoto/ Getty Images

and wrote on other aspects of radiation. Among his many popular books, perhaps his best were *The Universe Around Us* (1929) and *Through Space and Time* (1934). His important technical works include *The Dynamical Theory of Gases* (1904), *Theoretical Mechanics* (1906), *The Mathematical Theory of Electricity and Magnetism* (1908), and *Introduction to the Kinetic Theory of Gases* (1940).

SIR HAROLD SPENCER JONES
(b. March 29, 1890, London, Eng.—d. Nov. 3, 1960, London)

Sir Harold Spencer Jones was the 10th astronomer royal of England (1933–55) and organized a program that led to a more accurate determination of the mean distance between Earth and the Sun.

After studies at the University of Cambridge, Jones became chief assistant at the Royal Observatory in Greenwich in 1913. He was his majesty's astronomer to the observatory at the Cape of Good Hope from 1923 to 1933, and in the latter year he returned to Greenwich as astronomer royal. Jones's scientific work largely concerned determining more accurately the fundamental constants of astronomy and in particular the solar parallax—the angle subtended by Earth's radius as viewed from the Sun. Using information from observations of the asteroid Eros during its close approach to Earth in 1931, he computed in 1941 the solar parallax and from that the mean distance to the Sun, approximately 149 million km (93 million miles).

When the encroachment of the smoke and lights of London spoiled observation at the Royal Greenwich Observatory, Jones took steps to have the observatory moved. After World War II a new site was procured at Herstmonceux Castle in Sussex. The new observatory was completed in 1958. In 1990 it was moved to the Institute of Astronomy of the University of Cambridge, where it remained until its closure in 1998.

In 1943 Jones was knighted and received the Gold Medal of the Royal Astronomical Society and the Royal Medal of the Royal Society of London. He was created a Knight of the British Empire in 1955. His works include *Worlds Without End* (1935), *Life on Other Worlds* (1940), and *A Picture of the Universe* (1947).

JACOBUS KAPTEYN
(b. Jan. 19, 1851, Barneveld, Neth.—d. June 18, 1922, Amsterdam)

Jacobus Cornelius Kapteyn was a Dutch astronomer who used photography and statistical methods in determining the motions and distribution of stars.

Kapteyn attended the State University of Utrecht and in 1875 became a member of the staff of Leiden Observatory. In 1877 he was elected to the chair of astronomy and theoretical mechanics at the State University of Groningen.

Kapteyn was not the first to use photographic methods in astronomy, but his breadth of scientific vision and capacity for carrying through large programs made him a key figure in the development of photographic astronomy. Using measurements of the positions of star images on photographic plates made at the Cape of Good Hope by Sir David Gill, Kapteyn compiled the *Cape Photographic Durchmusterung*, (1896–1900; *Cape Photographic Examination*), a catalog of roughly 454,000 southern stars. He devised a sampling system in which the thorough counting of stars in small, selected areas gave an indication of the structure of the Milky Way Galaxy. While recording the motions of many stars, he discovered the phenomenon of star streaming—i.e., that the peculiar motions (motions of individual stars relative to the mean motions of their neighbours) of stars are not random but are grouped around two opposite, preferred directions in space. Many later investigations of the distances and spatial arrangement of the stars of the Milky Way Galaxy stemmed from his work.

ROY P. KERR
(b. May 16, 1934, Kurow, N.Z.)

New Zealand mathematician Roy Patrick Kerr solved (1963) Einstein's field equations of general relativity to describe rotating black holes, providing a major contribution to the field of astrophysics.

Kerr received an M.S. (1954) from New Zealand University (now dissolved) and his Ph.D. (1960) from Cambridge University. He served on the faculty of the University of Texas at Austin (1963–72) and, returning to New Zealand, became a professor of mathematics at the University of Canterbury, Christchurch, in 1972.

Kerr worked in the tradition of Karl Schwarzschild, who in 1916—shortly after the appearance of Einstein's general relativity theory—formulated from Einstein's field equations a mathematical description of a static, nonrotating black hole and the effect of its gravity on the space and time surrounding it. Scientists surmise, however, that black holes probably are not static. Since they are theoretically formed from the collapse of massive dead stars, and since virtually all stars rotate, black holes probably rotate also. Kerr's mathematical formula provides the sole basis for describing the properties of black holes theorists expect to find in space. His solution is called the Kerr metric, or Kerr solution, and rotating black holes are also called Kerr black holes. In later work (written jointly with A. Schild), he introduced a new class of solutions, known as Kerr-Schild solutions, which have had a profound influence on finding exact solutions to Einstein's equations.

NIKOLAY ALEKSANDROVICH KOZYREV
(b. Sept. 2, 1908, St. Petersburg, Russia—d. Feb. 27, 1983)

Russian astronomer Nikolay Aleksandrovich Kozyrev claimed to have discovered volcano-like activity on the Moon. His sightings of apparent gaseous emissions from the lunar surface challenged the long-held theory that the Moon is a dead and inert celestial body.

In 1931 Kozyrev joined the staff of the Pulkovo Astronomical Observatory, near Leningrad (St. Petersburg), where he studied the planets and auroral phenomena. These studies gained him distinction, but he was imprisoned by the Stalin regime in 1937 and was not released until 1948.

In 1954 Kozyrev made a much-disputed report of an aurora, similar to Earth's Aurora Borealis, on the planet Venus. The existence of such an aurora would mean that Venus has a magnetic field much like Earth's, and the study of Venerian phenomena would therefore provide much new information on geomagnetic storms. (The U.S. space probe Mariner 10, passing within 3,600 miles [5,800 km] of Venus in February 1974, found no detectable magnetic field.)

While investigating the lunar crater Alphonsus in 1958, Kozyrev reported a reddish mist covering part of it for a short time. He interpreted this as a volcanic eruption and confirmed his observations the following year, but his conclusion that volcanic activity was the cause of the disturbance has been disputed by astronomers. Nonetheless, his observations led to a new focus in lunar research for a time.

In 1963 Kozyrev startled astronomers with his spectroscopic discovery of hydrogen in the thin atmosphere of Mercury. This gas should have escaped Mercury's light gravitational field long ago. From further studies Kozyrev concluded that the hydrogen comes from the Sun in the form of hydrogen nuclei.

GERARD KUIPER

(b. Dec. 7, 1905, Harenkarspel, Neth.—d.
Dec. 23, 1973, Mexico City, Mex.)

Dutch-American astronomer Gerard Peter Kuiper was known especially for his discoveries and theories concerning the solar system.

Kuiper graduated from the University of Leiden in 1927 and received his Ph.D. from that school in 1933. That same year he moved to the United States, where he became a naturalized citizen (1937). He joined the staff of Yerkes Observatory of the University of Chicago in 1936, twice serving as director (1947–49 and 1957–60) of both Yerkes and McDonald observatories. Kuiper founded the Lunar and Planetary Laboratory at the University of Arizona in 1960 and served as its director until his death.

After conducting research in stellar astronomy, Kuiper shifted his focus to planetary research in the 1940s. In 1944, he was able to confirm the presence of a methane atmosphere around Saturn's moon Titan. In 1947 he predicted (correctly) that carbon dioxide is a major component of the atmosphere of Mars, and he also correctly predicted that the rings of Saturn are composed of particles of ice. That same year he discovered the fifth moon of Uranus (Miranda), and in 1949 he discovered the second moon of Neptune (Nereid). In 1950 he obtained the first reliable measurement of the visual diameter of Pluto. In 1956 he proved that Mars's polar ice caps are composed of frozen water, not of carbon dioxide as

had been previously assumed. Kuiper's 1964 prediction of what the surface of the Moon would be like to walk on ("it would be like crunchy snow") was verified by the astronaut Neil Armstrong in 1969.

In 1949 Kuiper proposed an influential theory of the origin of the solar system, suggesting that the planets had formed by the condensation of a large cloud of gas around the Sun. He also suggested the possible existence of a disk-shaped belt of comets orbiting the Sun at a distance of 30 to 50 astronomical units. The existence of this belt of millions of comets was verified in the 1990s,

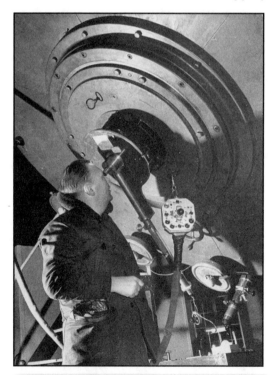

Gerard Kuiper, after whom the Kuiper belt is named, in 1948. Cornell Capa/ Time & Life Pictures/Getty Images

and it was named the Kuiper belt. Kuiper also initiated the use of high-flying jet aircraft to carry telescopes for infrared observations above the obscuring layers of the atmosphere. The Kuiper Airborne Observatory (1974) was named in his honour, as were craters on the Moon, Mercury, and Mars.

BERTIL LINDBLAD

(b. Nov. 26, 1895, Örebro, Swed.—d. June 26, 1965, Stockholm)

Bertil Lindblad was a Swedish astronomer who contributed greatly to the theory of galactic structure and motion and to the methods of determining the absolute magnitude (true brightness, disregarding distance) of distant stars.

After serving as an assistant at the observatory in Uppsala, Swed., Lindblad joined the Stockholm Observatory and in 1927 was appointed director, a post he held until 1965. He planned the observatory's relocation in 1931 to nearby Saltsjöbaden and modernized its facilities.

By the early 1920s the Dutch astronomer Jacobus C. Kapteyn and others had made statistical studies establishing that generally stars appear to move in one of two directions in space. In 1926 Lindblad successfully explained this phenomenon (called star streaming) as an effect of rotation of the Milky Way and thus became the first to offer substantial evidence that the Galaxy rotates. This theory was definitely proved soon after by Jan Oort of the Netherlands.

Lindblad also pioneered in studies to determine the absolute magnitude of distant stars from the stellar spectra (the characteristic individual wavelengths of light). Establishing his own spectral classification system, he used it to determine absolute magnitudes and, thence, the distance and transverse velocities of many distant stars.

Lindblad was president of the International Astronomical Union (1948–52).

MALCOLM LONGAIR

(b. May 18, 1941, Dundee, Scot.)

Scots astronomer Malcolm Sim Longair, noted for his scholarship and teaching, in 1980 was named astronomer royal for Scotland.

Longair was educated at the University of St. Andrews, Dundee, and at the University of Cambridge (M.A., Ph.D., 1967). In 1968–69 he went as an exchange fellow to the Soviet Union, where he worked in Moscow at the P. N. Lebedev Physical Institute of the Academy of Sciences of the U.S.S.R. He was a resident fellow of Cambridge from 1967 to 1971 and an official fellow from 1971 to 1980 and held positions of both demonstrator (1970–75) and lecturer (1975–80). He was a visiting professor for two years in the United States. His appointment to the position of astronomer royal brought with it the titles of regius professor of astronomy at the University of Edinburgh and director of the Royal Observatory on Edinburgh's Blackford Hill.

With others he edited a number of books, including *The Large Scale Structure of the Universe* (1978), *The Scientific Uses of the Space Telescope* (1980), and *Astrophysical Cosmology* (1982). He wrote *High Energy Astrophysics: An Informal Introduction* (1980), *Theoretical Concepts in Physics* (1984), and *Alice and the Space Telescope* (1986). He received the Britannica Award in 1986.

EDWARD MILNE
(b. Feb. 14, 1896, Hull, Yorkshire, Eng.—d. Sept. 21, 1950, Dublin, Ire.)

Edward Arthur Milne was an English astrophysicist and cosmologist best known for his development of kinematic relativity.

Milne was educated at the University of Cambridge and served as assistant director of the Solar Physics Observatory at Cambridge from 1920 to 1924. He then became a professor of applied mathematics at the University of Manchester, and from 1929 until his death he was a professor of mathematics at the University of Oxford.

Collaborating with Sir Ralph H. Fowler, Milne became known in the 1920s for their formulation of a reliable surface-temperature scale for stars of any spectral type. His theoretical studies of the balance between gravitational forces and radiation pressure in stellar atmospheres led him to study the escape velocities of molecules from stars, and he demonstrated that the Sun can eject atoms at speeds up to 1,600 km per second (1,000 miles per second). In 1929 he turned his attention to the structure and internal conditions of stars. His work eventually led to the theory explaining the highly dense white dwarf stars.

About 1932 Milne shifted his focus to cosmology, and he developed the theory of kinematic relativity. Like cosmologies based on Einstein's general theory of relativity, kinematic relativity featured an expanding universe, but it was nonrelativistic and used Euclidean space. Milne's theory met with opposition from his contemporaries on both scientific and philosophical grounds, but his work helped to sharpen mainstream ideas about space-time and also inspired the steady-state theorists. Milne's works include *Thermodynamics of the Stars* (1930), *The White Dwarf Stars* (1932), *Relativity, Gravitation and World-Structure* (1935), and *Kinematic Relativity* (1948).

MARCEL MINNAERT
(b. Feb. 12, 1893, Bruges, Belg.—d. Oct. 26, 1970, Utrecht, Neth.)

Flemish astronomer and solar physicist Marcel Gilles Jozef Minnaert pioneered in solar spectrophotometry and showed how such a technique could reveal much about the structure of the Sun's outer layers.

Minnaert was first a botanist, but his desire to understand more fully the effect of light on plants led him to study physics at the University of Leiden, in the Netherlands. Exiled from Belgium for his support of the nationalist Flemish movement before and during World War I, he became a staff member of the solar observatory at Utrecht in 1921.

After the invention of the microphotometer about 1920, Minnaert undertook the measurement of the intensities of dark lines in the solar spectrum. With the help of two pupils, he prepared the monumental Utrecht *Photometric Atlas of the Solar Spectrum* (1940), still a standard reference, which includes measurements of the absorption lines from 3,332 angstroms to 8,771 angstroms. Other works on the Sun's spectrum followed, but perhaps his most noted work is *Die Natuurkunde van't Vrije Veld*, 3 vol. (1937–42; Eng. trans. of vol. 1, *Light and Color in the Open Air*, 1954), on optical phenomena associated with meteorology.

From 1937 until his retirement in 1963 Minnaert was director of the Sonnenborgh Observatory at Utrecht, but during most of World War II he was interned in a Nazi concentration camp.

WILLIAM W. MORGAN

(b. Jan. 3, 1906, Bethesda, Tenn., U.S.—d. June 21, 1994, Williams Bay, Wis.)

In 1951 American astronomer William Wilson Morgan provided the first evidence that the Milky Way Galaxy has spiral arms.

Morgan studied at the University of Chicago (Ph.D., 1931) and then became an instructor at the Yerkes Observatory of the University of Chicago. He taught at that university from 1947 until his retirement in 1974, and he was director of the Yerkes and McDonald Observatories from 1960 to 1963. During his career he received many awards and honours.

Morgan was an astronomical morphologist who devoted his career to studying and classifying stars and galaxies. His first significant contribution was a correlation of the spectra of stars with their distances from Earth, published as the *Atlas of Stellar Spectra* (1943). After discovering the spiral structure of the Milky Way Galaxy, he focused on problems of star brightness, devising a system of classifying star magnitude and colour, discovering "flash" variable stars (stars that have quickly changing luminosity), and establishing the UBV (ultraviolet-blue-visual) magnitudes system for photometry. In 1956 Morgan began to study and classify galaxies, grouping them by stellar qualities, stellar population, and form.

JAN OORT

(b. April 28, 1900, Franeker, Neth.—d. Nov. 5, 1992, Leiden)

Dutch astronomer Jan Hendrik Oort was one of the most important figures in 20th-century efforts to understand the nature of the Milky Way Galaxy.

After studies at the University of Groningen, Oort was appointed astronomer to the Leiden Observatory in 1924 and became director in 1945, a position he held until 1970. In 1925 Bertil Lindblad of Sweden had advanced the theory that the Milky Way rotates in its own plane around the centre of the galaxy. Oort was able to confirm this theory in 1927 through his own direct observations of star velocities in the galaxy, and he modified the theory substantially into the form used thereafter.

Oort's subsequent work, as well as that of the school of astronomy he developed in the Netherlands, was directed toward strengthening and testing the Lindblad-Oort theory. Soon after having become a professor at the University of Leiden (1935), he determined by radio astronomy that the Sun is 30,000 light-years from the centre of the galaxy and takes 225 million years to complete an orbit around it. The discovery in 1951 of the 21-centimetre radio waves generated by hydrogen in interstellar space provided him with a new method for mapping the spiral structure of the galaxy.

In 1950 Oort proposed that comets originate from a vast cloud of small bodies that orbit the Sun at a distance of about one light-year, and the approach of other stars toward this cloud alters some comets' orbits so that they pass close to the Sun. The existence of this region, which was named the Oort Cloud, eventually came to be accepted by most astronomers.

From 1958 to 1961 Oort was president of the International Astronomical Union, of which he had been general secretary from 1935 to 1948.

ERNEST ÖPIK

(b. Oct. 23, 1893, Port-Kunda, Estonia, Russian Empire—d. Sept. 10, 1985, Bangor, County Down, N.Ire.)

Ernest Julius Öpik was an Estonian astronomer best known for his studies of meteors and meteorites, and whose life work was devoted to understanding the structure and evolution of the cosmos.

Öpik graduated with a gold medal from Tallinn University in Estonia in 1911, and in 1916 he received his degree in astronomy from Moscow University. In 1919 he joined the staff of the Tashkent Observatory (now in Uzbekistan) and from 1921 to 1944 worked at the Astronomical Observatory in Tartu, Estonia. The research he performed during the early 1920s elucidated the theory of the entry of high-speed bodies into the atmosphere and was fundamental to the understanding of ablation, the peeling back of meteor surfaces during vaporization. In 1922 he proposed the double-count method of tallying meteors, in which two observers work simultaneously. His work on meteors enabled him to correctly predict the frequencies of craters on Mars many years before these could be ascertained. He also contributed to cometary studies and proposed that a reservoir of comets orbit the Sun, providing the source of those few comets that assume orbits sufficiently eccentric to bring them so close to the Sun that they are visible.

In 1922 Öpik proved that the source of stellar energy was nuclear and heavily dependent upon temperature. At this time he also made an estimate of the distance of the Andromeda Nebula that was still valid a half century later. In the 1930s and '50s he made estimates of the age of the universe from meteorites and from galactic and extragalactic statistics. After World War II Öpik left his Baltic home land and joined the staff of the Armagh Observatory in Northern Ireland. From 1956 he held a position on the faculty of the University of Maryland, College Park, dividing his time equally between Armagh and Maryland.

SIR ROGER PENROSE
(b. Aug. 8, 1931, Colchester, Essex, Eng.)

In the 1960s British mathematician and relativist Sir Roger Penrose calculated many of the basic features of black holes.

After obtaining a Ph.D. in algebraic geometry from the University of Cambridge in 1957, Penrose held temporary posts at a number of universities in both England and America. From 1964 to 1973 he served as reader and eventually professor of applied mathematics at Birkbeck College, London. From 1973 he held the Rouse-Ball chair of mathematics at the University of Oxford. He was knighted for his services to science in 1994.

In 1969, with Stephen Hawking, Penrose proved that all matter within a black hole collapses to a singularity, a geometric point in space where mass is compressed to infinite density and zero volume. Penrose also developed a method of mapping the regions of space-time surrounding a black hole. (Space-time is a four-dimensional continuum comprising three dimensions of space and one of time.) Such a map, which is called a Penrose diagram, allows one to visualize the effects of gravitation upon an entity approaching a black hole.

SIR MARTIN RYLE
(b. Sept. 27, 1918, Brighton, Sussex, Eng.—d. Oct. 14, 1984, Cambridge, Cambridgeshire)

British radio astronomer Sir Martin Ryle developed revolutionary radio telescope systems and used them for accurate location of weak radio sources. With improved equipment, he observed the most distant known galaxies of the universe. Ryle and Antony Hewish shared the Nobel Prize for Physics in 1974, the first Nobel Prize awarded in recognition of astronomical research.

Ryle was the nephew of the philosopher Gilbert Ryle. After earning a degree in physics at the University of Oxford in 1939, he worked with the Telecommunications Research Establishment on the design of radar equipment during World War II. After the war he received a fellowship at the Cavendish Laboratory of the University of Cambridge, where he became an early investigator of extraterrestrial radio sources and developed advanced radio telescopes using the principles of radar. While serving as university lecturer in physics at Cambridge from 1948 to 1959, he became director of the Mullard Radio Astronomy Observatory (1957), and he became professor of radio astronomy in 1959. He was elected a fellow of the Royal Society in 1952, was knighted in 1966, and succeeded Sir Richard Woolley as astronomer royal (1972–82).

Ryle's early work centred on studies of radio waves from the Sun, sunspots, and a few nearby stars. He guided the Cambridge radio astronomy group in the production of radio source catalogues. The *Third Cambridge Catalogue* (1959) helped lead to the discovery of the first quasistellar object (quasar).

To map such distant radio sources as quasars, Ryle developed a technique called aperture synthesis. By using two radio telescopes and changing the distance between them, he obtained data that, upon computer analysis, provided tremendously increased resolving power. In the mid-1960s Ryle put into operation two telescopes on rails that at the maximum distance of 1.6 km (1 mile) provided results comparable to a single telescope 1.6 km in diameter. This telescope system was used to locate the first pulsar, which had been discovered in 1967 by Hewish and Jocelyn Bell of the Cambridge group.

CARL SAGAN

(b. Nov. 9, 1934, Brooklyn, N.Y., U.S.—d. Dec. 20, 1996, Seattle, Wash.)

Carl Edward Sagan was an American astronomer and science writer.

Carl Sagan, in 1974. Santi Visalli Inc./Hulton Archive/Getty Images

After obtaining his Ph.D. from the University of Chicago in 1960, Sagan taught at the University of California, Berkeley, and at Harvard University and was an astrophysicist at the Smithsonian Astrophysical Observatory (1962–68). There he divided his time between planetary astronomy and work on the Search for Extraterrestrial Intelligence (SETI) project. In 1968 he became director of the Laboratory of Planetary Studies at Cornell University, and he also worked on several U.S. unmanned space missions to Venus and Mars.

With the publication of *The Cosmic Connection: An Extraterrestrial Perspective* (1973), Sagan gained prominence as a popular science writer and commentator who was notable for his clear writing and enthusiasm for science. His *The Dragons of Eden: Speculations on the Evolution of Human Intelligence* (1977) won the Pulitzer Prize. He was a coproducer, as well as narrator, of the television series "Cosmos" (1980). In the 1980s he participated in research on the environmental effects of nuclear war and helped popularize the term "nuclear winter."

Sagan's writings include *Atmospheres of Mars and Venus* (1961), *Planetary Exploration* (1970), *Broca's Brain: Reflections on the Romance of Science* (1979), the novel *Contact* (1985), *Nuclear Winter* (1985), and *The Demon-Haunted World: Science as a Candle in the Dark* (1996).

MEGHNAD N. SAHA
(b. Oct. 6, 1893, Seoratali, near Dacca, India—d. Feb. 16, 1956, New Delhi)

Indian astrophysicist Meghnad N. Saha was noted for his development in 1920 of the thermal ionization equation, which, in the form perfected by the British astrophysicist Edward A. Milne, has remained fundamental in all work on stellar atmospheres. This equation has been widely applied to the interpretation of stellar spectra, which are characteristic of the chemical composition of the light source. The Saha equation links the composition and appearance of the spectrum with the temperature of the light source and can thus be used to determine either the temperature of the star or the relative abundance of the chemical elements investigated.

Saha became professor of physics at the University of Allāhābād in 1923 and was elected a fellow of the Royal Society in 1927. He went to the University of Calcutta in 1938, where he was instrumental in the creation of the Calcutta Institute of Nuclear Physics, of which he became honorary director.

In his later years Saha increasingly turned his attention to the social relation of science and founded the outspoken journal *Science and Culture* in 1935. In 1951 he was elected to the Indian Parliament as an independent. He co-authored *A Treatise on Heat* (4th ed., 1958) and *A Treatise on Modern Physics* (1934). One of his most important papers is "Ionization in the Solar Chromosphere," *Phil. Mag.* (vol. 40, 1920).

ALLAN SANDAGE
(b. June 18, 1926, Iowa City, Iowa, U.S.)

U.S. astronomer Allan Rex Sandage discovered the first quasi-stellar radio source (quasar), a starlike object that is a strong emitter of radio waves. He made the discovery in collaboration with the U.S. radio astronomer Thomas Matthews.

Sandage became a member of the staff of the Hale Observatories (now the Mount Wilson and Palomar Observatories), in California, in 1952 and carried out most of his investigations there. Pursuing the theoretical work of several astronomers on the evolution of stars, Sandage, with Harold L. Johnson, demonstrated in the early 1950s that the observed characteristics of the light and colour of the brightest stars in various globular clusters indicate that the clusters can be arranged in order according to their age. This information provided insight into stellar evolution and galactic structure.

Later, Sandage became a leader in the study of quasi-stellar radio sources, comparing accurate positions of radio sources with photographic sky maps and then using a large optical telescope to find a visual starlike source at the point where the strong radio waves are being emitted. Sandage and Matthews identified the first of many such objects in 1961. Sandage later discovered that some of the remote, starlike objects with similar characteristics are not radio sources. He also found that the light from a number of the sources varies rapidly and irregularly in intensity.

FRANK SCHLESINGER

(b. May 11, 1871, New York, N.Y., U.S.—d. July 10, 1943, Lyme, Conn.)

American astronomer Frank Schlesinger pioneered in the use of photography to map stellar positions and to measure stellar parallaxes, from which the most direct determinations of distance can be made.

From 1899 to 1903 Schlesinger was in charge of the International Latitude Observatory at Ukiah, Calif. He then was appointed astronomer at the Yerkes Observatory, Williams Bay, Wis., where he began developing a photographic method of determining parallaxes. With great care he worked to eliminate or compensate for all significant sources of error, with such success that his photographic parallax measurement techniques remain largely unchanged to the present day.

While serving as director (1905–20) of the Allegheny Observatory, Pittsburgh, Schlesinger obtained a long-focus refracting telescope especially designed for parallax determinations. He published the parallaxes of 7,534 stars in his *General Catalogue of Parallaxes* (2nd ed., 1935).

In addition to his parallax work at Allegheny, Schlesinger also pioneered in the use of wide-angle cameras for determining photographically stellar positions and proper motions (the apparent rates of change of position across an observer's line of sight), formerly measured by laborious visual methods. Fifteen volumes of the *Yale Zone Catalogues*, which were prepared under his direction, give results for about 150,000 stars.

Schlesinger became director (1920–41) of the Yale University Observatory and continued his parallax work. He also had a prominent role in the establishment of the International Astronomical Union (1919) and served as that organization's vice president (1925–32) and president (1932–35).

MAARTEN SCHMIDT

(b. Dec. 28, 1929, Groningen, Neth.)

Maarten Schmidt was a Dutch-born American astronomer whose identification of the wavelengths of the radiation emitted by quasars (quasi-stellar objects) led to the theory that they may be among the most distant, as well as the oldest, objects ever observed.

Schmidt was educated at the universities of Groningen and Leiden, receiving his Ph.D. from Leiden in 1956, and was scientific officer of the Leiden Observatory until 1959. He joined the staff of the Mount Wilson and Palomar Mountain Observatories (now Hale Observatories) in California in 1959, at the same time joining the faculty of astronomy at the California Institute of Technology. From 1978 to 1980 Schmidt was the director of the Hale Observatories. His early work included the creation of a mathematical model of the Milky Way Galaxy based on all the available data concerning the distribution of the stars and interstellar gas and dust. Schmidt's model led to greater understanding of the structure of the galaxy and its dynamical properties.

An even more important achievement, however, was Schmidt's study of an unusual extragalactic phenomenon, quasars. He and other astronomers in the 1960s came to believe were exceptionally distant from Earth and were receding from Earth with a velocity greater than that of any other known celestial object. In their searches through space, Schmidt and his colleagues found quasars receding so quickly and existing so far away that their light may have been traveling up to 13 billion years in order to reach Earth. Some astronomers, including Schmidt, theorized that these very distant and very old quasars are actually galaxies in the early stages of formation. Thus Schmidt's discovery and interpretation of quasars challenged many previously accepted theories of the origin and age of the universe.

KARL SCHWARZSCHILD
(b. Oct. 9, 1873, Frankfurt am Main, Ger.—d. May 11, 1916, Potsdam)

German astronomer Karl Schwarzschild's contributions, both practical and theoretical, were of primary importance in the development of 20th-century astronomy.

Schwarzschild's exceptional ability in science became evident at the age of 16, when his paper on the theory of celestial orbits was published. In 1901 he became professor and director of the observatory at the University of Göttingen, and eight years later he was appointed director of the Astrophysical Observatory at Potsdam.

While at Göttingen, Schwarzschild introduced precise methods in photographic photometry. The results of his studies clearly demonstrated the relationship between the spectral type and colour of a star. He pioneered in the use of a coarse grating (for example, a glass plate with closely spaced parallel lines etched into it) in the course of measurement of the separation of double stars. The technique has found widespread use in determining stellar magnitude and colour. He also developed certain basic methods for the analysis of solar spectra obtained during eclipses.

Schwarzschild enunciated the principle of radiative equilibrium and was the first to recognize clearly the role of radiative processes in the transport of heat in stellar atmospheres. His hypothesis of stellar motion is one of the most important results to come out of his fundamental work in modern statistical methods in astronomy. He also made theoretical studies of the pressure exerted on small, solid particles by radiation.

Schwarzschild made fundamental contributions to theoretical physics and to relativity. He was one of the great pioneers in developing the theory of atomic spectra proposed by Niels Bohr. Independently of Arnold Sommerfeld, Schwarzschild developed the general rules of quantization, gave the complete theory of the Stark effect (the effect of an electric field on light), and initiated the quantum theory of molecular spectra.

Schwarzschild gave the first exact solution of Albert Einstein's general gravitational equations, which led to a description of the geometry of space in the neighbourhood of a mass point. He also laid the foundation of the theory of black holes by using the general equations to demonstrate that bodies of sufficient mass would have an escape velocity exceeding the speed of light and, therefore, would not be directly observable.

While serving in the imperial German army during World War I, Schwarzschild contracted a fatal illness.

HARLOW SHAPLEY

(b. Nov. 2, 1885, Nashville, Mo., U.S.—d. Oct. 20, 1972, Boulder, Colo.)

American astronomer Harlow Shapley deduced that the Sun lies near the central plane of the Galaxy some 30,000 light-years away from the centre.

In 1911 Shapley, working with results given by Henry N. Russell, began finding the dimensions of stars in a number of binary systems from measurements of their light variation when they eclipse one another. These methods remained the standard procedure for more than 30 years. Shapley also showed that Cepheid variables cannot be star pairs that eclipse each other. He was the first to propose that they are pulsating stars.

Harlow Shapley, during a 1959 appearance on the television discussion show At Random. *Lee Balterman/Time & Life Pictures/Getty Images*

Shapley joined the staff of the Mount Wilson Observatory, Pasadena, Calif., in 1914. Employing the 1.5-metre (60-inch) reflecting telescope at Mount Wilson, he made a study of the distribution of the globular clusters in the Galaxy. These clusters are immense, densely packed groups of stars, some containing as many as 1,000,000 members. He found that of the 100 clusters known at the time, one-third lay within the boundary of the constellation Sagittarius. Utilizing the newly developed concept that variable stars accurately reveal their distance by their period of variation and apparent brightness, he found that the clusters were distributed roughly in a sphere whose centre lay in Sagittarius. Since the clusters assumed a spherical arrangement, it was logical to conclude that they would cluster around the centre of the Galaxy. From this conclusion and his other distance data Shapley deduced that the Sun lies at a distance of 50,000 light-years from the centre of the Galaxy. The number was later corrected to 30,000 light-years. Before Shapley, the Sun was believed to lie near the centre of the Galaxy. His work, which led to the first realistic estimate for the actual size of the Galaxy, was a milestone in galactic astronomy.

In addition to his studies of the Galaxy, Shapley studied the neighbouring galaxies, especially the Magellanic Clouds, and found that galaxies tend to occur in clusters, which he called metagalaxies. Shapley became professor of astronomy at Harvard University, later

director of Harvard College Observatory (1921–52), and was made director emeritus and Paine Professor of Astronomy at Harvard in 1952. His works include *Star Clusters* (1930), *Flights from Chaos* (1930), *Galaxies* (1943), *The Inner Metagalaxy* (1957), and *Of Stars and Men . . .* (1958).

WILLEM DE SITTER
(b. May 6, 1872, Sneek, Neth.—d. Nov. 20, 1934, Leiden)

Willem de Sitter was a Dutch mathematician, astronomer, and cosmologist who developed theoretical models of the universe based on Albert Einstein's general theory of relativity.

De Sitter studied mathematics at the State University of Groningen and then joined the astronomical laboratory there, where under J. C. Kapteyn's guidance he developed a liking for astronomy. He spent the years 1897–99 at the Cape Observatory in South Africa and devoted himself to astronomy thereafter. In 1908 de Sitter became professor of astronomy at the University of Leiden, and in 1919 he became director of the Leiden Observatory.

In his early career de Sitter analyzed the motions of Jupiter's four great Galilean satellites in order to determine their masses. His experience in celestial mechanics proved useful in 1916–17, when he published a series of papers in London in which he described the astronomical consequences of Einstein's general theory of relativity. His papers aroused

British interest in the theory and led directly to Arthur Eddington's 1919 expedition to observe a solar eclipse in order to measure the gravitational deflection of light rays passing near the Sun.

De Sitter's concept of the universe differed in some respects from that of Einstein. Einstein's relativistic conception of curved space led him to envision the universe as static and unchanging in size, but de Sitter maintained that relativity actually implied that the universe was constantly expanding. This view was later supported by Edwin Hubble's observations of distant galaxies and was eventually adopted by Einstein himself. De Sitter's calculations of the size of the universe and the number of galaxies contained in it subsequently proved to be too small.

VESTO SLIPHER
(b. Nov. 11, 1875, near Mulberry, Ind., U.S.—d. Nov. 8, 1969, Flagstaff, Ariz.)

Vesto Melvin Slipher was an American astronomer whose systematic observations (1912–25) of the extraordinary radial velocities of spiral galaxies provided the first evidence supporting the expanding-universe theory.

Born on an Indiana farm, Slipher studied at Indiana University (B.A., 1901; M.A., 1903; Ph.D., 1909). In 1901 he joined the staff of the Lowell Observatory at Flagstaff (though he returned to Indiana at times for graduate study), and he became its acting director in 1916 and director in 1926. There he organized and

guided the search that resulted in the discovery of Pluto in 1930. Slipher's extensive investigations led to the determination of the rotational periods of several planets. His discovery of dark absorption bands in the spectra of Jupiter, Saturn, and Neptune led to the identification of some of the chemical constituents of their atmospheres. He demonstrated that many diffuse nebulae (clouds of dust and gas) shine by the reflected light of nearby stars and discovered the bright radiations of the night sky and their changes in intensity. He also proved that sodium and calcium are scattered throughout interstellar space.

BENGT STRÖMGREN
(b. Jan. 21, 1908, Göteborg, Swed.—d. July 4, 1987, Copenhagen, Den.)

Danish astrophysicist Bengt Georg Daniel Strömgren pioneered the present-day knowledge of the gas clouds in space.

Son of the noted Swedish-born Danish astronomer Svante Elis Strömgren, he early developed an interest in astronomy. He collaborated with his father on several works of astronomy and in 1940 succeeded him as director of the Royal Copenhagen Observatory.

Strömgren served as an assistant and then associate professor at the University of Chicago from 1936 to 1938 and held a variety of positions in the United States during the late 1940s. In 1951 he was appointed director of Yerkes Observatory, Williams Bay, Wis., and McDonald Observatory, Fort Davis, Texas.

It had long been supposed that luminous gas clouds in space owe their luminosity to the radiation from stars within them. Strömgren found that many of the clouds consist of ionized hydrogen surrounded by un-ionized hydrogen and that the ionized hydrogen is confined to well-defined regions.

A versatile research scientist, Strömgren worked on a wide range of astronomical problems. His determinations of the abundance of hydrogen, helium, and other elements in space differ little from presently accepted values. He did research on the internal constitution of the stars and contributed to the understanding of the solar atmosphere. After 1951 he carried out an extensive program of measuring stellar spectra using photoelectric techniques. Before his efforts, the classification of stellar spectra was primarily a process of estimation.

In 1957 Strömgren joined the Institute for Advanced Study at Princeton, N.J., and 10 years later, he returned to the University of Copenhagen as professor of astrophysics.

OTTO STRUVE

(b. Aug. 12, 1897, Kharkov, Ukraine, Russian Empire [now Kharkiv, Ukraine]—d. April 6, 1963, Berkeley, Calif., U.S.)

Russian-American astronomer Otto Struve was known for his contributions to stellar spectroscopy, notably the discovery of the widespread distribution of hydrogen and other elements in space.

Struve was the last member of a dynasty of astronomers and a great-grandson of the noted astronomer Friedrich Georg Wilhelm von Struve. His studies at the University of Kharkov were interrupted for service in the Imperial Russian Army (1916–18) and, after the Russian Revolution, in the White Russian Army (1919–20). He endured months of privation in Turkey after the collapse of the White Army, but in 1921, he was able to immigrate to the United States. There, as a staff member at Yerkes Observatory, Williams Bay, Wis., he began the investigations in stellar spectroscopy (the study of the properties of stars through the analysis of the wavelengths of their light), which yielded his most notable contributions to stellar astrophysics. From his studies of Delta Orionis and other stars, he found that the spectrum of light from distant hot stars sometimes contains a dark (absorption) line corresponding to calcium, although this could not be caused by calcium present in the star itself. In 1925, he attributed this stationary calcium line to vast clouds of calcium found primarily in the galactic plane.

Struve became director of Yerkes Observatory in 1932, and in the same year he organized McDonald Observatory, Fort Davis, Texas, of which he later became director. In 1938, after a two-year search, he established the presence of hydrogen in interstellar space. That discovery later proved of prime importance in the development of radio astronomy. He demonstrated that many stars rotate rapidly on their axes, some with rotation periods of a day or less. His studies of many stars with variable luminosity and of the spectra of double, multiple, and peculiar stars were extensive.

In 1947 Struve retired as director of Yerkes and McDonald observatories and became chairman of the astronomy department of the University of Chicago. In 1950 he accepted the directorship of the Leuschner Observatory at the University of California, Berkeley, and from 1959 to 1962 he was director of the National Radio Astronomy Observatory, Green Bank, W. Va. As vice president of the International Astronomical Union from 1948 to 1952 and president from 1952 to 1955, he was instrumental in preventing Cold War tension from destroying that organization. A prolific writer, he published about 700 papers. His major books include *Stellar Evolution* (1950) and *The Universe* (1962).

POL SWINGS
(b. Sept. 24, 1906, Ransart, Belg.—d. Oct. 28, 1983)

Belgian astrophysicist Polidore F. F. Swings was noted for his spectroscopic studies of the composition and structure of stars and comets.

In 1932 Swings was appointed professor of spectroscopy and astrophysics at his alma mater, the University of Liège, Belgium. He taught there until 1976. He was a visiting professor at the University of Chicago (1939–43, 1946–52) and took part in war research (1943–45). He also

served as vice president (1952–58) and president (1964–67) of the International Astronomical Union.

During the early 1930s Swings studied the diatomic molecules of various metals. From his findings on the spectra of ionized neon, argon, and other elements, he furnished valuable insight into the significance of theretofore inexplicable lines in the spectra of some stars. With the Swedish physicist Bengt Edlén, Swings conducted an extensive study (1936–39) of the doubly ionized iron atom, which revealed the presence of iron in many stellar sources. While studying the spectra of comets, he discovered numerous radicals, including hydroxyl and cyanide. He showed that certain strong spectral bands (now called Swings bands) of comets are caused by tricarbon radicals. He also explained certain anomalies in cyanide spectra of the Sun by the Swings effect, the effect of the Fraunhofer lines and the Sun's radial velocity.

Swings's published works include *Considerations Regarding Cometary and Interstellar Molecules* (1942) and the *Atlas of Representative Cometary Spectra*, with Leo Haser (1956).

JOSEPH H. TAYLOR, JR.
(b. March 24, 1941, Philadelphia, Pa., U.S.)

American radio astronomer and physicist Joseph Hooton Taylor, Jr., with Russell A. Hulse, was the corecipient of the 1993 Nobel Prize for Physics for their joint discovery of the first binary pulsar.

Taylor studied at Haverford College, Pa. (B.A., 1963), and earned a Ph.D. in astronomy at Harvard University in 1968. He taught at the University of Massachusetts, Amherst, from 1969 to 1981 and then joined the faculty at Princeton University, where he became the James S. McDonnell professor of physics in 1986.

Taylor and Hulse conducted their prizewinning research on pulsars while Taylor was a professor at Amherst and Hulse was his graduate student. In 1974, using the large radio telescope at Arecibo, Puerto Rico, they discovered a pulsar (a rapidly spinning neutron star) emitting radio pulses at intervals that varied in a regular pattern, decreasing and increasing over an eight-hour period. They concluded from these signals that the pulsar must be alternately moving toward and away from Earth—i.e., that it must be orbiting around a companion star, which the two men deduced was also a neutron star.

Their discovery of the first binary pulsar, PSR 1913 + 16, provided an unprecedented test of Albert Einstein's theory of gravitation, which, according to the general theory of relativity, predicts that objects accelerated in a strong gravitational field will emit radiation in the form of gravitational waves. With its enormous interacting gravitational fields, the binary pulsar should emit such waves, and the resulting energy drain should reduce the orbital distance between the two stars. This could in turn be measured by a slight, gradual reduction in the timing of the pulsar's distinctive radio emissions.

Taylor and Hulse timed PSR 1913 + 16's pulses over the next few years and showed that the two stars are indeed rotating ever faster around each other in an increasingly tight orbit, with an annual decrease of about 75 millionths of a second in their eight-hour orbital period. The rate at which the two stars are spiraling closer together was found to agree with the prediction of the theory of general relativity to an accuracy of better than 0.5 percent. This finding, reported in 1978, provided the first experimental evidence for the existence of gravitational waves and gave powerful support to Einstein's theory of gravity. In the following years, Taylor continued making careful measurements of the orbital period of PSR 1913 + 16, and his research group went on to discover several other binary pulsars.

CLYDE W. TOMBAUGH

(b. Feb. 4, 1906, Streator, Ill., U.S.—d. Jan. 17, 1997, Las Cruces, N.M.)

American astronomer Clyde William Tombaugh discovered Pluto in 1930 after a systematic search for a ninth planet instigated by the predictions of other astronomers. He also discovered several clusters of stars and galaxies, studied the apparent distribution of extragalactic nebulae, and made observations of the surfaces of Mars, Venus, Jupiter, Saturn, and the Moon.

Tombaugh initially had no formal training in astronomy, only a keen interest that had been sharpened by his first glimpse of the heavens through his uncle's telescope. After finishing high school, Tombaugh built his own telescope according to specifications published in a 1925 issue of *Popular Astronomy*. Using this instrument, he made observations of Jupiter and Mars and sent sketches of these planets to Lowell Observatory in Flagstaff, Ariz., hoping to receive advice about his work. Instead, he received a job offer. Tombaugh's assignment was to locate the ninth planet, a search instigated in 1905 by astronomer Percival Lowell. To carry out this task, Tombaugh used a 33-cm (13-inch) telescope to photograph the sky and an instrument called a blink comparator to examine the photographic plates for signs of moving celestial bodies. On Feb. 18, 1930, Tombaugh pinpointed Pluto, and on March 13 Lowell Observatory announced the discovery of the new planet. (In 2006 Pluto was reclassified as a dwarf planet.)

After his discovery, Tombaugh attended the University of Kansas on a scholarship, returning each summer to the observatory until completing (1939) his M.A. in astronomy. Upon graduating, he returned to the observatory and continued his patrol of the skies, cataloging more than 30,000 celestial objects before he left in 1946. His observations of Mars led him to conclude in 1950 that the surface of the planet was pitted with craters

as a result of its proximity to the asteroid belt, a prediction borne out by images taken by the Mariner 4 space probe in the 1960s. Tombaugh also taught at Arizona State College and at the University of California, Los Angeles, and he worked as an astronomer and optical physicist at the White Sands Missile Range near Las Cruces, N.M., where he helped set up an optical tracking system to follow ballistic missiles. He joined the faculty of New Mexico State University in 1955 and there instituted a major program of planetary research. He retired in 1973 but remained involved as an observer and adviser at the university. Among his publications were *The Search for Small Natural Earth Satellites* (1959) and *Out of Darkness: The Planet Pluto* (1980), with Patrick Moore.

ROBERT TRUMPLER
(b. Oct. 2, 1886, Zürich, Switz.—d. Sept. 10, 1956, Berkeley, Calif., U.S.)

Robert Julius Trumpler was a Swiss-born U.S. astronomer who, in his extensive studies of galactic star clusters, demonstrated the presence throughout the galactic plane of a tenuous haze of interstellar material that absorbs light generally and decreases the apparent brightness of distant clusters.

Trumpler was educated in Switzerland and Germany, went to the United States in 1915, and joined the staff of Lick Observatory, Mount Hamilton, Calif., three years later. In 1922 he went to Wallal, W. Aus., Austl., on a solar eclipse expedition to test experimentally Albert Einstein's theory of general relativity by observing whether the Sun's gravitational field indeed would bend the light from nearby stars. His observations confirmed Einstein's theory, as had British astronomer Arthur Eddington's observations of the 1919 eclipse. Trumpler transferred to the astronomy department of the University of California, Berkeley, in 1938 and retired in 1951.

Trumpler's independent observations of galactic star clusters and the differences in them, which indicate their age, helped to provide the foundation of the present theory of stellar evolution. Probably the most successful scheme of classification of galactic clusters by appearance is Trumpler's. He also devised a method of classification in terms of magnitude and spectral type.

FRITZ ZWICKY

(b. Feb. 14, 1898, Varna, Bulg.—d. Feb. 8, 1974, Pasadena, Calif., U.S.)

Swiss astronomer and physicist Fritz Zwicky made valuable contributions to the theory and understanding of supernovas (stars that for a short time are far brighter than normal).

Zwicky received a doctorate in physics (1922) from the Swiss Federal Institute of Technology, Zürich, and served on the faculty of the California Institute of Technology, Pasadena, from 1925 to 1972.

During the early 1930s Zwicky contributed substantially to the physics of the solid state, gaseous ionization, and thermodynamics but soon turned to the study of supernovas, novas, and cosmic rays. In 1933 he discovered the existence of dark matter. In 1934, in collaboration with Walter Baade, he proposed that supernovas are a class of stellar explosion completely different from the ordinary novas and occur less often (two or three times every 1,000 years in the Milky Way Galaxy). Zwicky began conducting an extensive search of neighbouring galaxies for supernovas, and from 1937 to 1941, he discovered 18 of them. Only about 12 had been recorded previously in the history of astronomy.

As director of research (1943–46) of the Aerojet Engineering Corporation, Azusa, Calif., and technical adviser thereafter, he developed some of the earliest jet engines, including the JATO (jet assisted take-off) units used to launch heavy-laden aircraft from short runways.

antipodes The parts of Earth diametrically opposite from each other.

astrophysics The branch of astronomy that deals with the physics of the universe, including the physical properties of celestial objects and their interactions.

cosmic microwave background radiation A form of electromagnetic radiation filling the universe that is a residual effect of the big bang 13.7 billion years ago.

cosmological constant Term reluctantly added by Albert Einstein to his equations of general relativity in order to obtain a solution to the equations that described a static universe, as he believed it to be at the time.

cosmology Field of study that brings together the natural sciences, particularly astronomy and physics, in a joint effort to understand the physical universe as a unified whole.

empirical A term that denotes information gained by means of observation, experience, or experiment.

ephemeris Table giving the positions of one or more celestial bodies, often published with supplementary information.

epicycle A geometric model used to explain the variations in speed and direction of the apparent motion of the Moon, Sun, and planets.

equant A mathematical concept developed by Ptolemy in the 2nd century CE to account for the observed motion of heavenly bodies.

Euclidean geometry The study of plane and solid figures on the basis of axioms and theorems employed by the Greek mathematician Euclid.

geocentric system Any theory of the structure of the solar system (or the universe) in which Earth is assumed to be at the centre of all.

geodesy Scientific discipline concerned with the precise figure of Earth and its determination.

heliocentric system A cosmological model in which the Sun is assumed to lie at or near a central point (of the solar system or of the universe) while Earth and other bodies revolve around it.

homogeneity Having definite and consistent chemical composition and physical properties.

hypothetical Consisting either of a suggested explanation for an observable phenomenon or of a reasoned proposal predicting a possible correlation among multiple phenomena.

inertia Property of a body by virtue of which it opposes any agency that attempts to put it in motion or, if it is moving, to change the magnitude or direction of its velocity.

isotropy Uniformity in all directions.

kinematics Branch of physics and a subdivision of classical mechanics concerned with the geometrically possible motion of a body or system of bodies without consideration of the forces involved (causes and effects of the motions).

lunar eclipse An eclipse that occurs whenever the Moon passes behind the earth such that Earth blocks the Sun's rays from striking the Moon.

meteorology Scientific study of atmospheric phenomena, particularly of the troposphere and lower stratosphere.

nebula Any of various tenuous clouds of gas and dust in interstellar space.

neutrino elementary subatomic particle with no electric charge, very little mass, and 1/2 unit of spin.

nomenclature A system of names or terms, or the rules used for forming the names, as used by an individual or community, especially those used in science.

parallax The difference in direction of a celestial object as seen by an observer from two widely separated points.

perihelion The point in the path of a celestial body (as a planet) that is nearest to the Sun.

postulate A proposition that is not proved or demonstrated but considered to be either self-evident, or subject to necessary decision.

quantum Discrete natural unit, or packet, of energy, charge, angular momentum, or other physical property.

redshift Displacement of the spectrum of an astronomical object toward longer (red) wavelengths.

spectroscopy Study of the absorption and emission of light and other radiation by matter, as related to the dependence of these processes on the wavelength of the radiation.

superstring theory A theory that attempts to merge quantum mechanics with Albert Einstein's general theory of relativity.

wavelength Distance between corresponding points of two consecutive waves.

zodiac A belt around the heavens extending 9° on either side of the ecliptic, the plane of Earth's orbit and of the Sun's apparent annual path.

FOR FURTHER READING

Aughton, Peter. *The Transit of Venus: The Brief, Brilliant Life of Jeremiah Horrocks, Father of British Astronomy*. London, UK: Orion Publishing, 2005.

Barker, Andrew. *Scientific Method in Ptolemy's Harmonics*. New York, NY: Cambridge University Press, 2006.

Bartusiak, Marcia. *The Day We Found the Universe*. New York, NY: Pantheon, 2009.

Christianson, Gale E. *Isaac Newton*. New York, NY: Oxford University Press, 2005.

Christianson, John Robert. *On Tycho's Island: Tycho Brahe and his Assistants, 1570–1601*. New York, NY: Cambridge University Press, 2009.

Copernicus, Nicolaus, and Stephen Hawking. *On the Revolutions of Heavenly Spheres*. Philadelphia, PA: Running Press, 2004.

Einstein, Albert. *Relativity: The Special and the General Theory*. New York, NY: Penguin, 2006.

Farrell, John. *The Day Without Yesterday: Lemaitre, Einstein, and the Birth of Modern Cosmology*. New York, NY: Avalon Publishing Group, 2005.

Galilei, Galileo, and Maurice A. Finocchiaro (ed.). *The Essential Galileo*. Lancaster, UK: Hackett Publishing Co., 2008.

Gilder, Joshua, and Anne-Lee Gilder. *Heavenly Intrigue: Johannes Kepler, Tycho Brahe, and the Murder Behind One of History's Greatest Scientific Discoveries*. New York, NY: Anchor, 2005.

Gleick, James. *Isaac Newton*. New York, NY: Vintage, 2004.

Gregory, Jane. *Fred Hoyle's Universe*. New York, NY: Oxford University Press, 2005.

Hawking, Stephen W. *A Brief History of Time and the Universe in a Nutshell*. New York, NY: Bantam Dell, 2007.

Heath, Thomas Little. *Aristarchus of Samos: The Ancient Copernicus*. Boston, MA: Adamant Media Corp, 2007.

Herschel, William, and J. L. E. Dreyer (ed.). *The Scientific Papers of Sir William Herschel Volume 1*. Whitefish, MT: Kessinger Publishing, 2007.

Isaacson, Walter. *Einstein: His Life and Universe*. New York, NY: Simon & Schuster, 2008.

Johnson, George. *Miss Leavitt's Stars: The Untold Story of the Woman Who Discovered How to Measure the Universe*. New York, NY: W. W. Norton & Co., 2005.

Jones, Alexander, ed. *Ptolemy in Perspective: Use and Criticism of his Work from Antiquity to the Nineteenth Century*. New York, NY: Springer, 2009.

Koupelis, Theo. *In Quest of the Universe*. Sudbury, MA: Jones and Bartlett Publishers, 2007.

Lemonick, Michael. *The Georgian Star: How William and Caroline Herschel Revolutionized Our Understanding of the Cosmos.* New York, NY: W. W. Norton & Co., 2008.

Maran, Stephen P., and Laurence A. Marschall. *Galileo's New Universe: The Revolution in Our Understanding of the Cosmos.* Dallas, TX: Benbella Books, 2009.

Mitton, Gregory. *Conflict in the Cosmos: Fred Hoyle's Life in Science.* Washington, DC: Joseph Henry Press, 2005.

Naess, Atle. *Galileo Galilei: When the World Stood Still.* New York, NY: Springer, 2005.

Newton, Sir Isaac, and Stephen W. Hawking (ed.). *Principia.* Philadelphia, PA: Running Press, 2005.

Nicolson, Iain. *The Dark Side of the Universe: Dark Matter, Dark Energy, and the Fate of the Cosmos.* Baltimore, MD: The Johns Hopkins University Press, 2007.

Ohanian, Hans C. *Einstein's Mistakes: The Human Failings of Genius.* New York, NY: W. W. Norton, 2008.

Parker, Barry. *Einstein's Dream: The Search for a Unified Theory of the Universe.* Jackson, TN: Basic Books, 2001.

Penrose, Roger. *The Road to Reality: A Complete Guide to the Laws of the Universe.* New York, NY: Vintage Books, 2007.

Repcheck, Jack. *Copernicus' Secret: How the Scientific Revolution Began.* New York, NY: Simon & Schuster, 2008.

Sagan, Carl. *Cosmos.* New York, NY: Random House, 2002.

Siefe, Charles. *Decoding the Universe: How the Science of Information Is Explaining Everything in the Cosmos, from Our Brains to Black Holes.* New York, NY: Penguin, 2007.

Stoyan, Ronald, Stefan Binnewies, and Susanne Friedrich. *Atlas of the Messier Objects: Highlights of the Deep Sky.* New York: Cambridge, 2008.

Thoren, Victor E. *The Lord of Uraniborg: A Biography of Tycho Brahe.* New York, NY: Cambridge University Press, 2007.

Vollmann, William T. *Uncentering the Earth: Copernicus and the Revolutions of the Heavenly Spheres.* New York, NY: W. W. Norton & Co., 2007.

INDEX